Public Service Media Renewal

STUDIES IN COMMUNICATION AND POLITICS

Edited by Bogusława Dobek-Ostrowska and Michał Głowacki

VOL. 6

Notes on the quality assurance and peer review of this publication

Prior to publication, the quality of the work published in this series is reviewed by an external referee appointed by the editorship.

Michał Głowacki / Alicja Jaskiernia (eds.)

Public Service Media Renewal

Adaptation to Digital Network Challenges

PETER LANG
EDITION

Bibliographic Information published by the Deutsche Nationalbibliothek
The Deutsche Nationalbibliothek lists this publication in the Deutsche Nationalbibliografie; detailed bibliographic data is available in the internet at http://dnb.d-nb.de.
Library of Congress Cataloging-in-Publication Data
A CIP catalog record for this book has been applied for at the Library of Congress

Referees:
Karen Arriaza Ibarra, Minna Aslama Horowitz, Sandra Bašić Hrvatin, Charles Brown, Indrek Ibrus, Marta Jas-Koziarkiewicz, Stanisław Jędrzejewski, Andres Jõesaar, Matthias Karmasin, Beata Klimkiewicz, Katarzyna Konarska, Michał Kuś, Hannu Nieminem, Christian S. Nissen, Dariya Orlova, Tena Perišin, Natalya Ryabinska, Andrej Školkay, Barbara Thomass

English language editing by Derettens OÜ: http://derettens-english-language-editing.com

The publication was financially supported by the Faculty of Journalism, Information and Book Studies, University of Warsaw, Poland.

ISSN 2197-1625
ISBN 978-3-631-67728-5 (Print)
E-ISBN 978-3-653-07253-2 (E-PDF)
E-ISBN 978-3-631-70931-3 (EPUB)
E-ISBN 978-3-631-70932-0 (MOBI)
DOI 10.3726/b11680

Peter Lang Edition is an Imprint of Peter Lang GmbH.

Peter Lang – Frankfurt am Main · Bern · Bruxelles · New York · Oxford · Warszawa · Wien

This publication has been peer reviewed.

www.peterlang.com

Contents

Preface: Facing criticism and a new reality – the need for a new public service media mindset

Driven by technological innovation and the deployment of broadband networks, the media are currently undergoing many different changes that are making it an increasingly complex sector. The entire value chain, from content production to distribution and consumption, is being altered by new processes and emerging players.

The boundaries of traditional media are gradually dissolving, giving rise to an environment in which the life cycles of content accelerate and multiply, abundance appears unlimited, and new platforms and providers appear (and disappear) sudden and unexpectedly. Frontiers between sectors and countries are also becoming blurred, and national markets are now more interdependent than ever before. Such a context, together with the speed of change and the disruption capacity of external players, is forcing well-established business models of the media sector to be revised.

Furthermore, society and its citizens are changing, and so are their needs and expectations of media. Their consumption habits are evolving beyond traditional television viewing and radio listening as they rapidly embrace new media.

Public service media (PSM) are not an exception, and cannot ignore how the current transformation context creates new challenges for them to remain relevant, prominent and findable. Additionally, their future sustainability is certainly at stake.

Thanks to the overall perspective that working at the European Broadcasting Union provides, I would say that the main vectors of change PSM should tackle are:

- Globalization of the media sector, which has resulted in the rise of truly worldwide players that are gradually becoming more dominant,
- Consolidation of national media markets, which makes it difficult for non-profit organizations or new entrants to develop their service portfolios and meet new audience requirements,
- Arrival of new players and gatekeepers that disrupt the traditional media ecosystem by altering the structure of the value chain and shifting the balance of power,

- Fragmentation of the audience and the appearance of new consumption trends, which force broadcasters to redesign their media products, services and distribution strategies,
- Evolution towards a data paradigm that poses great challenges regarding the skills of those working for traditional media companies and jeopardizes the latter's position,
- Fast evolution and even radical disruption of the media content, which includes not only the evolution of formats and genres but also changes resulting from personalization, on-demand provision, addition of metadata and extended information layers, filtering, etc.,
- Uncertain role and value of regulation, which traditionally protected public service media but now seems to somehow hinder the evolution necessary if PSM is to keep pace with societal and industry changes.

In parallel, the ongoing economic crisis and the waning trust in public institutions across Europe have reinforced those contesting the remit, role and legitimacy of PSM and demanding a review of their activities and budgets.

It is clear that the current socio-economic conditions, aided by the dominant neoliberalism of western democracies, are very different from those that gave rise to public service media. The gradual commodification of media has reinforced the pre-eminence of its economic and industrial goals. Even more, the need for the media, and even their suitability, to contribute to the fulfilment of social and democratic goals have been questioned.

While concluding whether this evolution is positive or negative depends of course on each's ideology and values, it is clear that the current framework is not favourable for public service media. At least for the kind of public service media we are used to.

Criticism of PSM has been effectively expressed in various arguments:

- PSM legitimacy is challenged by neoliberal theses supporting the idea that the abundance of content and services, together with the choice enabled by technological innovation, empowers individuals to obtain whatever they need from the competitive and now convergent market.
- Public policy for the media and public service broadcasters are therefore considered totally unnecessary and even inappropriate, as they might distort competition and even hinder commercial or entrepreneurial success.
- Thanks to its self-regulation mechanisms, the market is portrayed to be the best arena for the free expression of ideas, values and interests, as well as capable of satisfying all users' needs.

Additionally, PSM organizations are also strongly questioned because of their:

- Structure, described as over-sized, inefficient and poorly governed,
- Accountability, seen as lacking in transparency and responsiveness to all stakeholders, especially citizens,
- Funding, claimed to be disproportional to their activities as well as a major cause of market distortion,
- Offer, for not being distinctive enough and often beyond the PSM remit, hindering private initiative.

The most elaborate positions against PSM bring together all these elements and manage to call into question the real value delivered by PSM companies. The latter are accused of being over-protected by regulations and wasting large amounts of public resources. In that way, PSM jeopardizes the development of the national industry, hinders competition and deprives national commercial operators of the opportunity to develop properly and maximize the value they could provide, preventing them from being competitive in the global scenario. In addition PSM's offer is questioned for not being good or distinctive enough, and therefore not providing good value for money.

PSM is somehow considered a Keynesian social welfare tool that has become obsolete. In fact, nowadays many commercial operators claim that they could even replace PSM organizations, providing greater value in a faster, more dynamic and more efficient way.

Independently from whether we agree or not with that rationale, it is a fact that those arguments have resulted in a mindset that is gaining strength in some countries. That is not at all beneficial for PSM organizations.

However, PSM could also be partly responsible for this situation. When basic questions, such as why PSM is needed, what they really do for us that others couldn't do, or how they operate and use public funding, are not answered with clear, concrete and understandable arguments, PSM are failing to build their own case.

While the traditional narrative about public service media is well known, it clearly has lost its ability to inspire or engage. And, even more worrying, PSM narratives are sometimes disconnected from current societal and political issues, which obviously results in a lower perception of value by their stakeholders. Additionally, due to the current adverse atmosphere and the sometimes preoccupying political interference that PSM organizations suffer, the latter forget or avoid pointing out their successes or the benefits and value they deliver.

It is then not a surprise that PSM legitimacy, role and remit are strongly contested, and their performance under close scrutiny. Additionally, the current economic crisis has made public service media a prime target of the austerity measures taken by national governments. This has not only resulted in a reduction in their resources, and therefore hindered their capability to perform, but it has somehow provided momentum for those advocating smaller PSM or their abolition altogether. Worryingly, proposals to close down public broadcasters, portraying the latter as old-fashioned and inefficient institutions, and suggestions to reallocate the public service mission and public funding among market players, are gaining traction and support in some countries.

In this context of change, and somehow hostility, it is the time for PSM organizations to take action and face the described criticism as well as the contextual challenges and threats.

First, PSM organizations need to adapt to the new context. Owing to the external forces listed above, public service media organizations must tackle increasingly complex changes in terms of their structure, corporate strategy, allocating resources, producing and distributing content and, no less important, acquiring and managing talent. While facing changes has always been part of the daily routine and strategy of PSM organizations, being too confident would be a fatal mistake. The current changes are happening with an unprecedented speed and towards new and unknown directions. While in the past PSM were able to own, appeal to and retain the key individuals, the state-of-the-art knowledge and the right skills, this is not the case anymore.

Nowadays, PSM companies face an enormous human resources challenge, which cannot be solved entirely by training, developing or replacing their staff but will force them to engage in new partnerships with a broad and diverse array of market players, private and public ones. The past isolation, even physical, of public service media is becoming a tremendous burden, hindering their adaptation to the networked society.

Secondly, PSM need to work on their legitimacy. Otherwise, any change and achievement in their evolution or adaptation will be useless. But addressing PSM's legitimacy goes beyond the constant discussion of the raison d'être of public service media that is very popular in academic or legal circles. In the current context, in order to maintain or even renew their legitimacy, public service media need more than ever to demonstrate their value and the benefits they deliver to their multiple stakeholders.

In fact, I would dare to state that this is the most critical problem for the future of PSM: politicians, market players and, most importantly, the citizens, do not understand what public service media stand for and what value they deliver. And while their intrinsic or moral values are still important, they are no longer enough for them to gain the political, market and social support they need. Nowadays, other types of value provided by PSM (individual, use, or exchange value) need to occupy a greater place in the public discussion about PSM's existence, role and scope.

Furthermore, PSM need to urgently understand that the concept of value is fairly relative, as it shaped by the consumers' perception, i.e. whether, in their eyes, that service meets a particular need. Consequently, finding out and understanding what the needs of PSM stakeholders are must be a priority.

As a result of the work that I have been carrying out at the Media Intelligence Service of the EBU in the last years, I am pretty convinced that public service media organizations still have a chance. However, acknowledging the current challenges and threats is the first requirement. Looking into another direction or continuing to preach the historical benefits of PSM will not bring any solution.

Secondly, a new mindset for PSM executives and staff is absolutely necessary. It is what we call the PSM Contribution to Society and it is based in three premises:

- **PSM have an impact on society**
  Beyond offering what might be regarded as quality content, and assessing its reach, PSM content and other activities have a positive impact on the communities they serve (on their economy, their culture, democracy, etc). Assessing that impact is essential to revamp PSM's legitimacy in the neoliberal networked societies we live in.
- **PSM's accountability to society as a whole**
  Based on the awareness of ongoing societal changes, PSM must not limit their activities to certain target groups but must embrace a strategy that strengthens their links to all their stakeholders, paying special attention to the citizens. While serving the citizens has been a key component of the traditional PSM narrative, the reality is that public service media organizations have on some occasions focused a bit too much on their relations with the political establishment and forgotten about the citizens.
- **PSM should stimulate the public debate on society's communication needs and how they should be satisfied**
  As key players in their national markets, and thanks to their non-profit orientation, PSM companies should lead the definition of the agenda on how the media system could deliver benefits to society as a whole, and become an active contributor to this debate. This will place them as a relevant societal asset.

This new mindset should result in internal changes, a new strategy, a new offer and a new approach to accountability that revamps not only the concept of public service media but the structure and performance of its providers. Parallel to this, and being essential to address the issue of PSM's legitimacy, the Contribution to Society mindset should also result in a renewed advocacy strategy. A key element of the latter will be a new narrative about PSM.

In order to address the scenario described above, respond to criticisms, renew their legitimacy, and bolster their political, market and social support, PSM organizations need to craft a comprehensive set of fact-based arguments about their remit, role and very importantly, their value. And this, together with a revamp of their communication strategies and techniques, should result in a renewed, inspiring and meaningful narrative about PSM that repositions it as a societal asset instead of the current picture of being an unnecessary cost.

This book addresses many of the challenges, opportunities, risks and obstacles that PSM faces nowadays. It provides an overall and comprehensive perspective, and points out some of the key steps that PSM organizations will need to take in the coming years and that could eventually result in the definition and adoption the new mindset we claim for PSM.

The editors have done a good job in the selection of the contributors, and thanks to the diversity in their origin and expertise the book offers a rich variety of perspectives, reflections and proposals. It is certainly a work that will contribute to closing a bit of the gap between academic scholar and professional practitioners, as the latter will find inspiring ideas in the following pages. And I hope that altogether this book will shed some light on how public service media, thanks to their values and performance, can continue to be an essential asset of the democracy, the culture, the technology and the economy of our European societies.

Dr Roberto Suárez Candel
Head of the Media Intelligence Service
European Broadcasting Union

Editors' introduction

Media organizations worldwide are currently challenged by the rise of digital and network practices. Technological change and adaptive users' behaviours are of particular concern to public service media (PSM), which originates from the pre-Internet era. PSM need to continually evolve in order to serve the traditional obligations of public service broadcasters: serving individual citizens and minority groups, fostering cultural diversity and supporting democratic processes.

Searching for the ways in which PSM might adapt to the new media and societal conditions has been the subject of several policy and academic debates. For instance, the Council of Europe and the European Broadcasting Union have argued for PSM to be more people centric and to overhaul their governance systems and operations in the digital space. The future of the fabric of PSM has also been recently discussed at the national level, with the examples of media reforms in Croatia, Italy, Latvia, United Kingdom, Poland and Romania. The technological and societal advances of the 21st century present an opportunity to embrace emerging post-broadcasting models typified by strategic re-organizations, transmedia forms, clustering of symbiotic businesses and collaborations with independent producers. Nevertheless, the process of developing new approaches and advanced PSM enterprises has in many countries proven to be problematic.

In this collection, we take a holistic approach to analyze public service media and its adaptation strategies to the digital network era. Referring to several case studies and research initiatives, involving a variety of methodological and theoretical approaches, we argue that the current changes in media and society are the right conditions for PSM renewal. A successful response to external and internal challenges might contribute to growth, competitiveness, innovation potential, better fulfilment of public service content delivery and ensure PSM becomes a key player in contemporary media landscapes. All of this is achieved while mapping the necessary conditions that might need to be put into force in order for public service media to evolve.

The collection begins with an exploration of the role of networks for accelerating media reforms. Bissera Zankova argues that current models of PSM regulation should be based on the principles of networks. The principles should maintain public service media independence, sufficient funding, participation, innovative leadership and ability to extend public service media operations beyond traditional broadcasting means.

Tim Raats and Karen Donders examine the value of the ecosystem approach and analyze policies that support collaboration between PSM and other stakeholders. An in-depth study of rhetoric and policy-making in Flanders helps to understand challenges for PSM relations going forward.

The opportunity to view PSM through the lenses of partnership systems and collaboration with high technology and creative media clusters is further explored by Michał Głowacki. Research in Estonia's capital, Tallinn, reveals the potential barriers and drivers for public service media ecology.

Mapping the public's attitude towards the programming of a PSM is one of the goals of study by Nicole Gonser, Markus Grammel, Johann Gründl and Gisela Reiter. Using this parameter as well as qualitative and quantitative data, the team examine Austria's PSM – ORF.

A call for participatory shift in public service media is explored and suggested in comparative study by Tiziano Bonini. The author argues that development of digital media has the potential of new forms of public engagement in the context of either or both terms of content creation and exploration of alternative models for funding.

An opportunity to maintain PSM function as a cultural facilitator is explored by Jonathon Hutchinson through the lenses of algorithmic culture. Hutchinson's study of Australia's national PSM, ABC, highlights the importance of engaging with broader audiences through social media.

Through examination of selected media firms (both public service and private) in the UK and USA, Lizzie Jackson argues for the need for PSM to engage with predictive analytics and behavioural targeting. The study showed that the potential of machine mediation requires new skills for PSM, such as data analytics and data management.

Anja Stević and Emil Čančar examine delays of new media strategy adaptation in Croatia. The chapter argues that the lack of technological awareness might be seen as a barrier for public social media development.

Political pressure, as an obstacle for the PSM renewal, is discussed in a study of shifts from public service to sovereign national media in Poland. Alicja Jaskiernia and Katarzyna Pokorna-Ignatowicz argue that recent changes in media law is a warning for PSM reforms in other countries.

The chapter by Päivi Maijanen explores PSM renewal from the organizational perspective. The study on managerial attitude and the mindset for being change-ready, in the case of Finland, maps internal conditions responsible for moving the concept of PSM away from traditional broadcasting.

Findings from the studies in this collection are summarized in the concluding sections where we argue for a multilayered analytical prism for the PSM change and renewal.

Several chapters included in this book were presented during an international conference, entitled "Public service media in the digital mediascapes", which took place at the University of Warsaw in June 2015. The meeting gathered policy-makers, public service media managers, scholars and representatives of international organizations to assist leaders of PSM enterprises with emerging genres of content and services in the digital realm. Other contributions were delivered during the conferences of the International Association for Media and Communication Research in Montreal (2015) and the International Communication Association in Fukuoka (2016).

Overall, we believe that this collection will contribute to current debates over public service media and will highlight a need for a new discourse in PSM. We hope that this book will attract the attention of researchers and scholars specialized in media policy, public service media and change management. In addition, we also hope that the studies presented here will be of great interest to policy-makers and practitioners of public service media and other enterprises exploring adaptation strategies in the network era.

Michał Głowacki and Alicja Jaskiernia

Bissera Zankova
Media21 Foundation, Bulgaria

Public service media regulation in the new media environment: the role of the networks for accelerating reforms

Abstract: The article deals with the topical issue of public service media (PSM) regulation in the digital environment, discussing the appropriate frameworks that have to be put in force. Reforms in PSM organizations and their transformation into modern and innovative enterprises merit particular focus. The role of networks in the new media landscape is considered as being beneficial for accelerating changes. At the same time the problems of network regulation vis-à-vis classical regulation are being debated. Three crucial areas for reforming PSM enterprises are identified, namely expanding public service functions on new services and platforms, creating a vibrant participatory public sphere and pursuing innovative leadership. In order for PSM reforms to be successful it is vital to strengthen their independence and to secure adequate funding for these central democratic and cultural institutions. The ultimate goal is to turn PSM into working enterprises matching the requirements of the digital age.

Keywords: public service media, regulation, public sphere, innovative leadership, networks.

Introduction

The future of public service media (PSM) and the appropriate regulatory frameworks that have to be put in place to assure their sustainability are topics that merit particular interest both on national and international policy-making levels. For instance, the Council of Europe (2013) states that "the preservation of the essential role of the media in the novel digital environment is premised on a well-funded, sustainable, independent, high quality and ethical public service media." Further to the policy documents related to PSM adopted by the Council of Europe[1] the European Broadcasting Union also published a series of papers analyzing in more

1 The most important of these documents being Recommendation CM/Rec(2007)3 of the Committee of Ministers to member states on the remit of PSM in the information society, Recommendation CM/Rec(2012)1 of the Committee of Ministers to member states on public service media governance, Declaration of the Committee of Ministers on public service media governance (2012).

depth the principles of regulation and governance of PSM in the digital environment.[2] Furthermore, policy makers, academics and media scholars have also observed that "the environment in which public service media in Europe currently operate is a turbulent one. One aspect of this changing context is technological change" (Nowak and Kuhn, 2015: 4). In line with this Raboy (2001: 182) at the beginning of the 21st century calls for a "forward-looking vision (…), reproducing the values of public service broadcasting but searching for new institutional forms for promoting these values."

Usually reforms in different spheres depend on particular values and are instrumental for the creation of "a value determined, and accepted as a possible for realization, model of development in particular social space and time" (Marinov, 2015: 41). This observation is all the more valid for the changes in PSM that are expected to improve and strengthen these enterprises in the highly competitive and dynamic modern setting. Values represent the corner-stone of PSM and finding the appropriate institutional design to reinforce them in the contemporary rapidly changing media landscape requires a new outlook and multiple efforts.[3] What are the best tools that can accelerate transformations in PSM in the digital age and particularly what type of regulation has to be implemented by policy makers? These are essential questions that demand consideration of various approaches and methods.

One of the ideas propounded by the literature in the sphere of regulation in recent years is that networks and networking have considerable impact over structures and processes. The idea stems from the premises of the networked society, in which we are immersed. Castells (2000: 2) claims that "new information technologies allow the formation of new forms of social organization and social interaction along electronically based information networks." The transition creates more abundant opportunities for innovation in all areas, but special "policies for activating innovation" (Soete, 2005: 128) are particularly needed. From a legal perspective, authors such as Craig (2006) believe these developments can generate opportunities for a more open, transparent and democratic regulation. Network regulation is viewed as an option for modernizing media regulation taking into account the democratizing role of the online space. Wider public involvement,

2 The series called Legal Focus build on the EBU Declaration on the Core Values of Public Service Media released to confirm the commitment of the EBU members to independence, diversity, high professional standards and innovation (EBU, 2012).

3 An example of such efforts is the EBU project "Connecting to a networked society – Vision 2020" published in 2014 starting the beginning of a permanent collaboration between the EBU and its Members on developing long term strategies (EBU, 2014, 2015).

openness to civil society, flexibility and close engagement with public demands through networks may successfully underpin a new regulatory approach to PSM. As Głowacki and Jackson (2014) explain, PSM created in the 20th century are nowadays located between two paradigms: the industrial broadcasting model and the network and post-industrial one requiring, in particular changes in production culture, leadership, organizational structures and regulation.

The aim of this article is to examine a set of the challenges for PSM regulation that support evolution and adaptation to the network of networks. The purpose is to point out some crucial areas, in which networks can be successfully deployed to speed up reforms. The changes entailed will pursue effective discharge of the public service remit in the digital environment and eventually more efficient PSM enterprises serving the public good. The three key areas that are the object of the analysis in this chapter comprise the transformation of public broadcasters into PSM through the full use of the new information and communications technologies, the invigoration of the public sphere through enhanced public participation and the implementation of new leadership as a guarantor and promoter of innovation policy. By doing so, the paper will discuss the application of networks and other aspects that could be considered by policy makers and legislators.

Mapping public media obligations

The purpose of the public service mission is to integrate various communities and people making them both feel owners of PSM. According to Eberle (2002: 1) public media represent specific organizations that fulfill functions of "essential importance for state and society." From the perspective of democracy and democratic principles Jakubowicz (2010: 225) states "there is thus, historically speaking, a growing association of public service media with democracy and civil society." Close bonds with the public which are typical for PSM acquire a new dimension in the digital environment. The organization – structure and functions – of these enterprises have to correspond to this role.

On the internet, PSM can be reliable navigators for information, education and culture serving the interests of all groups and generations. Public media content on new platforms and services is crucial for providing trustworthy information and diversity of opinion on a continuous basis (IRIS, 2015: 25). The internet enhances the contribution of PSM to the preservation and promotion of the European and world cultural heritage. Taking into account the versatile opportunities in the information society for creation and participation, Jakubowicz (2010: 226) proposes to reconstruct PSM into a platform for open societal communication and to establish "a new partnership with the public." This type of partnership could represent a new stage in the development of public media institutions after the paternalistic and the democratic-emancipatory stages and re-unite them with the civil society at large. The PSM and the public may come closer to each other via interactive platforms passing the institutional administrative barriers. The PSM–public partnership however, presupposes active interaction not only in content creation but in regulation and governance, too.

The implementation of the PSM's comprehensive remit and the adaptation of PSM to a networked society depends greatly on its relationships with all stakeholders and the public at large. Frameworks that govern these relationships should stimulate participation and regulation has to be tailored to respond adequately to the new position of PSM as essential public partner, navigator and collaborator to various stakeholders and communities. In the information society featuring a complex set of social, cultural and technological elements it is not sufficient to resort to regulation in general. It is necessary to apply regulatory models capable of managing risks and promoting changes in a multidimensional environment. Last but not least such policy should build on knowledge and aim at innovation or as Soete (2005: 127) explains it should activate "unexploited forms of knowledge."

The media field is not isolated from these regulatory demands, as PSM regulation has to provide for the broader remit of PSM and stimulate its discharge in an open and collaborative manner. More specifically the regulatory approaches have to search for adequate mechanisms for implementation which reflect the flexibility and openness of the networked society. Good regulation aims at effectiveness and efficiency and putting its principles into practice can turn public media organizations into modern and working enterprises.

Regulation and good regulation in a networked society

Regulation encompasses any government measure or intervention that seeks to impact the behaviour of individuals or groups. Some experts expounding public interest theories consider regulation necessary to remedy market failure. Others, including Craig (2015), contest the idea and emphasize that in most of the cases regulation serves private interests. In a complex environment, regulation is a term that signifies a process that develops among different bodies in a regulatory space.[4] The concept of the regulatory space as interdependence among

4 In the literature about regulation the regulatory state is said to have led to a more complex regulatory space (Scott, 2001; Hancher and Moran, 1989) of expansion of relationships across regulatory regimes, involving to a varying extent government departments, politicians, regulatory bodies, 'target populations,' firms, shareholders and

various subjects is akin to the networked approach in regulation. Both attempt at responding adequately to the transformations in the institutional structure due to globalization, which leads to new types of interaction at the level of governance (Maggetti and Gilardi, 2014). For Baldwin (2010: 275) modern regulation generally exhibits a "networked quality." In line with this idea, Scott (2010: 31) evidences that "networks are characterized by voluntary participation that frequently transcends both state/non-state distinctions and national boundaries." Featuring these characteristics networks (technical, institutional, expert) can structure important connections in the media field carrying the exchange of information, knowledge and expertise. Due to the internet they can also facilitate interaction between various types of regulation (national and international, regulation and self-regulation) and underpin the evolution of globally recognized rules and principles.

Institutional networks presuppose the development of relationships among organizations and bodies which expand beyond borders and allow for "pluralist, participatory form of control and accountability" (Craig, 2006: 179). Following this type of pattern, regulatory regimes are supposed to become more flexible and horizontally oriented. This poses a challenge for legal regulation, in which hierarchical structures dominate normally backed by national states. Another point raised by Magetti and Gilardi (2014) is the establishment of soft law rules as a consequence of transnational regulation which are not directly enforceable at a national level. Borzel (1998: 253 cited in Maggetti and Gilardi 2014: 1294) declaims that "after decades of wide use of the network metaphor among scholars and practitioners, it still remains to be systematically shown that policy networks do not only exist but are really relevant to policy-making." Further in the debate Craig (2015: 806) expresses concerns about the "circumvention of the normal rules of representative democracy."

Against the backdrop of these debates the theory of regulation and administrative law in particular has to clarify how networks influence the quality of regulation, whether they really bring better coordination, transparency and efficiency to the regulatory impact and eventually whether they enrich democracy. The OECD's guiding principles for regulatory quality and performance adopted in 2005 can serve as a fruitful basis for such investigation. Without referring to network or new modes of regulation these principles generally encourage innovative regulation, i.e. "regulation that promotes innovation through market

---

the wider public. This theory has risen with the deconcentration of the state power and the mushrooming of regulatory agencies including media regulatory bodies. For more see: Ayres and Braithwaite (1992) Baldwin and Cave (1999), Baldwin, Scott and Hood (1998), Hancher and Moran (1989), Lodge (2004), Scott (2001) and Zankova (2013).

incentives and goal-based approaches" (OECD, 2005). They prescribe concrete steps to be undertaken towards reforms premised on "a dynamic approach to improve regulatory systems over time, to improve the stock of existing and the quality of new regulations, and ensure that reforms are carried out in a logical order" (OECD, 2005). An unalienable element of good regulation is the ex-post evaluation taking into account the public interest (OECD, 2005). In some countries improving regulation is a goal of national importance. In the UK for instance, the Better Regulation Task Force was set up in 1997 to promote the principles of proportionality, accountability, consistency, transparency and targeting for measuring and raising the quality of regulation and its enforcement.

Good regulation also provides for better governance of enterprises. According to the OECD principles their realization in practice pursues efficiency and transparency in various sectors to assist the accomplishment of other publicly relevant goals. This inference gives a clue as to how good regulation could support good governance as an array of standards that encourage better management of resources and risks within organizations (Zankova, 2014: 127).

Another point is that governance possesses internal and external dimensions. The latter pertains to those elements going beyond the purely internal managerial issues that overlap with regulation representing by and large "regulatory/steering issues such as civil society, owner relations, control regimes, competition and co-operation, institutional setup and outsourcing of production" (Nissen, 2011: 10). The interplay between governance and regulation can promote transformations within PSM organizations (internal changes) as well as innovative regulatory solutions (external changes). It helps to view the process as an interrelationship between internal and external factors that complement each other and create the necessary conditions for reforms. Besides, the criteria for good regulation have changed over time. In order to be adapted to the 21st century, regulatory policies and tools have to become cross-sectoral, pro-active and more responsive to public demands. New issues come to the fore such as multilevel coordination, market openness, risk awareness and effective implementation (OECD, 2005). These rules go hand-in-hand with the general principles that encourage innovation such as introducing technological change, boosting competition, abolishing administrative burdens and streamlining effectiveness and striving to greater harmonization and compatibility internationally (OECD, n.p.).[5] The application of all these

5 On a practical scale the OECD/Eurostat OSLO Guidelines for Collecting and Interpreting Innovation Data, 3rd Edition (2005) is a useful tool which provides advice how data on innovation activities have to be collected and assessed.

guidelines inevitably have a bearing on the external and internal relationships of PSM, which have to be redesigned along the principles of good regulation. Amongst them, streamlining innovation and creativity is considered crucial for carrying out reforms. With respect to PSM, it is a widely shared opinion that boosting innovation is a fundamental factor in order for PSM to develop in the digital environment. Moreover Głowacki and Jackson (2014: 277) point out that innovation practices in a multiple and mixed platform mediascape can turn PSM enterprise into an international "potential stakeholder network in itself." However, specific schemes how to make innovation viable are missing. Efforts towards innovation presuppose the undertaking of a complex array of scientific, technological, organizational, financial and commercial steps. While the availability of scientific and technological conditions seems clear, it is important how organizational, financial and commercial measures will be triggered for the accomplishment of innovation oriented policy within the organization. Establishing organizational conditions for innovation is vital because it creates the necessary internal climate for efficient innovation activities. As OECD/Eurostat (2005) notes, a general preparation is needed for the adjustment of the structure and functions along the lines of innovation and creativity and it includes getting external knowledge, technical equipment and training. The new model of PSM regulation has to provide for the conditions that can turn the regulatory principles and innovation above all from a hollow word into live practice.[6]

Towards a new model of PSM regulation

For the media self-regulation is crucial as it supports media independence from within and reduces the risks of excessive administrative interference of regulatory bodies. Balancing the interests of the public and the private sector co-regulatory models provide for more industry involvement. However important these tools they cannot surmount regulation as there are media areas that cannot rely on self- and co-regulation only. Jaskiernia (2015: 23) argues that "leaving the media with no regulations and counting only on self-regulation does not ensure good governance." An argument fundamental for democracy is that through regulation, freedom of expression which is not an absolute right is balanced to other rights and its exercise is overseen by an independent body. Media regulation has to be perceived as the process of creating sufficient political, legal and social

6 From the perspective of PSM values Vision 2020 perceives this a multistage process of connecting to a networked society in which the focus shifts from "standardized workflows" to a greater emphasis on dialogue, innovation and flexibility (EBU, 2014: 11).

guarantees for the proper implementation of freedom of expression through any means and on any service and platform (Zankova, 2013). Historically in Europe, media regulation has been justified by and graduated having regard to its potential high impact on society and on individual rights; regulation has also been a means of managing scarce resources in the public interest. Given the importance of standard-setting activities for democracy, the Council of Europe introduced them to ensure the highest protection of media freedom and to provide guidance on duties and responsibilities. With regard to freedom of expression and freedom of the media, regulation has to be treated with restraint. The European Court of Human Rights (ECtHR) has stated on many occasions that any regulatory measure in the media field should be based on art. 10 of the European Convention of Human Rights and the relevant case law of the Strasbourg Court. The Council of Europe recommendation on a new notion of media also reiterates this precept (Council of Europe, 2011).

In his contribution to the First Ministerial Conference on Media and New Communications Services, in Reykjavik, Jakubowicz (2009: 27) expressly points out a need for a new regulatory framework for the media, particularly for the new media rooted in the Council of Europe human rights documents. Jakubowicz further concludes that "regulation often serves protection of freedom of expression, rather than imposes restrictions on that freedom" (Jakubowicz, 2009: 28). This idea has to be a guiding principle when discussing any new regulatory mechanism in any environment.

The protective function of regulation can be jeopardized by political majorities or economic groups. Analyzing PSM regulation, Krewel (2015) juxtaposes autonomy of PSM and regulatory frameworks in four European countries concluding that major threats to PSM autonomy stem from politics as political actors can put limitations on the autonomy through the legal instruments they pass (Krewel, 2015: 143). Economic groups, however, can also interfere via lobbies and political allies. Craig (2015: 3) makes similar observation when referring to the different schools explaining the rationale of the regulatory foundations. Political majorities can propose regulation matching narrow political and economic interests or be passive without taking adequate measures to assure the proper funding or management of PSM. In a rapidly developing society, the lack of timely and forward-oriented reforms can also be perilous for the future of these organizations. Bearing all of this in mind, the goal of PSM regulation is to focus on several essential problems the solving of which can strengthen the position of public media as a central democratic, social and cultural institution in the digital age. This includes extension of PSM operations to new platforms and devices, enhancing public debate and participation as well as turning PSM organizations into innovative and result-oriented enterprises. All of these can be workable when securing funding and fostering sufficient level of independence, which is of critical importance for any regulation of PSM going forward.

Fostering PSM independence

A report of the Committee on Culture, Science, Education and Media of the Parliamentary Assembly of the Council of Europe (PACE) titled "The state of media freedom in Europe" gives examples of interference with PSM independence in many parts of Europe including both established and new democracies, such as France, Italy, Bosnia and Herzegovina, Croatia, Kosovo (PACE, 2012). The issue of independence is fundamental for the successful transition of public service broadcasters and for the fully fledged operation of PSM in the digital age. The EBU points out that "without a sufficient level of independence, PSM cannot sustain their credibility and will lose popular support" which is crucial in a networked open society (Wagner and Berg, 2015: 9). At the same time, "PSM cannot act in isolation but only in interaction with other stakeholders or they have to be connected" (ibid.). In this respect "absolute" independence is "not a realistic or justifiable objective" (Wagner and Berg, 2015: 9).

In a network environment, PSM independence depends on a multitude of relationships with institutions, bodies and other subjects and the policy framework should specify these relationships setting "the responsibilities of the different parties involved: government, parliament, regulatory authorities (including auditing and other inspectorates) and the public service media themselves, as well as any specified engagement from designated third parties (civil society, market representatives, etc.)" (Council of Europe, 2012b). Independence has to be understood as a set of links with relevant stakeholders which allow PSM to discharge successfully their broader remit. Frameworks have to be structured in an open dialogue with stakeholders and the public-at-large, forestalling any attempts of political majorities or economic conglomerates to stifle or take advantage of the reforms.

Securing sufficient funding

The discharge of a broader remit in the digital environment could be challenging for those PSM organizations, which do not have at their disposal adequate financial and human resources[7]. The EBU's guiding principles on PSM funding particularly stress that PSM funding should reflect the dynamics of the developing broadcasting markets with increasingly more interactive digital services (Burnley, 2015: 9). Public media funding has relied on a complementary set of sources but nowadays has to be adjusted to the new digital requirements (Burnley, 2015). The cited principles do not approve of a specific financial mechanism and it is up to the countries to find new financial sources that could secure PSM sustainability. The network paradigm can be useful here as a model of possible sources of funding benefiting from the opportunities of the net such as crowdsourcing, for instance. Karmasin and Kraus (2014: 74) suggest a combination of stakeholder management and crowdsourcing and the redefinition of the internal and external communication of the company switching from "one-way communications to interconnected communications." Taking stock of the network relationships, Karmasin and Kraus are of the opinion that such relationships can transform the overall PSM management along new lines of operation. Such a challenging exercise presupposes also change in the corporate culture and management of organizations (Karmasin and Kraus, 2014). Policy makers have to consider these innovative approaches that take a complex outlook of PSM management and funding, and engage larger public involvement not only through the traditional license fee but through networks' channels as well.

Extension of PSM operations to new channels and platforms

The regulation of PSM should facilitate the transition towards more advanced and participatory PSM model and the availability of their content on all services and platforms. Though it is expected that PSM has replaced public service broadcasting across Europe, this has yet to occur. In 2012 the Committee of Ministers of the Council of Europe adopted two groundbreaking documents – a declaration and a recommendation on PSM governance (Council of Europe, 2012a, 2012b) which formulated principles of good governance indispensable to the "positive public perception of PSM and their acceptance by society" (Wagner and Berg,

7 The threat of financial collapse of Bosnian PSM is instructive in this respect. The case became widely known in December 2015 but the OSCE representative has warned about the lack of sustainable funding already in 2013 issuing recommendations to the authorities "to establish mechanisms for regular reviews of public broadcasters financial needs and provide public funds to enable broadcasters to operate in the digital environment" (*Media Landscape South East Europe*, Press review, Retrieved March 1, 2016 from www.kas.de/medien-europe).

2015: 7). In addition, the acts also formulate some conclusions about the state of PSM in Europe. The picture is varied as it represents European PSM being at different stages of development. There are still public service broadcasters that have not accomplished the objectives laid out in the Recommendation on the remit of public service media in the information society (Council of Europe, 2007). The instrument formulated three major goals the PSM regulation should pursue:

- To guarantee the fundamental role of the public service media in the new digital environment, setting a clear remit for public service media (…);
- To include, where they have not already done so, provisions in their legislation/regulations specific to the remit of public service media, covering in particular the new communication services, thereby enabling public service media to make full use of their potential and especially to promote broader democratic, social and cultural participation (…);
- To guarantee public service media, via a secure and appropriate financing and organisational framework, the conditions required to carry out the function entrusted to them by member states in the new digital environment, in a transparent and accountable manner (…) (Council of Europe, 2007).

The fact that in Europe there still exist public media organizations that have not been transformed into PSM serves as a proof that regulation has not been attuned properly to the requirements of the digital environment. Digitization as a process can alleviate the situation to some extent but special measures are needed to adapt the PSM remit to the demands of the Internet age.

A recent survey on the online activities of PSM, has an optimistic view about the future of PSM on the web, basing its conclusions on the experience in 16 European countries where the legislation not only "empowers but instructs the public service operators to provide content online" (IRIS, 2015: 26). However, despite these 16 advanced countries there are many others where transition is difficult due to social and political reasons where much more efforts on the part of society are needed to complete reforms. According to the same survey, the legal instruments in force in some countries provide for the PSM online remit in very general or vague terms (IRIS, 2015: 27). From the perspective of PSM digital offerings, Leurdijk (2006) argues that though public service broadcasters expand their activities to digital platforms still existing legal limitations and modest budgets undermine the stability of these projects.

Exploring PSM functions, Lund and Nissen (2014) emphasize three challenges in the process of adjusting to digital conditions – adapting PSM production to the new internet formats and interactive discussions, stepping into the internet distribution of content and providing free news services on highly ranked portals and changing consumption habits of audiences orienting them towards "personalized services provided in non-linear, interactive Internet environments" (Lund and Nissen, 2014: 32–33). These are more specific objectives which require additional internal organizational measures. Lund and Nissen (2014) rightly observe that the central position of the PSM institution depends on clearly defined policies and approaches. A regulatory framework building on the principles of good regulation and reflecting the demands of the information society with respect to people, organizations and communities is essential to assure the implementation of such policies.

Participation and the public sphere

Any regulatory frameworks in the digital environment should foster public input and participation. Moreover, wider public involvement in various spheres makes possible networking to become a real driving force. The future of the public sphere "is with the digital media, which offer exciting possibilities as digital networks enhance and change social structures" (Boeder, 2005: n.p.). In line with this, Jakubowicz (2013: 193) argues that PSM has to create an international/global public sphere to compensate for the democratic deficit at local and regional level. Such an ambitious project transcends national borders and requires intense international collaboration. In the digital environment, the accomplishment of this objective can count on the capacity of the networking arrangements.

In the same direction of thought, the Council of Europe (2012b) explicitly refers to the broader democratic function of PSM in the digital age aiming at creating a vibrant European public sphere and fostering democratic citizenship within European societies. These goals are interrelated and mutually reinforcing. An active public sphere can be constructed through the plurality of voices of active citizens that openly state their position on matters of public concern. Keane (1992) shares the view that big public service institutions have to be replaced by a multitude of public service broadcasters that can function independently from the public and commercial realm supported by civil society. The realization of this idea calls for strong legal and political guarantees for the independent status, stable organization and financial assurance of these media. Keane's suggestion is similar to some extent to the concept of distributed public service according to which, the public function and not the institutional structure matters for the achievement of PSM goals[8]. However, what Keane apparently had in mind is a

---

8 In the contemporary pluralist environment, the public service can be carried out for instance, by platforms and services performing as media fulfilling a range of socially

new type of PSM which is more open, flexible and participatory and represents the civil society at large. This type of ideal democratic model seems more plausible to be successfully accomplished in a network setting where diverse participants at various levels contribute to the achievement of the public service mission. In practice the reforming of the existing PSM institutions making them more publicly oriented could lead to a similar outcome. EBU's Vision 2020 project states "we must reinvent PSM, in the sense that we translate the values and the remit to inform, educate and entertain, within the new context of a networked society. We must develop new roles, we must empower, curate and share, and connect with audiences, public institutions, cultural industries and areas of civic society that deliver public value" (EBU, 2014: 7). The document outlines the novel functions and possible allies of PSM in the digital society, which have to be reflected by regulation.

In order to preserve the PSM central position in the multidimensional media environment, frameworks have to provide for concrete channels for public participation in the creation of content and in the decision-making processes at all levels – public consultations, hearings, content contribution, programme proposals, platforms for public input, etc. Public involvement in content creation is of particular importance. Users as citizens have the right and obligation to monitor programme making and to decide whether content satisfies their needs and eventually embodies their values. The constitution of programming and advisory councils of a new kind operating on a constant or an ad hoc basis and being connected with the public via specific platforms or the social media is an example of the larger public involvement in decision-making.

The Council of Europe recommendation (Council of Europe 2012b) proposes international cooperation on a pan-European scale enhancing the exchange of best practice and best content to accomplish a pluralist and vibrant public sphere in Europe. The concepts of best practice and best content embrace both organizational ideas and co-production. This type of professional communication can generate the potential to turn PSM into a "developmental enterprise" (Lowe, 2016) and contribute to the establishment of a working public sphere based on values. Craig distinguishes among various types of networks ranging from government networks to national networks, of a horizontal and vertical character and asserts

relevant obligations. They can cooperate and complement each other. It is problematic, however, if the public service is distributed whether the media subjects can have the capacity to discharge an integrated and comprehensive remit typical for traditional PSM.

that networks prevail in international relations facilitating greatly international cooperation (Craig, 2015: 570–571).

There are various networks supporting the media, including emerging PSM. Some of them are evolving on the basis of conferences and meetings or are promoting scholarly and journalistic sharing (as the popular @RIPE initiative of the RIPE Global PSM network or the recently structured, in 2015, Mediapowermonitor.com). These networks are valuable centres for exchange of ideas and research and they can elaborate novel approaches to PSM regulation. By and large, the networks can promote collaboration for the construction of an efficient international public sphere and PSM can become a central factor sustaining such public sphere. Due to its unique role and membership, the EBU can serve as a centre of the networks' based exchange encouraging dialogue and professional, information and harmonization cooperation among different stakeholders.

Innovative leadership

Harnessing innovation at all levels – e.g. legal drafting, governance, human resources, and in leadership is crucial for the establishment of new PSM regulation. The already cited OECD/Eurostat (2005) covers a broad range of forms of innovation. Essentially, innovation comprises the implementation of a significantly improved or totally new product, process, method, organization or practice. In the organizational context that encompasses structures and culture, innovation is linked to positive changes in efficiency, productivity and quality (OECD/Eurostat, 2005: 206).

From an internal perspective the purpose of any organization is to find the appropriate approaches and means to transform innovative activity into tangible performance improvements and to reach better results. Externally to apply innovative regulation means to implement more advanced regulation which counts on novel ideas and practices. Innovative regulatory approaches with regard to PSM presume good understanding of the technology impact over regulation, enhancing efficiency and competitiveness of the enterprise, streamlining regulations in the field by removing administrative burdens and boosting managerial culture.

However, the accomplishment of these objectives is not an easy task. Experts claim that creative and effective organizations do not emerge by accident. These types of organizations rely on leaders to contemplate the changes, to find adequate tools for implementing them and to bring them to completion (Agbor, 2008: 39). Without creative leaders, reforms cannot be successfully brought to fruition. Leadership should not be perceived as a one-person initiative. In a complex society, like the information society, one of the trends adopted by leaders should be to "spread leadership capacity throughout the organization and democratize leadership" (Petrie, 2014: 6). With the technological and social shifts an innovative regulatory culture relying on effectiveness and creativity in an era of general uncertainty and financial difficulties is considered a powerful factor for reforms. PSM regulation should embrace such new regulatory culture (Council of Europe, 2012b).

PSM organizations should represent structures that stimulate innovative ideas and support creative effort. These aspirations are rooted in the public service values that underpin regulatory, managerial and production activities. Vision 2020 underlines that PSM should become more open, creative and decentralized and in order to achieve this it needs new managerial procedures and different leadership styles (EBU, 2014). In greater detail this means that "it's clearly vital today for PSM managers and makers to become masters in handling relations with the people they are required to serve in their varied identities – as consumers, as citizens, as audiences, as users, as communities, and so forth" (Lowe, 2016: 9). Regulatory frameworks should promote all these new paths to innovation at all PSM management levels – organizational, relationships with stakeholders, at the level of leadership, staff relationships, decision-making and relations with multiple stakeholders. Networks (personal, expert, academic) can support innovative leadership activating latent knowledge and making popular individual experiences and solutions.

Conclusions

Public service media (PSM) regulation should be modernized to suit the digital age and to respond adequately to the challenges of a dynamic environment. The network paradigm is an option for the democratization of traditional regulation and its orientation towards more intensive cooperation at a national and global level and informal communication. The network paradigm has been used in various contexts signifying a more open, participatory-oriented and connected regulation. However, this approach needs more consistent research to ascertain whether or not it is really viable. Another point is how networks in regulation relate to the mechanisms of the democratic state and to what extent they enhance the efficiency of these mechanisms or undermine them. What PSM need today are genuine reforms, which regulatory frameworks have to facilitate. However, changes can bring results if PSM independence and funding are preserved and sustained in the digital environment, and digitization does not serve as a pretext for switching back to governmental control.

In the article three challenging areas for the new PSM regulation have been discussed – expanding the PSM mission to reach various services and platforms, wider public involvement through a vibrant international public sphere and innovative leadership. Networks can be efficient channels for public input and participation and they can bring in new ideas and practices giving impetus to innovative solutions and innovative leadership in particular. On the one hand, the network approach can enrich regulatory mechanisms transcending states and bodies and on the other, networks can complement traditional forms of regulation providing additional expertise, involvement and inspiration for changes. Notwithstanding their democratizing effect, it is naive to think that the network paradigm alone can promote positive changes in the PSM sector without applying the classical regulatory tools. However, networks can successfully avoid the administrative burdens, speed up information exchange and generally improve regulation.

In the context of regulation in the light of the reforms in the PSM sector, which are deemed inevitable for the advancement of PSM organizations, there are shortcomings of the approaches. The overall problem with regulation is that to a great extent regulatory inertia creates a state of mind that avoids or delays reforms. In a time of rapid global change and transformation in economic and social conditions, the old type of regulation can become a serious obstacle to achieving economic and social well-being in the given sphere for which it is intended. Besides, new paradigms, such as the network paradigm, are not well known among policy makers and are not considered reliable alternatives for improvement. Still a division exists between the technical approach, which depends on digital technologies, and the administrative approach backed by legal norms, which in the digital world exist as two dimensions that have to complement each other and operate together. Another obstacle to rapid and timely reforms pertains to the lack of clear vision how to make knowledge in all spheres and at all levels a real force. More specific problems comprise impediments to innovation, barriers to economic efficiency, influence of vested interests seeking protection from competition and generally outdated or ill designed regulations that fail to accomplish policy goals. The precise cost of failure to reform is hard to measure but its impact can be substantial. In the case of PSM, these disadvantages of regulation are combined with the protectionism and politicization that have been looming over these organizations for many years, and in some countries have been continuing. In the European countries, various regulatory experiences exist and good models are not always transferable from one state to another due to the different traditions, cultures and state of democracy. The contribution of PSM to democratic development, culture and education is huge but the time has come when these conservative institutions have to be replaced by dynamic and efficient enterprises through frameworks promoting new governance and active public attitude.

Last but not least, paradigms and frameworks are of benefit, but most important is their implementation. What really matters at the end of the day is who will turn these frameworks into live practice, and how. In order for a novel regulation matching the needs of the digital environment to become effective, we need new leadership, enlightened minds, unbiased people with clear understanding and courage that are capable of carrying out radical transformations in the PSM sector. A strong will, creativity and openness are necessary, particularly at the level of policy making to attune it to the requirements of the digital age.

References

Agbor, E. (2008). Creativity and innovation: the leadership dynamics. *Journal of Strategic Leadership*, Vol. 1, N. 1, 2008: 39–45. Retrieved July 20, 2016 from http://www.regent.edu/acad/global/publications/jsl/vol1iss1/JSL_Vol1iss1_Agbor.pdf.

Ayres, I., and J. Braithwaite (1992). *Responsive regulation*. New York: Oxford University Press.

Baldwin, R. (2010). Better regulation: the search and the struggle. In: R. Baldwin, M. Cave, and M. Lodge (eds.), *The Oxford Handbook of Regulation*. Oxford, New York: Oxford University Press, 259–279.

Baldwin, R., and M. Cave (1999). *Understanding regulation*. Oxford: Oxford University Press.

Baldwin, R., C. Scott, and C. Hood (1998). Introduction. In: R. Baldwin, C. Scott, and C. Hood (eds.), *Reader on regulation*. Oxford: Oxford, University Press, 1–55.

Better regulation task force. Principles of good regulation. Retrieved July 20, 2016 from http://webarchive.nationalarchives.gov.uk/20100407162704/http:/archive.cabinetoffice.gov.uk/brc/upload/assets/www.brc.gov.uk/principlesleaflet.pdf.

Boeder, P. (2005). Habermas' heritage. The future of the public sphere in the network society. *Press – Reviewed Journal on the Internet,* Volume 10, N 9 – 5, September 2005. Retrieved July 20, 2016 from http://firstmonday.org/ojs/index.php/fm/article/view/1280/1200#p8.

Borzel, T. (1998). Organizing Babylon – on the different conceptions of policy networks. *Public administration*, Vol. 76 (2): 253–273.

Burnley, R. (2015). *Legal focus: Public funding principles for public service media*. Geneva: European Broadcasting Union.

Castells, M. (2000). Toward a sociology of the Network Society. *Contemporary Sociology*, Vol. 29 (5): 693–699.

Council of Europe (2007). *Recommendation CM/Rec (2007)3 of the Committee of Ministers to member states on the remit of public service media in the information society (Adopted by the Committee of Ministers on 31 January 2007at the 985th meeting of the Ministers' Deputies)*. Retrieved July 20, 2016 from https://wcd.coe.int/ViewDoc.jsp?id=1089759.

Council of Europe (2011). *Recommendation CM/Rec(2011)7of the Committee of Ministers to member states on a new notion of media (Adopted by the Committee of Ministers on 21 September 2011 at the 1121st meeting of the Ministers' Deputies)*. Retrieved July 20, 2016 from https://wcd.coe.int/ViewDoc.jsp?id=1835645.

Council of Europe (2012a). *Declaration of the Committee of Ministers on public service media governance (Adopted by the Committee of Ministers on 15 February 2012 at the 1134th meeting of the Ministers' Deputies)*. Retrieved July 20, 2016 from https://wcd.coe.int/ViewDoc.jsp?id=1908241.

Council of Europe (2012b). *Recommendation CM/Rec(2012) 1 of the Committee of Ministers to member Stateson public service media governance (Adopted by the Committee of Ministers on 15 February 2012 at the 1134th meeting of the Ministers' Deputies)*. Retrieved July 20, 2016 from https://wcd.coe.int/ViewDoc.jsp?id=1908265.

Council of Europe (2013). *Resolution N2: Preserving the essential role of media in the digital age, Council of Europe Conference of Ministers responsible for Media and Information Society "Freedom of expression and democracy in the digital age: opportunities, rights, responsibilities"*, November 7–8, 2013, Belgrade. Retrieved July 20, 2016 from http://www.coe.int/fr/web/secretary-general/speeches/-/asset_publisher/gFMvl0SKOUrv/content/council-of-europe-conference-of-ministers-responsible-for-media-and-information-society?_101_INSTANCE_gFMvl0SKOUrv_viewMode=view/.

Craig, P. (2006). *EU Administrative law*. Academy of European Law, European University Institute: Oxford; New York, USA: Oxford University Press.

Craig, P. (2015). *UK, EU and global administrative law. Foundations and challenges*. Cambridge: Cambridge University Press.

Eberle, C.E. (2002). *The regulation of public service broadcasting*. Retrieved July 20, 2016 from http://www.epra.org/attachments/ljubljana-plenary-1-the-regulation-of-psb-keynote.

EBU (2012). *Empowering society. A Declaration on the Core Values of Public Service Media*. Geneva: European Broadcasting Union.

EBU (2014). *Connecting to a networked society – Vision 2020 Continuous improvement of trust and return on society*. Retrieved July 20, 2016 from https://www3.ebu.ch/files/live/sites/ebu/files/Publications/EBU-Vision2020-Full_report_EN.pdf.

EBU (2015). Vision 2020. *Connect, grow and influence*. Retrieved July 20, 2016 from https://www.ebu.ch/files/live/sites/ebu/files/Publications/EBU-Vision2020-Connect_EN.pdf.

Głowacki, M., and L. Jackson (2014). Towards a twenty-first century public media: conclusions. In: M. Głowacki, and L. Jackson (eds.), *Public media management for the Twenty-first Century: Creativity, innovation and interaction*. New York and London: Routledge, 271–289.

Hancher, L., and M. Moran (1989). Organising regulatory space. In: L. Hancher and M. Moran (eds.), *Capitalism, Culture and Economic Regulation*. Oxford: Clarendon, 271–299.

IRIS (2015). *Online activities of public service media: remit and financing*. Strasbourg: European Audiovisual Observatory.

Jakubowicz, K. (2009). *A new notion of media?* Media and Information Society Division, Directorate General of Human Rights and Legal Affairs: Council of Europe.

Jakubowicz, K. (2010). From PSB to PSM: A new promise for public service provision in the information society, In: B. Klimkiewicz (ed.), *Media Freedom and Pluralism. Media Policy Challenges in the Enlarged Europe*. Budapest – New York: CEU – Press, 193–227.

Jakubowicz, K. (2013). *Media and democracy in the 21st Century. Searching for new models. Special edition*. Warsaw: Poltext Ltd.

Jaskiernia, A. (2015). Co-decision and legitimization. In: A. Jaskiernia, and M. Głowacki, *Democratization of media policy in the digital ecosystems – the case of Poland*. Report from scientific seminar at the University of Warsaw (October 17, 2014). Warsaw: ASPRA-JR.

Karmasin, M., and D. Kraus (2014). Strategies for stakeholder management and crowdsourcing. In: M. Głowacki, and L. Jackson (eds.), *Public media management for the Twenty-first Century: Creativity, Innovation and Interaction*. New York and London: Routledge, 59–77.

Keane, J. (1991). *The media and democracy*. Cambridge: Polity Press.

Krewel, M. (2015). Autonomy and regulatory frameworks of public service media. Diverging scenarios in a Europe of different levels. In: K.A. Ibarra, E. Novak and R. Kuhn (eds.), *Public service media in Europe. A comparative approach*. London and New York: Routledge, 126–146.

Leurdijk, A. (2006). *Public service broadcasting dilemma's and regulation in a converging media landscape*. Paper for RIPE conference. Retrieved July 20, 2016 from http://ripeat.org/wp-content/uploads/2010/03/Leurdijk.pdf.

Lodge, M. (2004). *Accountability and transparency in regulation: critiques, doctrines and instruments*. Retrieved July 20, 2016 from http://regulation.upf.edu/reg-network/papers/lodge2.pdf.

Lowe, G.F. (2016). *PSM in the 21st century: What value and which values?* Retrieved July 20, 2016 from https://www3.ebu.ch/files/live/sites/ebu/files/Publications/EBU-MIS%20-%20PSM%20in%20the%2021st%20Century%20-%20What%20Value%20and%20Which%20Values.pdf.

Lund, A.B., and C. Nissen (2014). Three challenges and a fine kept balance. In: *Public value report 2013/14*. Vienna: ORF: 31–33.

Maggetti, M., and F. Gilardi (2014). *Network governance and the domestic adoption of soft rules*. Retrieved July 20, 2016 from http://www.fabriziogilardi.org/resources/papers/Maggetti-Gilardi-JEPP-2014.pdf.

Marinov, O. (2015). Public values and administrative reforms. *Conservative quarterly*, Institute for right policy, year 1, volume 3/4: 20–53 (in Bulgarian).

Nissen, C. (2011). Innovation – a sketch for discussion. In: *Appendix, Ad hoc advisory group on public service media governance (MC-S-PG)*. Strasbourg: Council of Europe.

Nowak, E., and R. Kuhn (2015). Public service media in Europe: Diversity as a challenge. In: K. Arriaza Ibarra, E. Novak, and R. Kuhn (eds.), *Public service media in Europe. A comparative approach*. London and New York: Routledge, 3–8.

OECD (2005). *Guiding principles for regulatory quality and performance*. Retrieved July 20, 2016 from http://www.oecd.org/fr/reformereg/34976533.pdf.

OECD/Eurostat (2005). *Oslo Manual Guidelines for Collecting and Interpreting Innovation Data, 3rd Edition*. Retrieved July 20, 2016 from http://www.keepeek.com/Digital-Asset-Management/oecd/science-and-technology/oslo-manual_9789264013100-en#page97.

OECD (n.p.). *Regulatory reform and innovation*. Retrieved July 20, 2016 from http://www.oecd.org/sti/inno/2102514.pdf.

PACE (2012). *Report: The state of media freedom in Europe*. Retrieved July 20, 2016 from http://assembly.coe.int/nw/xml/XRef/X2H-Xref-iewPDF.asp?FileID=19177&lang=en.

Petrie, N. (2014). *Future trends in leadership development*. Retrieved July 20, 2016 from http://insights.ccl.org/wp-content/uploads/2015/04/futureTrends.pdf.

Raboy, M. (1997). Public service broadcasting in the context of globalization. In: D. Atkinson, and M. Raboy (eds.), *Public service broadcasting: the challenges of the 21st century*. UNESCO Publishing, 77–91.

Raboy, M. (2003). National, transnational and global approaches to public service media. In: M. Price, and M. Raboy (eds.), *Public service broadcasting in transition. A documentary reader.* Kluwer Law International, The Hague/London/New York, 180–195.

Scott, C. (2001). Analysing regulatory space: Fragmented resources and institutional design, *Public law*, Summer: 329–252.

Scott, C. (2010). Regulatory governance and the challenge of constitutionalism. In: D. Oliver, T. Prosser, and R. Rawlings (eds.), *The regulatory state: constitutional implications*. Oxford: Oxford University Press, 15–33.

Soete, L. (2005). Innovation, technology and productivity: why Europe lags behind the United States and why various European economies differ in innovation and productivity. In: M. Castells, and G. Cardoso (eds.), *The network society. From knowledge to policy*. Washington, DC: Johns Hopkins Center for transatlantic relationships, 125–148.

Wagner, M., and A.K. Berg (2015). *Legal focus: Governance principles for public service media.* Geneva: European Broadcasting Union.

Zankova, B. (2013). *Regulation in the new media environment – problems, risks and challenges from the perspective of the experience in five European democratic countries*. Retrieved February 20, 2016 from http://liternet.bg/publish28/bisera-zankova/reguliraneto-en.htm.

Zankova, B. (2014). Governance, accountability and transparency of public service media in a contemporary mediatised world: the case of Bulgaria. In: M. Głowacki, and L. Jackson (eds.), *Public media management for the Twenty-first Century: Creativity, innovation and interaction*. New York and London: Routledge, 125–142.

Tim Raats and Karen Donders
Vrije Universiteit Brussel, Belgium

Public service media and partnerships: analysis of policies and strategies in Flanders

Abstract: In recent years media policy-makers, scholars and public broadcasters (PSB) have increasingly been defining their role in relation to the surrounding media ecosystem. The chapter evaluates to what extent the policy rhetoric and actions within this ecosystem approach are driven by public value or rather market sustainability arguments, and to what extent they provide a case for sustainability of public service media in a networked environment. The chapter therefore contextualizes the ecosystem approach within the broader perspectives of the media welfare state and the Digital Commons, and presents an in-depth case study of Flanders, where the role of PSB has been increasingly tied to partnerships and ecosystems. The authors argue that an exploration of value beyond PSB merits further attention. However current ecosystem provisions are mainly driven by protecting existing players' business models rather than by broader public objectives and an assessment of the content worth sustaining in the ecosystem.

Keywords: public service media, media policy, ecosystems, partnerships and collaboration, VRT.

Introduction

The remit of public service broadcasting (PSB) has traditionally been defined from a public interest perspective. Public service broadcasters were granted government funding and legitimacy based on a public remit, which consisted of a combination of core tasks for PSB – information, education, entertainment, etc. – and a series of core values (diversity, universality, quality, trust, etc.) (Blumler, 1992; Raboy, 1996; Tracey, 1998; McCauley et al., 2003; Lowe and Martin, 2014). This status grants and obliges PSB to indulge in services for specific target groups or to invest in cost-intensive specialized content for relatively small audiences. Adopting a case for public service media (PSM) in a multiplatform era, media scholars highlighted the need for large-scale reforms, while staying true to this traditional PSB rationale (Bardoel and d'Haenens, 2008; Debrett, 2010; Steemers, 2015).

In recent years however, media policy-makers, scholars and most notably PSBs, have increasingly been defining their role in relation to the surrounding media ecosystem. In such a perspective, PSM should use their position to sustain or strengthen market activities, stretching their role from the public interest to the surrounding ecosystem, with PSM serving as standard for quality of the output of other broadcasters and producers,[1] and as a 'lever' for market innovation, developing creativity and sustaining a flourishing production sector (Barwise and Picard, 2014; EBU, 2014; Donders and Raats, 2015; Raats and Donders, 2015). In the United Kingdom for example, ever since its Second Public Broadcasting Review, Ofcom continuously emphasized PSM's indispensable role in maintaining the amount, originality and quality of domestic television fiction in the UK. In recent work of, among others, Barwise and Picard (2014) (see also Davies, 2005, 2013; Doyle and Paterson, 2008; BBC, 2013) acknowledged this pivotal role of PSM in sustaining domestic programming, as their research convincingly argues that the consequences of decreased PSM spending on television fiction would be detrimental for the entire UK audiovisual sector. In line with other PSBs in Europe, Norway's NRK recently increased its commitments towards the creative industries, most commonly articulated in an uptake of external commissioning. RTE in Ireland on the other hand, increased its commitments towards innovation, aiming to serve as a hub for creative, media and technological innovation, amongst others through collaboration with universities and startups.

This chapter questions to what extent the idea of an ecosystem approach merely serves a rhetoric purpose and pragmatic agenda aimed at sustaining market activities, or to what extent it provides a case for PSM's role in a networked society and market.

The chapter therefore firstly, aims to ground the idea of an ecosystem to more theoretical ideals of PSB in a networked media society (i.e. Graham Murdock's Digital Commons perspective) and the conceptualization of value from a market player perspective (i.e. the Media Welfare perspective, Syvertsen et al., 2014). Second, setting out from an in-depth case study of Flanders, we analyze how ecosystems are articulated and motivated in policy rhetoric, and the domains and types of action that are listed in policymakers strategic and policy notes and management contracts following from them. We build on evidence from Flanders, that has over the past decade undergone a shift in policy and strategy towards partnerships, coined under the label of an ecosystem approach. Thirdly, the chapter evaluates to what extent the aformentioned policy rhetoric and actions are driven by public value or rather market sustainability arguments and to what extent they can be linked with broader views on public service media's role and legitimacy in the current media landscape.

---

1 This is an often repeated argument in 2015/2016 debates on the Charter renewal in the UK.

In Flanders (the Dutch-speaking part of Belgium, comprising approximately 6 million inhabitants), the public service remit is the responsibility of the Vlaamse Radio- en Televisieomroep (VRT). The ecosystem approach was heavily promoted during the terms of the previous Minister of Media (2009–2014) as well as the current (2014–2019). As such, we investigate which arguments in Flanders have been made in order to make the case for an ecosystem approach, and which voices have been mostly articulated and how an ecosystem approach is translated into practice. The Flemish market displays the characteristics of small nations (restricted number of players, limited export and small domestic market, language differences) (Puppis et al., 2009; McElroy and Noonan, 2016), but at the same time shows high proportions of domestic programming and viewing, has a flourishing production sector and a strong position of its PSB – VRT (Raats et al., 2016).

The case study builds on a qualitative document analysis (close reading) (Karppinen and Moe, 2012), including various sources related to official policy, regulation and strategy statements. Our analysis is based on a selection of key policy and VRT documents relating to the management contract and its renewal. The VRT management contract is negotiated every 5 years and stipulates the mission, tasks, and financial and programatoric obligations of the VRT. The document analysis includes two consultations conducted in preparation of the management contract (2010, 2015), the four management contracts of the VRT (2002–2006, 2007–2011, 2012–2016, 2016–2020), two 'vision notes' prepared as part of the negotations process in 2010 and 2015, and reports of two 'States-General for Media' that took place during the previous legislative periods. Aside from the policy documents of Flanders, the chapter draws on a literature review and further includes documents, press statements and policy reports in other markets, such as the Netherlands and the United Kingdom.

The chapter argues that an exploration of public value beyond public broadcasting merits attention. However, a focus on market sustainability and economic relevance of PSB could, when insufficiently tied to public interest ambitions and a broader notion of ecosystem, pave the way for a strict market failure approach whereby the public remit is merely instrumental and public interest objectives are gradually eroded. In such a perspective, an ecosystem approach fosters a market oriented approach whereby public value is considered 'pivotal' as long as it does not distort market players' activities.

Contextualizing the ecosystem approach

What we coin as the ecosystem approach in this chapter is based on the use of the term in Flemish policy rhetoric. The term is not systematically pinpointing to a specific set of guidelines or obligations; nor does it refer to a fixed set of policy actions or clearly spelled-out form of media governance. Nevertheless, what could be considered part of an ecosystem approach is discernable in the policy discourse of various Western European markets, whereby partnership is often the common denominator. Consequently, in order to pinpoint what could be considered part of that approach, it is most helpful to look at the underlying motives that are being put forward, as well as the types of actions proposed as part of the ecosystem 'toolkit.'

On the initial level, the emphasis on PSM's role towards market players stems from increasing criticism on the position and activities of public broadcasters, which are according to most private players – especially in a digital environment – considered to be market distortive. Using PSB dominance as a lever rather than a break then fuels a pragmatic answer to respond to external criticism of third parties while at the same time preventing public broadcasters from radical curtailment. Especially when being confronted with large-scale transformations in their business models, cut-backs in advertising expenditure, new market entrants and shifted media use, policy-makers have been sensitive to arguments from traditional media players, most notably the publishers, producers and private broadcasters. As such, an ecosystem logic also follows a larger shift in media governance towards multi-stakeholderism and evidence-based policy-making (Aslama and Clark, 2013; Donders and Raats, 2012; Iosifidis, 2013). The BBC Trust for example commissioned large-scale consultancy reports estimating the net value of the BBC and its operations in the market (BBC Trust, 2008; Department of Culture, Media and Sport, 2015) and the European Broadcasting Union (2014) stresses the importance of measurable societal value.

On a second level, the articulation of an ecosystem approach follows a series of recent cutbacks on the level of PSBs. Often under the umbrella of increased improved collaboration and synergies, partnerships are being enforced as part of large-scale restructuring agendas. The BBC's 2010 license fee settlement, whereby the latter was frozen, partly came with increased partnership and joint ventures between the BBC and the Welsh S4C, Scottish STV and Gaelic Television. In the Netherlands, collaboration and efficiency were put forward in policy rhetoric to motivate an integration of local and regional broadcasters, previously operating autonomously, under the overarching structure of the NPO (Ministry of OCW, 2012a; 2012b; Raats, 2012).

On a third level, the ecosystem logic corresponds with a view where public value does not solely derive from public broadcasters alone, but by all players in the media market. The latter has been motivating decisions to explore forms of additional distributed public service provisions in the UK (see plans of the Public Service Publisher in 2007), or to provide additional funding for market players for broadcasting minority services, subtitling or children's and youngster's news programming (Donders and Raats, 2015; Raats and Donders, 2015). With regard to specific genres, such as regional news, TV drama and documentary or children's programming, policy-makers have launched mechanisms to sustain its provision. Especially the latter meaning, makes the ecosystem approach relevant for PSM scholars to further develop and explore to what extent it might benefit the continued provision of public value as well as the sustainability of high-quality, domestic and creative content.

As already noted above, while treating an ecosystem approach in its entirety to mainly serve a rhetorical use, it also refers to various commitments being proposed by policymakers, market players and public broadcasters as part of sustaining or strengthening market activities. These commitments are most clearly spelled out by private players, understandably as they set out from direct and short-term needs and requirements. Based on the demands made in stakeholder consultations in the Netherlands (Donders et al., 2010; Donders and Van den Bulck, 2012; Ministry of OCW, 2010; Raats et al., 2015; 2016; Van den Bulck and Donders, 2014), as well as proposals articulated by media regulators and policy-makers, such as Ofcom, the BBC Trust and the House of Commons Select Committee in the United Kingdom (see e.g. Ofcom, 2009; House of Commons, 2015), several types of commitment can be discerned (see Table 1).

Table 1: Commitments ecosystem approach

Type of commitment	Activities	Targeted market players
Content sharing	Sharing of audio-visual news, entertainment, documentary clips	Private broadcasters Publishers
Infrastructure sharing	Sharing of production facilities, studios, personnel, etc. for example with local and regional news providers	Publishers Broadcasters Producers
Platform and service sharing	Opening up on-demand services for other players; sharing standards and services with private players	Broadcasters Distributors
Strengthening independent production sector	Increased investments in external commissioning	Independent producers

Type of commitment	Activities	Targeted market players
Dialogue and consultation	Dialogue with various stakeholders (music industry, producers, right holders, distributors, etc.)	All actors in PSM value chain
Investments in technological innovation	Supporting start-ups	Technological players, broadcasters, distributors

Source: Authors.

Theoretical foundations for media ecosystems: public interest vs. market sustainability

Graham Murdock re-envisaged the cultural commons by connecting the role of PSM explicitly to a Digital Commons, which he describes as "a linked space defined by its shared refusal of commercial enclosure and its commitment to free and universal access, reciprocity, and collaborative activity" (Murdock, 2005: 227). From such a perspective, public broadcasters function as a "principal node in an emerging network of public and civic initiatives that taken together, provide the basis for a new shared cultural space (…)" (Murdock, 2004: 2). This idea of public broadcasters functioning as hubs has been clearly articulated in EBU's Vision2020 project. According to EBU (2014: 11):

> We must reinvent PSM, in the sense that we translate the values and the remit to inform, educate and entertain, within the new context of a networked society. We must develop new roles, we must empower, curate and share, and connect with audiences, public institutions, cultural industries and areas of civic society that deliver public value.

The EBU highlights collaboration with cultural organizations, public institutions and other actors to enlarge the scope of delivery and increase return-on-society. The organization sees the shift towards collaboration strongly coinciding with a shift "from a closed, or fortress-like institution to one that is open and connected to networks of people, communities, cultural organizations and civic society" (EBU, 2014: 12).

The aspect the Digital Commons perspective has in common with an ecosystem approach that it expands the role of PSM outside of the PSM institutions, amongst others by connecting public broadcasters with other public value content and information that is already – sometimes hidden – available on the web. A renewed partnership, both with the audience and public players is pivotal to achieve this Digital Commons. However, contrary to an ecosystem approach, Murdock stresses the importance of cooperation with museums, library, education and public institutions alike, to create this shared, public space (Murdock

2004; 2005). Indeed, the Digital Commons is rooted in forms of non-commercial collaboration and, more importantly, it sets out from a strong holistic and centralized public service institution that runs counter to models proposing distributed public service or that align market strengthening with limiting PSM. The question is whether a Digital Commons could be extended to include private, as well as commercial players (see Donders, 2011: 38). While seemingly presented here as an unproblematic alliance of public players, recent research has shown that, in practice, public broadcasters entering into partnerships with public players are also confronted with thresholds on legal, social and organizational levels, as well as power asymmetries between all players involved (Raats, 2014).

Aslama and Clark (2013: 171) also aimed to conceptualize media governance from the perspective of an ecosystem. They distinguish between an instrumental rationale for collaboration, pointing to the outcomes by sharing expertise and a process-based rationale, pointing to "the process of collaboration (as) desirable to enhance commitments and ownership." The latter builds on the work of Murdock in the sense that public value is not necessarily restricted to public broadcasters, but could be achieved by and in collaboration with other players (see also Moe and Van den Bulck, 2014). The argument furthermore hints at PSM being required to collaborate in the benefit of the whole ecosystem, with the former creating value that would not have been possible without collaboration. Lastly, from a strategic point of view, the argument also implies that public broadcasters could be involved in operations that do not necessarily benefit the public broadcaster, but the whole ecosystem.

To bypass dichotomous conceptions of public versus private, Collins (1998; 2011) introduces a public service communication perspective, stressing the importance of public value which newspapers and private broadcasting provide, and thereby legitimizing additional funding for public delivery, as was proposed by Ofcom in its 2006 Public Service Publisher (PSP) plans. Plans for the PSP were scrapped in 2010 following criticism concerning the questionable impact it might have, as well as the underlying premise it set out from. Freedman (2009: 110) described the PSP as "a way of seeing public service content not as a cultural or social phenomenon in its own right and with its own logic and values, but instead viewing it primarily in relation to the impact which it has on the wider media market." Nevertheless, in many countries, private broadcasters already secure funding for subtitling of news and other programming. Also the production of fiction, animation and documentary is supported by dedicated funds. More recently, the crisis of the newspaper industry, seeing advertising revenues migrate to the internet while online news aggregators are investing little to nothing in journalism, has provoked debates on the necessity of public funding for the press (see Collins, 2011; Pauwels and Picone, 2013; Schweizer et al., 2014).

A similar focus, where media value is approached from the totality of all media output provided by the sum of all media players in the landscape, was followed in the media welfare state project (Syvertsen et al., 2014), which set out to analyze media systems in the Nordic countries. More than a theoretical perspective, the media welfare state is a way to describe the media system in the Nordic countries, which is characterized by Interventionist cultural and media policies as well as strong social welfare. As such, it follows a regulatory approach where the public value of private broadcasters, production companies, telecom providers, and publishers, is also recognized by governments. As such, the media welfare state perspective makes a distinction between stakeholder and shareholder interests to pinpoint differences between private and public interests. Private media companies can also contribute to broader public interests. The perspective furthermore shows how media policy is inextricably linked to broader policy discussions and often reflects overarching values in society laid out in more generalist policies. Syvertsen et al. (2014) refer to the universality of key aspects reflected in PSB regulation: egalitarianism, the gender ratio in grants attributed, etc., 'personal liberties' (i.e. a strong editorial freedom and independence, as well as access to information), transformative policies, (i.e. in the sense of redistributive policies, considered as vehicles to transform society), and a cooperative/consensual culture (i.e. the explicit ideal that as many parties should agree on policies, that policies must include a broad variety of stakeholders).

Flanders and the ecosystem approach

Introducing the case of Flanders

In Belgium, the Flemish, French-speaking and German Communities are autonomously responsible for public service broadcasting (Voorhoof, 1995: 198), a separation that reflects the differences in market structure and cultural consumption in Belgium (Coppens, 2003: 148). In Flanders, VRT operates under a management contract agreed upon by the Flemish Government and VRT, which is renewed every 5 years. This contract determines a combination of qualitative (relating to quality and diversity of offers) and quantitative (notably key performance indicators relating to audience reach) obligations (Coppens and Sayes, 2003). With an average market share of 40 percent for television and 60 percent on radio, VRT holds a dominant position in the Flemish media landscape.

VRT operates in a small market next to its private competitors Medialaan and SBS Belgium (each having one popular generalist channel and one or more thematic channels), with a relatively small number of players. While independent production is fragmented heavily – consisting of more than 40 relatively small companies and a select number of key producers mostly linked to international brands or that are part of larger broadcasting conglomerates (e.g. Studio 100, Woestijnvis, Eyeworks) – the private broadcasters and publishers are highly concentrated. The main cable distributor Telenet (owned by US player Liberty Global) is the dominant shareholder of SBS Belgium. The proportion of domestic viewing and programmes in Flanders is considerable (Raats et al., 2016). Netflix was introduced at the end of 2014 and cable distributor Telenet has a relatively large number of pay-tv subscriptions (VRM, 2015).

From pax media to digital friction

The rhetoric of an ecosystem approach in Flanders should be understood in relation to a reconfiguration of power balances in the Flemish media market, following the start of gradual, but large-scale, shifts in the business models of traditional media players. For a relatively long time, broadcasters and media companies were still Belgian-owned and due to the importance of cable in the Flemish market, as well as its lack of scale, no significant pay-tv channels were operating in Flanders. The focus on balances, collaboration and dialogue actually predate an ecosystem approach and was already characteristic in policy discourse when the public monopoly was replaced with a comfortable duopoly allowing only one commercial broadcaster in Flanders. In the 1990s, following years of fierce competition between the public broadcaster and its sole competitor VTM (now Medialaan), an artificial 'pax media' was promoted in media policy and broadcasting rhetoric (Raats and Pauwels, 2013).

Today the pax media is rarely included in policy and broadcasting rhetoric, but the private broadcasters and public broadcasters share an understanding of healthy competition. This is apparent in their rhetoric as well, with VRT stating the importance of a strong private television competitor and Medialaan openly valuing qualitatively strong productions of its public counterpart, thereby portraying the VRT as a sort of 'necessary evil' in Flanders. However, there are still conflicts between the public service broadcaster and its commercial rivals, but they remain anecdotal or relate to areas for which there is a silent agreement to disagree. For example, on the legality of subsidies and the scope of the remit such an agreement to disagree exists and Medialaan (owning VTM) has not refrained – to the dislike of VRT – from filing a complaint against the funding of VRT with the European Commission's Directorate General for Competition (Donders, 2012).

Digitalization gradually changed the roles of cable distributors and telecom operators in Flanders, allowing them to include content packages and channels in their portfolio and leading to increased competition with traditional broadcasters. In 2008, heated debates on the lack of remuneration for transmission fees (Donders and Evens, 2010) caused tensions between all broadcasters and the cable distributor Telenet. With a media landscape increasingly confronted with this hybridization of roles and power positions, with new players potentially entering domestic markets, a shift in media use and a decline on advertising revenue, the focus on the ecosystem as a whole and not just the sum of its parts was gradually introduced by policymakers.

An ecosystem approach driven by collaboration

The VRT management contract 2002–2006 (VRT and Flemish Government, 2001) already mentioned specific areas for dialogue and collaboration (sports, science and culture), but remained very modest in terms of specific action. The 2007–2011 management contract more clearly formalized commitments for investments with the independent production sector, and added an ambitious partnership with the cultural sector as part of a multi-platform cultural delta, a plan that later proved more difficult to realize in practice and that resulted in a cultural website based on collaboration (VRT and Flemish Government 2006; 2007).

It was not until the policy letter launched by the Minister for Media, Ingrid Lieten, in 2009 that the idea of an ecosystem approach was launched in rhetoric. The policy letter emphasized collaboration to the benefit of the whole Flemish media landscape, highlighting amongst other partnerships those for technological innovation and sufficient investment in independent production (Ministry of the Flemish Government, 2009). These ideas were undoubtedly informed by increasing pressure from the third party private competitors of the VRT. In another vision note 2010, preceding the negotiations for the 2012–2016 management contract, the role of VRT was explicitly tied to its surrounding ecosystem and was henceforth described as both challenger and partner in the Flemish media landscape (Lieten, 2010). The vision note proposed a stakeholder strategy to address the challenges of today's media landscape, emphasizing the strength of the VRT as driving force for audio-visual production, as a standard for quality and services. Furthermore, the note emphasized the need for a multi-stakeholder approach in defining the tasks of VRT, in order to respect the role and values of private players' activities, and thirdly, it emphasized partnership as key (Lieten, 2010).

Two aspects were characteristic in policy rhetoric. The first is a focus on dialogue and consensus as part of the policy-making process. This resulted amongst others in the instalment of the Flemish Sector Council for Media mid-2000s, fostering dialogue amongst all important media players, independent academic experts and civil society organizations, as well as the launch of stakeholder consultations as part of each management contract renewal of the VRT. However, neither actions stemmed directly from a clear-cut decision to include partners, but from the national adaptation of new regulation in the European Broadcasting Communication (Donders and Raats, 2012; Donders and Van den Bulck, 2012).

The second aspect is a clear focus on partnerships and collaboration on the level of PSB. In contrast to, for example, the BBC (Raats, 2012; BBC, 2009), a call for more collaboration was proposed by government and third parties rather than the public broadcaster itself, most notably resounded in calls from the cultural sector, education, and civil society organization. However, market players such as regional broadcasters (private-owned in Belgium), publishers and private broadcasters gradually called for a VRT that is more open for collaboration as part of supporting market initiative.

Interestingly, the emphasis on partnerships also reflects a defensive attitude of the incumbents towards digitalization and convergence as part of maintaining the strong positions in the market, and safeguarding revenue from advertising and content, from going to foreign players as Google, YouTube and Netflix. Concerns amongst Flemish players for the advent of Netflix and the loss of advertising revenue to third party players such as YouTube were key concerns at the three Staten Generaals voor de Media [State General for Media], which were gatherings organized by the Minister for Media. Collaboration was considered essential to face the challenges and the idea of a shared fate, common adversaries and common challenges (Lieten, 2010; Staten-Generaal 2011). Here, collaboration with private players was put forward as a means to foster consensus rather than conflict in the media landscape, by using the position of VRT as lever for private players and calling for collaboration in domains where private players claimed the VRT was market distortive or too dominant. This was for example the case for the online news provision, where publishers felt the online free access news offer of the VRT is market distortive for the online offer of newspapers. Collaboration in the form of sharing of audio-visual content was hence proposed on various occasions.

The call for collaboration was re-confirmed a short while later in a large-scale consultation of 85 stakeholders (including press, producers, private broadcasters and regional broadcasters) (Donders et al., 2010) that underpinned an unambiguous demand for more partnerships from the VRT. Based on this consultation, the Sector Council for Media launched its formal advice that amongst others demanded sharing of content with private players, and collaboration in the eco-system for media-innovation. Since then, the term ecosystem (and its alternatives, such as media ecology) was picked up widely in policy discourse and press coverage (Sectorraad Media, 2010: 13–14).

It is not, therefore, a surprise that the 2012–2016 management contract that resulted from these negotiations, put partnership to the forefront. Collaboration was considered one of the core pillars of the VRT (next to quality, innovation, transparency, and so on). Much attention is devoted to a formalization of dialogue and consultation in the form of stakeholder management. However, the contract revealed much more than a clear and strategic key objective in everything VRT does. A series of proposed partnerships were included in various parts of the management contract, with the domains of partnerships clearly reflecting the voices of the ones heard most in the negotiations. Dialogue with stakeholders in culture, sports, regional broadcasting, youth organizations, diversity representatives, music, producers and creative talent, universities and archive institutions, are all included to have some sort of annual dialogue. While commitments with the cultural sector were clear and elaborately described, much less clear are the various commitments with private players. The contract emphasizes that collaboration with regional players 'should be explored' (*translated citation*), where possible news content should be shared with other private partners, and VRT should increase transparency towards its private counterparts. Consequently, the management contract can be seen as the ultimate compromise between VRT and its opponents, with a management contract where every stakeholder finds some concessions and with the VRT maintaining control – reflected in the vagueness of its formulations – over strategic decisions to collaborate with private players.

The media cabinet pushed that an on-demand iPlayer-like service from VRT would be developed in a collaborative model with private players, rather than VRT launching the service on its own. However, conflicting interests and legal boundaries caused this to be more difficult than presumed, and lead to a more modest service Stievie that presented on-demand offer on tablets and smartphones. Collaboration was also put to the forefront in the establishment of the Media Innovation Expertise Center (MIX) that decentralized part of the VRT R&D department and replaced it with a call-based research programme based on collaboration with and between market players. Again, while backed by practically all private players, the outcome and impact of MIX was relative, and the centre ceased existence in 2015.

From collaboration to market strengthening and distinctiveness

Similar to the previous stakeholder consultation, in the 2015 consultation conducted prior to the negotiations on the new VRT management contract, collaboration resounded from regional and private broadcasters, publishers, producers, and media startups. Clearly, media players touched upon the role of VRT as a 'market strengthen-*er*.' The term was picked up in public hearings by parliamentarians and lobbyists during the negotiations, and was even picked up by VRT as well in communicating its core priorities with the media Cabinet (Raats et al., 2016). On a first level it can be considered an articulation of the VRT as a lever for sustaining valuable content and services within the ecosystem, on a second, underlying level, market strengthening unmistakably aims to restrict the activities of the VRT in specific domains (e.g. specific commercial audiences as youngsters, online news offering, commercial activities, regional broadcasting, etc.), a demand that matched the large-scale cut-backs that paralleled the negotiations of the new management contract.

The negotiations resulted in a more focused management contract that did preserve the necessary leeway for VRT in programming and development of new services. However VRT should more clearly articulate distinctiveness in its programming (amongst others by focusing more clearly on culture and education). Market strengthening was picked up as one of the core six strategic objectives (VRT and Flemish Government, 2016). Commitments include collaboration with newspapers, distributors, the music sector and various forms of collaboration aimed at technological innovation. Interestingly, an ecosystem approach is seemingly commensurable with a more clear emphasis on distinctiveness, while at the same time one could say partnerships, market strengthening and the likes, if not sufficiently tied to requirements and safeguards, could be hazardous for the distinctive status (independence, non-commercial character) of PSB (see Collins, 1998).

Evaluation: an ecosystem approach reinforcing the status quo?

Based on the Flemish case, a series of important observations can be made with regard to the translation of the ecosystem logic in policy commitments that point to the problematic nature of its current use. The ecosystem approach for defining the role of PSM has some important advantages. One aspect is that the pragmatism central to the ecosystem results in a broader basis and support for proposed public broadcasting regulation, an aspect that is shared by supporters of multi-stakeholder governance in media policy and that could also be found in the governance structures of ideals as the media welfare state model or a digital commons.

Consensus and comprise, when insufficiently tied to a long-term vision on the role of PSM, might however end up with the status quo hampering rather than supporting long-term sustainability of PSM and their stakeholders. It is clear that the current policy approach that sets out to sustain the Flemish ecosystem is mostly oriented towards sustaining the (power) positions of traditional media players, rather than the content and services they produce and are – from a policy point of view – worthy to sustain for society. This is problematic for a number of reasons.

Firstly, the interests of private players are not always identical with the sustainability they set out to defend. For example, it might well be that, in order to sustain an ecosystem for high-end TV drama, the ecosystem would benefit from having a smaller number of stronger production companies than various small producers scattered over the media landscape that become extremely dependent on subsidy mechanisms. Moreover, decisions in Flanders that called for PSM to partner up or share its services and/or content in various domains, were often informed by claims of market distortion made by a selective number of private players, that are only exceptionally backed by evidence.

Secondly, putting the emphasis on maintaining existing positions of players in the ecosystem might render the current ecosystem approach somehow conservative, and blind players for potential interesting other collaborations with new market entrants. Consequently, in some cases the partnership logic even presents a naive interpretation of the willingness of market players to contribute to the long-term sustainability, as these players mostly search for quick wins in the short term. Indeed, it could be questioned to what extent independent producers would refrain from interesting options with Netflix or Apple as part of sustaining their own activities.

Thirdly, an ecosystem approach presupposes responsibilities for all players in the market, however in its current form it is presented as an approach with one-sided responsibilities from the PSM towards its surrounding ecosystem. These aspects blinds policymakers to the fact that other market developments such as increased vertical integration, partly cannibalizing on other competitors in a small market, might be more distortive for the ecosystem than a strong public service broadcaster.

Fourthly, and most problematic, an ecosystem approach creates the perception that all content created by traditional media players is valuable enough to sustain and that it is supposedly interchangeable with the content and services produced by the public broadcasters. The approach circumvents discussions on the lack of access of multimedia and information offers of traditional players or discussions on the lack of diversity in news coverage of newspapers websites.

Lastly, an ecosystem approach seemingly presents itself as sustaining all media players. However, in practice, commitments towards partnerships are restricted to just a few, larger media players, or the ones whose criticism at the moment resounds loudest. Additionally, the ecosystem approach is strictly oriented towards partnerships with private players. It is here that the ecosystem logic presents itself as relatively restricted to the financial sustainability of private partners, rather than the content and value they produce. The potential for large-scale, cross-media and cross-sector projects with libraries, archives and educational institutions that might benefit from surfing on the government support to stimulate ecosystems is easily overlooked. Partly explanatory is the fact these types of partnerships are more complex and supersede different policy domains, but it also relates to the fact that these projects import additional costs rather than decrease costs by collaboration. Consequently, the most crucial stakeholder, and admittedly the least organized stakeholder, i.e. the audience, is not included in the ecosystem approach, and it could be argued that sustaining an ecosystem does not always reflect the best interest of the audience. For example, if sustaining means limiting access, introducing various artificial boundaries for consumption or reducing the quality of experience is not in the audience's best interest.

Another observation from the analysis of Flanders relates to the problematic nature of enforcing partnership in regulation, obligations and measurable criteria for PSM. The previous and current management contracts of the VRT show the difficulties of balancing between arbitrary obligations and providing flexible leeway for fruitful collaboration. Indeed neither the Flemish management contracts (2012–2016, 2016–2020) that clearly promoted an ecosystem approach, nor the policy notes of the Minister, propose large-scale alliances with concrete specific partnership commitments. Often commitments towards collaboration remain restricted to formulating the actual commitment, and consequently the operational and substantive aspects to the deals remain restricted. Mutual understanding and shared objectives and interests have proven to be an obvious but often forgotten key aspects of partnerships (Raats, 2012; 2014). Those between stakeholders and public broadcaster cannot be artificially forced, particularly because the public broadcaster is dependent on the willingness of its stakeholders to effectively participate. Thus, current commitments only rarely touch upon the true essence and value of the partnership idea. A focus on partnerships and balances might enforce the partnerships for the sake of the partnerships rather than maintaining the value of services and content provided by media players.

Conclusions

This chapter addressed a widespread shift in policy discourse to increasingly emphasize market objectives in defining the role for public service media, and did so by analyzing the translation of an ecosystem approach in Flemish media policy. Bear in mind that at no point during the process was an ecosystem approach actually formalized into specific policy regulation. Rather it should be seen as an overall shift in media policy-making and rhetoric. We can, therefore, observe a shift in policy rhetoric where the role of the public broadcaster is not only linked to public interest objectives, but also to sustaining and strengthening the market.

Increased interdependence of all players within a digital value chain as well as cutbacks and a shift in revenue have increasingly tied PSM's legitimation and role to its surrounding ecosystem. Current discussions in Flanders, as well as in the UK, Norway and Denmark on the importance of PSM outsourcing sufficient productions to sustain or foster an independent creative sector are prime examples. As the British case has markedly demonstrated, this also had an effect on arguments in favour of legitimizing PSM, with public broadcasters (as well as the EBU) increasingly emphasizing their economic role in society and hence contributing to legitimizing public services based on evidence and measurable indicators, which could also be seen in operationalizing the remit and aspects of public value and distinctiveness.

On the one hand, the ecosystem discourse provides a rhetorical instrument to legitimize cut-backs and efficiency, and to appeal to demands of private players. On the other hand, the ecosystem might be a valuable approach towards media value created in domestic markets, one where value supersedes public broadcasting value, and one that takes into account shifting business models and the challenges of other players.

The ecosystem approach's main advantage is that it enlarges the basis for proposed policies by including more stakeholders' concerns and demands in the policy process. The approach rightfully acknowledges the need for collaborations between media companies and PSM to address the challenges of shifts in media markets, especially for smaller media ecologies. However, an ecosystem approach that starts out from defending existing power positions might succeed in remediating existing frictions but not in anticipating new ones. An ecosystem approach that is solely aimed at aligning all players in the same direction will prove counterproductive to addressing the challenges of a digital era.

Defending sustainability of media content instead of players might in the long run strengthen consumer value as well as PSB's legitimacy. However this would only succeed when an ecosystem approach is tied to content and delivery of quality services rather than safeguarding the position of existing players, which is often, but not necessarily, overlapping. More sustainable therefore is the search for an overarching framework for partnership and collaboration developed by government, public broadcaster(s) and private players, that is tied to a series of overarching values and qualities within the ecosystem as part of defending it in the long run, and which could most notably linked to issues of pluralism, diversity of opinions and identities. In that respect, VRT in 2017 developed a framework for collaboration with third-party private players in the ecosystem. It provides an instrument to evaluate the potential benefits for VRT and the ecosystem, and lists a series of criteria under which partnerships need to take place. However, the framework explicitly refrains from defining the objectives of an ecosystem approach for Flanders (i.e. what services, quality, and value to sustain and what to develop?) as it considers that a shared responsibility of all media players and government. Future research will have to assess to what extent the framework has proven valuable for VRT and private media players.

References

Armstrong, M. (2005). Public Service Broadcasting. *Fiscal Studies*, 26(3): 281–299.

Aslama, M.A., and J. Clark, (2013). Multi-stakeholderism. Value for Public service media. In: G.F. Lowe, and F. Martin (ed.), *The Value of Public Service Media*. Göteborg, Nordicom, 165–183.

Bardoel, J., and G.F. Lowe (2008). From Public Broadcasting to Public Service Media. The Core Challenge. In: J. Bardoel, and G.F. Lowe (eds.), *From Public Service Broadcasting to Public Service Media. RIPE@2007*. Göteborg: Nordicom, 9–29.

Barwise, P., and R. Picard (2014). *What If There Were No BBC Television? The Net Impact on UK Viewers*. Oxford: Reuters Institute for the Study of Journalism.

BBC (2009). *Public service partnerships. Helping sustain UK PSB*. London: British Broadcasting Corporation.

BBC (2013). *Public and private broadcasters across the world – the race to the top*. London: BBC.

BBC Trust (2008). *The BBC Trust Conclusions: The economic impact of the BBC on the UK creative and broadcasting sector*. London: BBC.

Blumler, J. (1992). *Television and the public interest. Vulnerable Values in West European Broadcasting*. London: Sage Publications.

Collins, R. (1998). Supper with the devil – A case study in private/public collaboration in broadcasting: The genesis of Eurosport. *Media, Culture and Society*, 20(4): 653–664.

Collins, R. (2011). Content online and the end of public media? The UK, a canary in the coal mine? *Media, Culture and Society*, 33(8): 1202–1219.

Coppens, T. (2003). Digital public broadcasting in Flanders: walking the tightrope. *Telematics and Informatics*, 20(2): 143–159.

Coppens, T., and F. Saeys (2006). Enforcing performance: new approaches to govern public service broadcasting. *Media, Culture and Society*, 28(2): 261–284.

Davies, G. (2005). The BBC and public value. In: J. Heath, and D. Levy (eds.), *Can the market deliver? Funding public service television in the digital age?* Eastleight: John Libbey Publishing, 129–150.

Davies, G. (2013). A 2020 Vision for the BBC. In: R. Picard, and P. Siciliani (eds.), *Is there Still a Place for Public Service Television?* Oxford: Reuters Institute for the Study of Journalism, 70–78.

Debrett, M. (2010). *Reinventing Public Service Television for the Digital Future.* Bristol: Intellect.

Department of Culture, Media and Sport (2015). *BBC Charter Review. Public Consultation*. London: DCMS, July 16, 2015.

Donders, K. (2012). *Public service media and policy in Europe*. New York: Palgrave Macmillan.

Donders, K., and T. Evens (2010). *Broadcasting and its distribution in Flanders, Denmark and the United States: an explorative and future-oriented analysis: A research report for SBS Belgium*. Brussel/Gent: IBBT-SMIT, VUB/ MICT, UGent.

Donders, K., and T. Raats (2012). Analyzing national practices after European State aid control: are multi-stakeholder negotiations beneficial for public service broadcasting? *Media, Culture and Society,* 34(2): 162–180.

Donders, K., and T. Raats (2015). From Public Service Media Organisations to De-centralised Public Service for the Media Sector: A Comparative Analysis of Opportunities and Disadvantages. *Javnost, The Public*, 22 (2): 145–163.

Donders, K., T. Raats, A. Moons, and N. Walravens (2010). *De toekomstige plaats en rol van de openbare omroep in Vlaanderen: een stakeholderbevraging. Onderzoek in opdracht van de Sectorraad Media van de SARC en het Departement Cultuur, Jeugd, Sport en Media van de Vlaamse Gemeenschap* [The future role and position of public broadcasting in Flanders: a stakeholder inquiry. Research commissioned by the SARC and Department of Culture, Youth, Sports and Media]. Brussels: IBBT/SMIT/IES.

Donders, K., and H. Van Den Bulck (2012) (eds.). *De VRT in de 21ste eeuw. Overbodige luxe of maatschappelijke meerwaarde* [The VRT in the 21st Century, more obsolete or more relevant]. Antwerpen: UPA.

Doyle, G., and R. Paterson (2008). Public Policy and Independent Television Production In the UK. *Journal of Media Business Studies*, 5(3): 17–33.

Elstein, D. (2000). The Future of broadcasting. Competing with the Public Sector in Broadcasting. *Economic Affairs*, 20(4): 13–20.

European Broadcasting Union (2014). *Connecting to a networked society*. Geneva: EBU.

Freedman, D. (2009). The Public Service Publisher – an Obituary. *Journal of British Cinema and Television* 6(1): 103–121.

Freedman, D. (2010). Media Policy Silences: The Hidden Face of Communications Decision Making. *The International Journal of Press/Politics*, 15(3): 344–361.

House of Commons Culture, Media and Sport Committee (2015). *Future of the BBC Fourth Report of Session 2014–15*. London: House of Commons.

Iosifidis, P. (2013). *Global Media and Communication Policy*. Basingstoke: Palgrave.

Lieten, I. (2010). *De VRT als uitdager en partner in het Vlaamse medialandschap. Visienota Media beheersovereenkomst tussen de Vlaamse Regering en de VRT 2012–2016* [The VRT as challenger and partner in the Flemish media landscape. Vision note]. Brussels: Vlaamse Regering, December 14, 2010.

Lowe, G.F., and F. Martin (eds.) (2014). *The Value of Public Service Media*. Göteborg: Nordicom.

McCauley, M.P., E.E. Peterson, B. Lee Artz, and D. Halleck (eds.) (2003). *Public Broadcasting and the Public Interest*. New York: M. E. Sharpe.

McElroy, R., and C. Noonan (2016). Television drama production in small nations: Mobilities in a changing ecology. *The Journal of Popular Television*, 4(1): 109–127.

Ministerie van Onderwijs, Cultuur en Wetenschap (2010). *Onderwerpen en vragen toekomstverkenning landelijke publieke omroep* [Subjects and questions for future public broadcasting]. Den Haag: Ministerie van OCW.

Ministerie van Onderwijs, Cultuur en Wetenschap (2012a). *Uitwerking regeerakkoord Rutte II onderdeel Media* [Roll-out of the government agreement, part Media]. Den Haag: Ministerie van OCW, December 6, 2012.

Ministerie van Onderwijs, Cultuur en Wetenschap (2012b). *Wijziging van de Mediawet 2008 teneinde het stelsel van de landelijke publieke omroep te moderniseren. Voorstel van wet* [Changes in the Media Law 2008. Proposal for law]. Den Haag: Ministerie van OCW.

Ministry of the Flemish Government (2009). *Beleidsnota Media (2009–2014)*. Policy letter Media (2009–2014). Brussels: Ministry of the Flemish Government.

Moe, H., and H. Van den Bulck (2014). *Some Snowden, A Lettuce Bikini and Grumpy Cat? Searching for Public Service Media Outside the Boundaries of the Institution*. Paper presented at RIPE@2014 Conference, Tokyo, Japan.

Murdock, G. (2004). *Building the Digital Commons: Public Broadcasting in the Age of the Internet. The 2004 Spry Memorial Lecture*. Vancouver, 18 November; Montreal, 22 November.

Murdock, G. (2005). Building the Digital Commons. Public Broadcasting in the Age of the Internet. In: G.F. Lowe, and P. Jauert (eds.), *Cultural Dilemmas in Public Service Broadcasting*. Göteborg: Nordicom, 213–230.

Puppis, M., L. D'Haenens, T. Steinmaurer, and M. Künzler (2009). The European and Global Dimension Taking Small Media Systems Research to the Next Level. *International Communication Gazette*, 71(1–2): 105–12.

Raats, T. (2012). Public Service Media and partnership practices. Matching public policy with broadcasting policy. *International Journal for Media and Cultural Politics*, 8(1): 105–125.

Raats, T., and C. Pauwels (2013). Best friennemies forever? Public and private media in Flanders. In: K. Donders, C. Pauwels, and J. Loisen (eds.), *Private television in Western Europe: Content, markets and policies*. Basingstoke, Palgrave, 199–213.

Raats, T. (2014). *And now for something completely different. The role and position of public service broadcasting in a networked media constellation. A geographic-comparative analyze setting out from PSB's cultural remit*. Unpublished PhD thesis, Brussels: Vrije Universiteit Brussel.

Raats, T., and K. Donders (2015). From centralized to distributed public service media: An analysis of market and public value driven arguments. *International Journal of Digital television*, 6 (2): 103–124.

Raats, T., T. Evens, A-S. Vanhaeght, S. Ruelens, and J. Loisen (2015). *Stakeholderbevraging ter voorbereiding van de nieuwe beheersovereenkomst van de VRT met de Vlaamse Regering* [Stakeholder inquiry in preparation of the new VRT Management contract]. Brussel en Gent: iMinds-SMIT en iMinds-MICT.

Raats, T., T. Evens, and S. Ruelens (2016). Challenges for sustaining local audiovisual ecosystems. Analysis of financing and production of domestic TV fiction in small media markets. *Journal of Popular Television*, 4 (1): 129–147.

Raats, T., H. Van den Bulck, and L. d'Haenens (2016). *Een VRT voor morgen, of morgen geen VRT meer?* [A VRT for tomorrow, or no VRT tomorrow]. Kalmthout: Pelckmans.

Raboy M. (ed.) (1996). *Public broadcasting for the 21st century*. Luton: Luton Press.

Schweizer, C., M. Puppis, M. Künzler, and S. Studer (2014). *Public Funding of Private Media.* LSE, Media policy brief 11.

Sector Council for Media (2010). *Advies SARC-Sectorraad Media. Beheersovereenkomst tussen de openbare omroep en de Vlaamse Gemeenschap voor de periode 2012–2016.* [Advise of the SARC Sector Council for Media on the Management agreement between VRT and the Flemish Government 2012–2016]. Brussels: Strategic Council for Culture, Youth, Sports and Media.

Staten-Generaal van de Media (2011). *Sterker door samenwerking* [Stronger through collaboration]. Brussels: Department of Culture, Youth, Sports and Media, 6th May 2011.

Steemers, J. (2015). Broadcasting is dead. Long live television: perspectives from Europe. In: J. Steemers, J. Trappel, and B. Thomass (ed.), *European media in crisis: values, risks and policies.* London: Routledge, 64–81.

Syvertsen, T., G. Enli, O. Mjos, and H. Moe (2014). *The Media Welfare State: Nordic Media in the Digital Era.* Ann Arbor: University of Michigan Press.

Tracey, M. (1998). *The Decline and Fall of Public Service Broadcasting.* Oxford: Oxford University Press.

Van den Bulck, H., and K. Donders (2014). Of Discourses, Stakeholders and Advocacy Coalitions in Media Policy: Tracing Negotiations towards the New Management Contract of Flemish Public Broadcaster VRT. *European Journal of Communication,* 29(1): 83–99.

Vlaams Parlement (2011). *Voorstel tot resolutie betreffende betreffende de nieuwe beheersovereenkomst tussen de Vlaamse Radio- en Televisieomroeporganisatie (VRT) en de Vlaamse Gemeenschap, 1154 (2010–2011) – Nr. 1.* Brussel: Vlaams Parlement, Commissie voor Cultuur, Jeugd, Sport en Media, 18 mei.

Vlaamse Regulator voor de Media (2015). *Rapport mediaconcentratie 2015* [Report on media concentration in 2015]. Brussels: VRM.

Voorhoof, D. (1995). Mediabeleid en mediarecht in Vlaanderen [Media policy and media law in Flanders]. In: J.C. Burgelman, D. Biltereyst, and C. Pauwels (eds.), *Audiovisuele media in Vlaanderen: analyse en beleid* [Audiovisual media in Flanders]. Brussel: VUB Press, 187–212.

VRT and Flemish Government (2001). *Beheersovereenkomst tussen de VRT en de Vlaamse gemeenschap 2002–2006* [Management contract between VRT and Flemish Government].

VRT and Flemish Government (2006). *Beheersovereenkomst 2007–2011 tussen de VRT en de Vlaamse Gemeenschap: De taken van de openbare omroep in het digitale tijdperk* [Management contract between VRT and Flemish Government].

VRT and Flemish Government (2007). *Addendum Beheersovereenkomst inzake het openbare omroepdomein cultuur* [Addendum to the management contract on culture].

VRT and Flemish Government (2011). *Beheersovereenkomst 2012–2016 tussen de Vlaamse Gemeenschap en de VRT* [Management contract between VRT and Flemish Government].

Michał Głowacki

University of Warsaw, Poland

Public service media ecology: Tallinn, Estonia

Abstract: The evolution of media enterprises calls for the clustering of symbiotic businesses. New practices for sharing knowledge, skills, mobility and building partnership relations with creative industries, high technology clusters and media hubs generate new opportunities for the renewal of public service media, which cannot be analyzed in isolation anymore. In order to fully understand the challenges, as well as the ways in which the fabric of public service media might evolve, one needs to take a wider public service media ecology perspective. This study aims to investigate the value of partnership in the capital city of Estonia, which is regarded as one of the most advanced models of digital solutions in Europe. Through semi-structured interviews with public service media staff, policy-makers, and experts in the Tallinn area (June 2016), the study examines drivers and barriers for collaborations between public service media, universities, creative initiatives and high technology firms.

Keywords: public service media ecology, creative media clusters, high technology clusters, collaboration, networks, partnership relations, adaptation and change.

Introduction

The development of new media and digital technologies followed by user-engagement practices, prosumerism, crowdsourcing, swarming and the increasing distribution of media and communications via networks (the Internet and the World Wide Web) has widely changed the production practices of contemporary businesses, as well as their overall structures and organizational systems. The most successful enterprises in high technology and culture are the most collaborative, with observable clustering of symbiotic businesses and partnership relations in certain locations (see for instance Tech City UK in London and Soho Factory in Warsaw). The clustering is proving to be useful to support mobility, and also practices for sharing the infrastructure, knowledge, skills and so on (Karlsson and Picard, 2011). Clusters and hubs – comprised of particularly innovative individuals or businesses, which act as agents of change (Creativeworks London, 2016; NESTA, 2016), may contribute to the success and growth of the overall ecology. For public service media (PSM), competition is therefore no longer only about keeping pace with private media firms but also with high technology and creative media clusters. Overall, the suggestion is that partnering with such concentrations might be of benefit for PSM.

Policy-making initiatives and studies have already identified a need for reinvention and extension of public service media beyond traditional broadcasting (Bennett et al., 2012). Overall, experts have argued for a more people-centric approach to PSM (Jakubowicz, 2008), the extension of public service tasks (Brown, 2014), changes in management systems (Lowe and Brown, 2016) and the opening up of public service media to multiple stakeholders (Karmasin and Kraus 2014, EBU, 2014). Although some experts have called for reconsidering PSM through the lenses of the ecosystem approach (Raats, 2012; Aslama and Clark, 2012; Głowacki and Jackson, 2014), very few have deconstructed the position of PSM within emerging high technology and creative media clusters.

In this chapter, I argue that in order for PSM to be fit for the digital era and to remain relevant and accessible, the expertise found within clusters of media firms may support a reinvention of PSM. I also suggest that proximity to commercial high tech firms has the potential to improve internal and external conditions for being adaptive and change-ready and is not necessarily counter to PSM distinctiveness. Through collaboration and development of partnership systems PSM might become a catalyst for innovation and a key player in contemporary mediascapes.

Tallinn – the capital of Estonia – has long been regarded as one of the most advanced and successful models of disruptive innovation practices. The city has vigorously supported the development of a digitally-oriented society. The City Hall has schemes promoting e-residence and i-voting, and has encouraged the aggregation of creative and high-tech companies. The publicly funded Eesti Rahvusringhääling (ERR), Estonia's public broadcaster enjoys a stable level of public trust and market position. At the same time, as with PSM in other countries, ERR is searching for ways to respond to changing market conditions. Evolution towards digital media forms has often proven to be problematic. By looking at the Estonian case study the questions to be addressed are: what drives the development of partnership systems within PSM ecology? What are the potential barriers for collaboration between PSM, creative media and high technology clusters?

The outcomes presented here are a small section of the indicative findings of a three-year international study "Organizational culture of public service media: people, values and processes" (2015–2018). Michał Głowacki (the lead author of this paper) is working collaboratively with Professor Lizzie Jackson from London South Bank University, UK. The overall aim is to analyze the internal cultures and practices of high technology clusters in North America and Europe. Practices that might be beneficial to assist the evolution of PSM will be disseminated for their consideration. The study will, however, also be of great interest to all media firms.

Public service media ecology

The complexity of today's media calls for fresh ideas and new discourses in relation to assisting PSM to surmount the challenges and to develop suitable models for the Information Age. One future scenario is PSM as part of a wider ecology where there is no longer any separation between traditional and new media. This ecology might include a range of creative industry firms, and also, high-tech firms which might supply new platforms or communication systems. In order to find a framework for the analysis of high technology clusters the researchers drew data from creative industries, media clusters and network theory.

The existing literature argues that the rise of creative industries contributes to contemporary knowledge-based economies. Several typologies and conceptualizations stress the societal importance of activities, which generate both cultural goods and revenue through the exploitation of intellectual property (Hesmondhalgh, 2013; UNESCO, 2009). One argument holds that human knowledge, talent, skills and creativity are among the most important economic resources (Florida, 2002). According to a definition of creative industries, by the UK's Department for Culture, Media and Sport, which other countries including Estonia have adopted, the list of sectors within the creative industries includes advertising, architecture, design, publishing, music, visual arts, museums, galleries and libraries as well as IT, software, computer services and broadcasting media (DCMS, 2015). In the United Kingdom, the clustering of creative industries is regarded as one of the most critical drivers of innovation (NESTA, 2010; 2016).

In the media sector, Karlsson and Picard (2011) evidence that concentrations of media firms "promote and improve production of entertainment and content by connecting producers through private and public partnerships and projects, i.e. making media production more efficient" (Karlsson and Picard, 2011: 4). Most recently, a team of researchers from three universities in Belgium have launched a collaborative project to explore the development of media clusters. In addition to looking at the location of media organizations within clusters, they will also examine the structure and dynamics, the skills and mobility of the workforce, and lastly the communities of practice, understood as "social and communicational environments that foster learning within/across clusters" (Media Clusters Brussels, 2016). In the course of the study, they intend to look at different aspects of media clustering such as place, proximity, population, profile, path-dependency, cluster performance and policy-making. Such factors support the aggregation and eventual concentration of media firms (Komorowski, 2016). According to Picard (2009: 879) there is a significant difference between media clusters and high technology clusters, since "firms in media clusters tend to have more limited facility, equipment, personnel needs compared to those in both industrial and high tech clusters and they tend to rely more on services than goods in their production processes."

Finally, the aggregation of media firms within clusters requires the development of partnership, relationship and collaboration systems, which might be further analyzed under the umbrella of network theory, for example, network dynamics and network culture (Terranova, 2004; Rainie and Wellman, 2014; Vitale, 2014).

Partnership and collaboration between public service media and other agents is much older than the high technology clusters themselves. Indeed, PSM in many countries have established long-term partnerships with a range of different cultural institutions to support democratic participation and cultural activities. The PSM model has also served as a platform for the promotion of exhibitions, plays, events and so on. Collaborations with education have supported the media literacy programmes or other educational content. The PSM have also commissioned content from independent producers or produced co-productions. Public service media companies have started to engage with entrepreneurs specializing in high technology. In Flanders, PSM is facilitating start-up communities through "Sandbox" an international joint platform for collaborative innovation (VRT, 2016). Also in Austria PSM aims to encourage young entrepreneurs to become involved in innovation and research and development (ORF-Mediaservice, 2016).

In this paper we introduce the term **public service media ecology** to emphasize PSM's need to interact with a wider range of agents (Figure 1). These may be located within high technology clusters, which include universities, policy-makers (city municipalities/authorities included), accelerators, social spaces, co-working spaces, architecture, transportation systems, and the high-tech firms themselves. One of the subsectors of high technology clustering is further framed under the 'umbrella' of creative media clusters, which builds on activities of cultural institutions, creative cities and hubs, traditional and online-born media firms as well as other enterprises connected with social innovation and emerging types of media, for instance gaming and virtual reality. All these connections might be formal vs. informal, project-based, as well as obligatory vs. voluntary.

Figure 1. Public service media ecology

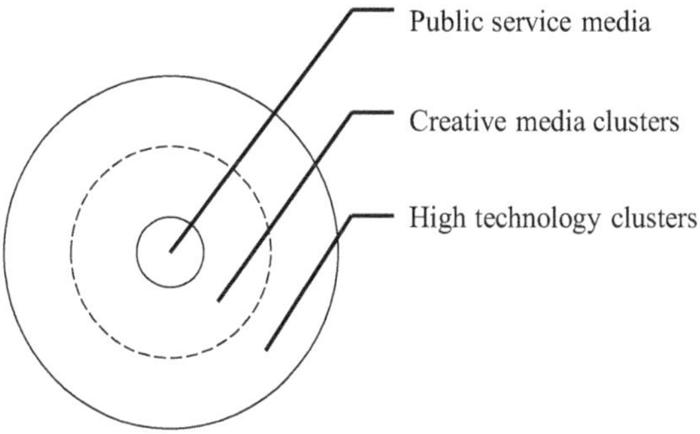

Source: Author.

Public service media as a key player of high technology and creative media clusters might strengthen both the overall ecology and PSM itself. Collaboration and partnership networks might improve either or both of the economic and societal value of PSM services and the visibility and reach of such platforms. Being part of an ecology will certainly contribute to staff mobility and the development of new skills. Involvement in transmedia projects such as the development of pan-platform branded content might increase the competiveness of PSM. Partnership systems with emerging hubs and clusters might also result in the evolution of PSM organizational structures creating opportunities for new models to emerge. The PSM has traditionally been involved in the development of new forms of cultural and local activity as well as initiatives relating to technology and content innovation. Finally, the development of public service media ecologies might assist strategies to counter the dominance of the large transnational corporations currently risking the domination of national media, which is especially important in small countries.

The development of a strong public service media ecology relies on a variety of criteria, from being open and inclusive to having sufficient institutional and regulatory support to be collaboration-ready. Building effective partnership networks is also connected with setting limitations, negotiation, exploring expectations, business models and the understanding of what might be very different working patterns (editorial standards included). Another factor is whether PSM is an attractive partner for collaboration. Finally, the goal is to elaborate on public-private partnership taking into account geographic proximity and the effects of partnership relations on the distinctiveness and competitiveness of PSM and clusters.

Bearing in mind that public service media ecology reflects a unique societal, cultural, economic and political environment, one of the ways is to analyze its phenomenon by using a case study approach.

Methodology

The ideas presented and advanced here build on indicative findings from the afromentioned three-year international study looking at high technology clusters in ten cities in North America (Austin, Boston/Cambridge, Detroit, Toronto) and Europe (Brussels, Copenhagen, London, Tallinn, Vienna, Warsaw). The overall goal is to indicate whether there are strategies, values and processes in high technology clusters which are likely to foster development, collaboration, and risk-taking in PSM. The study will offer insights into governance structures, production infrastructures, and funding schemes.

The study used a holistic approach of qualitative research combining semi-structured interviews with analysis of corporate documentation and observations, for example of the location and of social spaces in each city. Fifteen interviews in Tallinn were conducted in June 2016. The interviewees were PSM professionals at ERR, the Ministry of Economic Affairs and Communications and Enterprise Estonia – one of the largest institutions within the national support system for entrepreneurship in the country. Additionally, interviews were held with representatives from Tallinn University (TLU), Tallinn Creative Hub, Telliskivi Creative City and the Estonian ICT Cluster. The interview questions included orientations to innovation, arrangements covering research and development (R&D), organizational and after work culture, as well as the nature of any partnership relations. In order to protect the interviewees, they were coded by the interview no., date of the interview and institution: the public service media (PSM), the high technology cluster (HTC) or one of the creative media clusters in Tallinn (CMC).

The findings presented here show selected factors that are likely to have either a positive or negative impact on a public service media ecology (Table 1). The list includes the examination of regulatory frameworks, funding schemes and the overall dynamics. In addition, we argue that collaboration and partnership networks also depend on the level of innovation capacity present, which derives, for example, from knowledge exchange as well as a strong afterwork culture. We contend that staff will collaborate with each other if they have common interests, expectations, ethical standards and working patterns, and also when they do not see collaboration as a threat to their own development. Finally, the rise of any public service media ecology will depend on geographic proximity, organizational structures and shared infrastructure. Taken together, the presence of these factors are likely to indicate whether different enterprises are attractive partners for each other.

Table 1: Public service media ecology: potential drivers and limitations

	Potential drivers	**Potential barriers**
1.	Dynamics of high technology and creative media clusters development, strong market position of PSM	The lack of dynamics of high technology and creative media clusters development, weak market position of PSM
2.	Supporting regulation for entrepreneurs and PSM	Insufficient support for entrepreneurs, outdated regulation for PSM
3.	The existence of funding schemes and support structures, sufficient funding for PSM	Insufficient financial support to entrepreneurs and PSM
4.	Strong innovation capacity of PSM and public service media ecology	Weak innovation capacity of PSM and public service media ecology
5.	Shared knowledge, skills and mobility	Separation of knowledge, skills, the lack of mobility
6.	Common interests, expectations, ethics and working patterns	Separate interests, expectations, ethics and working patterns
7.	Informal and horizontal communication	Formal and vertical communication
8.	Shared infrastructure, proximity of PSM to high technology and creative media clusters	The lack of shared infrastructure, distance between PSM and high technology and creative media clusters
9.	Organic organizational structures, strong after work culture	Mechanistic organizational structures, weak afterwork cultures
10.	Mindset for being open, adaptable and change-ready	Mindset for being self-sufficient, not adaptable and change-ready
11.	Collaboration seen as value for the overall public service media ecology	Collaboration seen as a threat for PSM distinctiveness
12.	High technology, creative media clusters and PSM are attractive partners for collaboration	High technology, creative media clusters and PSM are not attractive partners for collaboration

Source: Author.

Public service media in the advanced digital environment: the case study of Estonia

Located in Northern Europe with 1.3 million citizens, Estonia has reached a high level of digital and technological evolution. The post-Soviet country has successfully transformed its media and it is currently regarded as one of the most advanced models from the perspectives of innovation, technology and entrepreneurship (The Economist, 2013; e–Estonia, 2016a). The Estonian digital society, where the access to the Internet is regarded as a social good, has advanced due to the nature of the infrastructure and interconnectivity, as well as several initiatives introduced to limit bureaucracy and make citizens' lives easier. For example, an e-identity (ID-card and mobile-ID), digital signature, i-voting systems and e-residency arrangements (Hammersley, 2015). As noted by Ross (2016: 211):

> Estonia has demonstrated how innovation in the industries of the future can do more than just generate wealth and employment; it can enhance our civic and political life. In this respect we should stop asking about the next Silicon Valley and start asking about the next Estonia.

The progress of Estonian digital business is due to several factors such as supportive regulation (e.g. easy tools to start a business), the role models for new companies offered by Skype and Transfer Wise, and forward-looking policy-makers, who

> created the general understanding in society that things can be done quickly. [#12 HTC, June 27, 2016]

Other factors include openness, low hierarchy and a particular mindset that argues that nothing is impossible. As noted by one interviewee, the overall attitude is that

> (…) the outsiders are considered to have more knowledge in many ways and in many fields. It is not like that we know everything. It is more about coming here and sharing. We are listening. [#11 CMC, June 27, 2016]

Estonian Public Broadcasting and its ecology

The ERR, Estonia's public broadcaster is regulated by the broadcasting law and funded by the state budget. The ERR has played a significant role in the media market since 2007, when PSM was reconstructed by the merger of radio and TV (Jõesaar, 2009; Lõhmus et al., 2010; Loit and Siibak, 2013). With approximately 700 employees and a location in the center of Tallinn, ERR fulfilled its mission by supporting social cohesion, celebrating Estonian history and culture, and by running important events (Estonian Public Broadcasting Act, 2007). The ERR enjoys a stable level of public trust (EBU, 2016). The challenges the organization had, relate to having insufficient public funds as well as carrying the additional burden of an expectation that the ERR will play a new role in innovation coordination (Ibrus, 2015). There is also the problem of dealing with outdated media regulation:

> Imagine you have very well defined goals and tasks which is based on old media. But it is not the same. There is no regulation or requirement for the Internet, this has been quite spontaneous for all the time. [#8 PSM, June 21, 2016]

The Tallinn area achieved a ranking of being in the 18th and 28th positions for startups and scale-ups (European Digital City Index, 2016). High positions in the ranking are mostly based on evidence of having an advanced digital infrastructure, a strong entrepreneurial culture and easy access to early stage funding (EDCi, 2016). Estonia approached the development of Estonia's creative industries through the use of European Union structural funds (2007–2013). These funds covered production costs, the building of support structures and so on. The aggregation of creative industries alongside firms related to IT, production, culture, film and the audiovisual sector is a relatively new phenomenon. This is the result of changing market conditions and the presence of such support structures and systems (Ibrus et al., 2013; Enterprise Estonia, 2016). Companies in Estonia are clustering in order to survive due to a previous lack of market opportunities and to take advantage of a global marketplace. An innovation cluster is:

> (…) a cooperation platform where the companies are coming to win something. They are stronger together. [#14 HTC, June 28, 2016]

The ERR is approximately a 15 minute walk from Tallinn University with its Baltic Film, Media, Arts and Communication School. The area is easily accessible by public transport and is located next to the sea. In contrast the ICT Cluster is approximately three kilometers from the ERR in the suburban area of Ulemiste City, in new buildings. The reason for this is that rents are lower there. However, when looking at the Tallinn creative media clusters, it is debatable whether location has any significance:

> I think in Estonia we cannot speak about cluster in a way it is location-based. In the cluster theory companies are in the circle of 200 km, it takes whole Estonia then (…) We are responsible for the whole country, this means we should be everywhere not just in the center of Tallinn. [#14 HTC, June 28, 2016]

The size of the creative media cluster matters when looking at the potential and the nature of potential collaborations as the relationships and networks associated with these clusters, are often informal and trust-based:

> Estonia is a very small country which means that all the people know each other, we don't have to have formal contracts for doing cooperation. We just go there and say: let's do it together. [#9 PSM, June 21, 2016]

Relations with high technology clusters

The Baltic Film, Media, Arts and Communication School at Tallinn University is one the leading centers specializing in the film industry, cross-media production, media innovations and transmedia projects. In addition to the study programs, courses and training offered the center offers support for startups and young entrepreneurs. Tallinn University is one of the founders of the Estonian Digital Center and a host of the Digital Creative Media Incubator (DIGIX). The school runs several projects that aim to facilitate cooperation within the media industry as well as to encourage collaboration between organizations in the audiovisual industry. Collaborations are also encouraged with tourism companies, healthcare and education providers and so on:

> Our idea is to push for this kind of innovation happening (...) making these industries familiar with each other, helping them to work with each other. [#6 HTC, June 20, 2016]

Overall cooperation between clusters, the various business accelerators and universities in Estonia works more on a company to university level rather than the university being fully integrated in the cluster. As noted by one interviewee from the ICT Cluster, partnership relationships with such research and science centers might be problematic due to the different project timeframes:

> (...) There is always a mis-match between universities and companies, because companies are always in rush with things. They want to have results today, better yesterday. Researchers and universities want to think and have time. But after two years this is already an old idea. [#14 HTC, June 28, 2016]

The list of activities between Tallinn University and the ERR includes staff exchange and mobility (public media professionals running courses at Tallinn University). Tallinn University and the ERR also organize joint conferences. The ERR provides training opportunities for students whom they frame as future media professionals. A high proportion of the ERR's new staff are from Tallinn University and these relationships often start during their studies. According to #13 PSM (June 27, 2016), having internship programs at the ERR for university students is very important. This is particularly the case as the University does not provide teaching in entrepreneurship. The attitude of young people towards the internship opportunities has recently changed:

> They actually don't want to come, young people are changing, they want to have money and we cannot offer it. [#9 PSM, June 21, 2016]

On the other hand, there is the sense that:

> (…) for many people a proper career prospect is still getting the salaried job (…). In the media fields there are two ways, either you are public media salary person or you are through that. [PSM] is a stable business, all the rest of the staff is project-based. [#12 HTC, June 27, 2016]

There is the sense that staff from the ERR are key to acceleration and incubation programs at DIGIX through their work as mentors. The way that the Digital Creative Media Incubator works helps to explain the informal relationships with experts:

> (…) we look at what companies and incubators want. They are more than willing to cooperate, deliver seminar because of curiosity (…) we don't pay them anything. [#12 HTC, June 27, 2016]

The Estonian ICT cluster supports cooperation, development and the export of e-solutions that have been successfully developed in Estonia. The help available therefore includes areas such as human resource development, cooperation with other economic sectors inside Estonia, and the exportation of digital goods. The various initiatives provide support to 86 companies through different kinds of projects that bring extra funding to the high-tech sector. This includes encouragement to put in bids for funding to the European Union's Horizon 2020 program. Collaboration within the cluster has had positive effects, firms and partnerships with the Cluster have created 75 percent of the turnover of the Estonian ICT sector (e-Estonia, 2016b).

Representatives of the ICT Cluster see their role as being facilitators of partnership within the cluster in the City district of Ulemiste. They believe this success is due to the high level of proximity between firms that – we are finding – is often quoted in terms of density. Proximity and the resulting density of firms and staff is also amplified by a strong afterwork culture facilitated in part by the city location and its bars and cafes. More widely the cluster has developed partnerships with universities and media organizations:

> Our role is to give companies more idea how the universities can help them and can be useful (…) We have done meetings/workshop with media companies. We put together in one room ICT and media companies (…) Media companies are speaking about their business, daily life, how it goes; ICT sector explains them their business. [#14 HTC, June 28, 2016]

The interviews evidence that there are very few connections between the ERR and the companies within the ICT Cluster. This might be due to the limitations of the public-private partnership structure, and regulation that does not support engagement between PSM and private entrants. It may also be due to working methods, as the majority of the work in high-tech is project-based. Lastly, it may be due to a low capacity to undertake research and development in the public media firms themselves. This might also include the ability to gain commercial benefit from R&D. This raises the question of whether ICT companies in the cluster consider ERR as a potential partner in technology innovation. As one interviewee explained:

> In order to develop IT systems you need resources, and our budget has not changed in years. Then again it is a question to the management – do they value how much innovation matters? [#9 PSM, June 21, 2016]

Both funding restraints and innovation capacity have an impact on the position and role of the PSM in the overall media ecology. If PSM does not evolve – and this depends on its capacity to evolve – it might not be able to continue and compete.

Relations with creative media clusters

Like many other countries, the Estonian PSM has played a significant role as a content commissioner and events facilitator. According to one of the interviewees (#6 HTC, June 20, 2016) the ERR has had an undisputed effect over the last ten years on revitalising the Estonian popular music scene including its commercial aspects. The ERR has achieved this by using different program formats on TV and radio. In turn this has also positively influenced innovation and experimentation in the audiovisual sector – pushing companies to evolve new kinds of storytelling themselves.

Let us now look at the range of potential opportunities for partnership working that might interest PSM. The Tallinn Creative Hub is one of the accelerators facilitating cultural activities in the capital city of Estonia. Funded by the city municipalities the Hub offers spaces for a wide range of cultural events, such as concerts, theatre performances, conferences, learning clubs, workshops, and exhibitions and festivals. In addition there are a range of focussed activities for creative people and entrepreneurs, such as a MakerLab, a recording studio and the Creative Hub Garden that opens each summer (Kultuurikatel, 2016).

For those who work in the Tallinn Creative Hub collaboration is critical. They view their role as an aggregator and partnership-builder seriously, considering it absolutely critical; it is not merely establishing linkages between different sectors but building long-term transdisciplinary interactions:

> My personal aim as well as the aim of Tallinn Creative Hub is to inspire and motivate which means it is very important to show different innovative or brand new ideas (...) For example [the] food industry is not really considered as part of [the] creative industries but it is (...) My personal agenda is that food is not only food, it connects politics, social entrepreneurship. [#11 CMC, June 27, 2016]

Another important element that encourages efficient partnership working is having a shared or similar set of working practices:

> It goes down to people, whether people really have similar – if not the same work – ethics and working system. [#11 CMC, June 27, 2016]

In addition, having fluid organizational structures that enable a responsive approach to projects and a transdisciplinary mind-set and skill-set help the Tallinn Creative Hub accelerate long-term successful partnerships.

Telliskivi Creative City, a private independent business hub – also supports innovative partnership projects for the culture and creative industries in Estonia. The city consists of 10 buildings, and almost 200 different companies employing more than 1,500 creative industries professionals. The city comprises offices, ateliers, studios, workshops, rehearsal spaces, shops and clubs. It also hosts a bike shop, bread factory, print shop, concert hall, theatre stage, and several cafes, galleries, bars and restaurants (Telliskivi, 2016). The initiative was incubated in an old industrial area which was previously considered anti-social and in decay has now become one of the most vibrant and safe places in the Tallinn area. All of this has been made possible through the development of innovative ideas on how business, culture and creative communities can co-support each other:

> Telliskivi has always been the type of enterprise that I hope all enterprises will be in 20 years-time. It is not fully [a] business or fully social enterprise, it has to be somewhere in the middle. [#15 CMC, June 28, 2016]

The interviewee was keen to point out the importance of the involvement of the creative community:

> Since the beginning the idea was to create an environment for creative industries that will be community-driven, not usual top down management, to turn it around – that the community decides what matters. [#15 CMC, June 28, 2016]

Telliskivi Creative City builds its relationships with creative professionals and entrepreneurs by renting adaptive and reasonably priced spaces to architects, graphic designers, dancers, recording studios, musicians, photographers, and painters. This arrangement supports young professionals and their start-ups at a critical point in their career. Approximately 45 percent of the 500 cultural events in 2015 were hosted at the City for no cost. Telliskivi is a self-sustaining enterprise and for this reason few instances of partnership working with other agents – such as the City of Tallinn and the Tallinn Creative Hub – were observed. As argued by one interviewee:

> We have very little cooperation with the city of Tallinn or the state because we never ask them for their support. The fact that we are so successful in [the] cultural field and creative industry incubation in one way it proves that they fail in this field (…) It just shows the lack of efficiency that the public sector has. [#15 CMC, June 28, 2016]

There is some evidence of PSM collaboration in Estonia. The Tallinn Creative Hub partners with the ERR to broadcast a classical music radio program and performances from the studio and hall. Public-private partnerships, however, between PSM and commercial firms have largely been problematic. The issue is largely connected with the regulatory framework since PSM cannot give such projects or initiatives any kind of publicity; even product placement is not allowed. In the main the links tend to be between the ERR and cultural organizations that are either publicly or state funded such as operas, theatres. There is a closer match from the perspective of the organizational and regulatory structures, the organizational cultures, and the work practices, as one PSM interviewee explained:

> (…) Maybe [the] interests are different, cooperation with [the] private sector is always complicated because you will lose independence and neutrality, you can't be critical being as a partner (…) This is why we might not be very much interested to cooperate with [the] private sector. It is always some complication. [#13 PSM, June 27, 2016]

The importance of having matching values, processes and organizational systems has now become clear. This, together with any regulatory constraints, might be regarded as the key challenge and barrier to the public service media's ability to embed within creative media and high technology clusters.

Conclusions

The aim has been to map the position and relationships between the Estonian PSM within the overall ecology of Tallinn and to evidence the value of partnerships. We have also looked at the positive and negative factors that affect such collaboration. It has been argued that in order for public service media to benefit from such collaborations it will be necessary to ensure their working practices, values and organizational structures are able to 'match' those of the commercial sector. The case study of the high technology and creative media clusters of Tallinn in Estonia has been useful in identifying some of the organizational and cultural factors that are critical for co-operation and joint working.

Estonia is an advanced European digital society experimenting with innovative solutions to exploit their creative and digital economy. For example, they have recently introduced digital citizenship schemes to attract entrepreneurs from other countries. Estonia's success is partly due to the ease with which businesses can startup. There are low cost, attractive places to work. These businesses have adaptive organizational structures and a 'can do' mindset – nothing is impossible. This cocktail is enabling digital orientations to work to flourish in the culture, education and ICT sectors. The result has been the production of innovative e-solutions and strong export activity due to supportive regulation and funding frameworks, including the availability of external funding.

The density and proximity of firms located in the ICT Cluster supports networking and networking results in the amplification of knowledge and skills. This is accelerated by staff mobility, partnership building and a strong afterwork culture. Knowledge building and knowledge exchange is further amplified through partnerships with schools and universities, including the Baltic Film, Media, Arts and Communication School at Tallinn University. Tallinn University's ability to build linkages and interactions with creative individuals and entrepreneurs in the media has been evidenced though the establishment of a Digital Creative Media Incubator to support new talents and entrepreneurship in the media and communications and creative industries. Regardless of different types of ownership (public vs. private) building collaboration with creative individuals and communities is of critical importance and is facilitated through flat management, as well as similar values, expectations, ethics and the working standards, which are often project-based. As a result, there is a strong emphasis on mixed media working and this increases the possibility of new forms of media and cultural goods. The mindset is to be open and collaborative which results in the emergence of long-term interactions supported by initiatives such as the Tallinn Creative Hub and Telliskivi Creative City.

The strong development of both high technology and creative media clusters offers a wide range of opportunities for partnership systems with PSM. Supportive conditions in terms of infrastructure, location and the size of the overall cluster, together with informal and trust-based connections offer a space for PSM to be a central agent of the public service media ecology. The Estonian Public Broadcasting enterprise has established relationships with a variety of state-owned and publicly funded cultural institutions, such as galleries, museums and theatres. Collaboration with Tallinn University is also strong, although in recent years some young people are less enthusiastic about training and forms of internship in the PSM. Still, many future employees at the ERR graduate from different study programs offered by Tallinn University; work at the ERR is regarded as being stable rather than project-based. So far, only a few attempts have been made to strengthen the ICT companies, which were often explained in the PSM by funding limitations for innovation activities. In addition to this, there are regulatory constraints that hinder PSM engagement with commercial firms. It is much easier for them to partner with similarly organized cultural institutions. The collaboration of the ERR with the Tallinn Creative Hub to produce radio and television programs is encouraging, but it is a simple supplier-distributor model. All of this might restrict PSM activity to organizational systems and cultures that may also be struggling to evolve.

One thing that is of critical importance is the awareness of the need for change within the PSM. Although the interviews with people from the PSM evidenced an urgency to evolve and adapt there was a low level of awareness that the current organizational structures might not be suitable for the digital information age. The need for partnership working has not been fully recognized; in fact, there may be resistance:

> If all creative ideas come from the outside it raises a big question why public service media exists if it is not able to provide something new. [#1 PSM, June 16, 2016]

The prevailing orientation appears to be protectionist. The predominant focus remains on how to make broadcasting successful:

> ERR is still competing, and it is all about the ratings, while my argument has been they should really re-orientate themselves as a kind of environment creator – ecology facilitator for all the production industries (…) I think they are too closed (…) They should have some formats or mechanisms to invite people with good ideas. [#6 HTC, June 20, 2016]

Lessons from Estonia show that public service media in Europe need to find a way to benefit from others, through knowledge exchange and development of innovation and entrepreneurial skills, in order to be the central player of the overall media, communications and cultural and creative ecology. This case study has shown that among the most important factors for successful collaboration are regulation, funding, similar working practices, a can-do approach and complementary skills in a high-density cluster. In order to benefit from opportunities offered by partnership systems and collaboration policy-makers, as well as leaders and managers, need to realize that PSM is not an individual enterprise anymore and they need to stimulate the current organizational setting to change. As evidenced in the case of Tallinn, some of the mission-led initiatives supporting creative individuals have become self-sufficient, which does not leave much room for the operations of public service media. The lack of proper reaction to the rise of high technology and creative media clusters might result in the marginalization of PSM in the future. This in turn might have a negative effect for the PSM remit related to universal access and being a part of the innovation ecology and creative communities to whom public service media is mandated to serve.

Acknowledgements

The paper presents indicative findings from 3-year international study (2015–2018), entitled "Organizational culture of public service media in the digital mediascapes: people, values and processes" which is funded by the Polish Science Foundation (NCN), SONATA 8. For more information: www.creativemediaclusters.com.

References

Aslama, M., and J. Clark (2012). *Circuits of stakeholders. How to foster collaboration for Public Service Media?* Paper presented at RIPE@2012 Conference: Value for Public Money – Money for Public Value. Sydney, University of Sydney, September 5–7, 2012.

Bennett, J., N. Strange, P. Kerr, and A. Medrado (2012). *Multiplatforming Public Service Broadcasting: The Economic and Cultural Rose of UK Digital and TV Independents*, London: Royal Holloway, University of London, University of Sussex, London Metropolitan University.

Brown, Ch. (2014). Public service content provision. New models, new partnerships, new skills. In: M. Głowacki and L. Jackson (eds.), *Public media management for the Twenty-first Century: Creativity, innovation and interaction*. London and New York: Routledge, 198–215.

Creativeworks London (2016). http://www.creativeworkslondon.org.uk/the-hub/.

DCMS (2015). *Department for Culture, Media and Sport. Creative Industries Economic Estimates January 2015*. Retrieved April 30, 2016 from https://www.gov.uk/government/uploads/system/uploads/attachment_data/file/394668/Creative_Industries_Economic_Estimates_-_January_2015.pdf.

EBU (2014). *Connecting to a networked society*. Geneva: European Broadcasting Union.

EBU (2016). *Trust in Media*. Geneva: European Broadcasting Union.

EDCi (2016). *European Digital City Index 2016*. Retrieved December 30, 2016 from https://digitalcityindex.eu/city/30.

Enterprise Estonia (2016). *About Enterprise Estonia*. Retrieved April 16, 2016 from http://www.eas.ee/eas/?lang=en.

Estonian Public Broadcasting Act (2007). Retrieved April 30, 2016 from https://www.riigiteataja.ee/en/eli/509012014002/consolide.

e-Estonia (2016a). Estonia is a Digital Society. Retrieved July 31, 2016 from http://www.visitestonia.com/en/why-estonia/estonia-is-a-digital-society.

e-Estonia (2016b). *ICT Cluster.* Retrieved April 30, 2016 from https://e-estonia.com/meet-the-industry/ict-cluster/.

Florida, R. (2002). *The rise of the Creative Class. And how it's tranforming work, leisure and everyday life.* New York: Basic Books.

Głowacki, M., and L. Jackson (2014). Towards a Twenty-first Century public media: Conclusions. In: M. Głowacki and L. Jackson (eds.), *Public media management for the Twenty-first Century: Creativity, innovation and interaction.* London and New York: Routledge, 271–287.

Hammersley, B. (2015). Why you should be an e-resident of Estonia. *WIRED*, July 2015. Retrieved March 1, 2016 from http://www.wired.co.uk/article/estonia-e-resident.

Hesmondhalgh, D. (2013). *The Cultural Industries.* 3rd Edition. London, Thousand Oaks, New Delhi, Singapore: SAGE.

Ibrus, I. (2015). Audiovisual Policymaking in Estonia at Times of Convergence: An 'Innovation System' as a Policy Rationale. *Baltic Screen Media Review*, Vol. 3: 103–115.

Ibrus, I., K. Tafel-Viia, S. Lassur, and A. Viia (2013). Tallinn Film Cluster. Realities, expectations and alternatives. *Baltic Screen Media Review*, Vol. 1: 7–27.

Jakubowicz, K. (2008). *Participation and partnership: a Copernican revolution to re- engineer public service media for the 21st century.* Retrieved July 30, 2016 from http://ripeat.org/~qasvminy/library/2008/6731-participation-and-partnership-copernican-revolution-reengineer-public-service.

Jõesaar, A. (2009). Formation of Estonian broadcasting landscape 1994–2007: Experience of the transition state. *Central European Journal of Communication*, Vol. 2, no. 1: 43–62.

Karlsson, Ch., and R. Picard (eds.) (2011). *Media clusters. Spatial agglomeration and content capabilities.* Cheltenham: Edward Elgar.

Karmasin, M., and D. Kraus (2014). Strategies for stakeholder management and crowdsourcing. In: M. Głowacki and L. Jackson (eds.), *Public media management for the Twenty-first Century: Creativity, innovation and interaction.* London and New York: Routledge, 59–81.

Komorowski, M. (2016). *Untangling media clusters: Towards a new typology.* Paper presented at the European Media Management Association (emma) annual conference: Creativity, Coopetition and Uncertainty in Media, Porto, Porto University, June 2–5, 2016.

Kultuurikatel (2016). *Tallinn Creative Hub.* Retrieved April 30, 2016 from http://kultuurikatel.ee/en/tallinn-creative-hub/kultuurikatel/.

Lõhmus, M., H. Tiikmaa, and A. Jõesaar (2010). Duality of Estonian public service media in reflection of the world and positioning society. *Central European Journal of Communication*, Volume 3, no. 1: 95–113.

Loit, U., and A. Siibak (2013). *Mapping Digital Media: Estonia. A Report by the Open Society Foundation*. Retrieved August 1, 2016 from https://www.opensocietyfoundations.org/sites/default/files/mapping-digital-media-estonia-20130903.pdf

Lowe, G.F., and Ch. Brown (eds.) (2016). *Managing media firms and industries. What's so special about media management?* Switzerland: Springer International Publishing.

Media Clusters Brussels (2016). *The Project.* Retrieved August 15, 2016 from http://mediaclusters.brussels/our-research/the-project/.

NESTA (2010). *Creative clusters and innovation. Putting creativity on the map.* Retrieved April 30, 2016 from https://www.nesta.org.uk/sites/default/files/creative_clusters_and_innovation.pdf.

NESTA (2016). *The geography of creativity in the UK. Creative clusters, creative people and creative networks*. Nesta and Creative England. Retrieved August 12, 2016 from https://www.nesta.org.uk/sites/default/files/the_geography_of_creativity_in_the_uk.pdf.

ORF-Mediaservice (2016). Retrieved December 15, 2016 from http://www.ots.at/t/orf-mediaservice.

Picard, R. (2009). Media Clusters and Regional Development: Reflections on the Significance of Location in Media Production. In: E. Bernhard (ed.), *The Geography of Innovation and Entrepreneurship: revised papers presented at the 12th Uddevalla Symposium, 11–13 June, 2009, Bari, Italy / Uddevalla Symposium 2009*. Trollhättan, Sweden: University West, 877–886.

Raats, T. (2012). Public Service Media and partnership practices. Matching public policy with broadcasting policy. *International Journal for Media and Cultural Politics,* 8(1): 105–125.

Rainie, L., and B. Wellman (2014). *Networked. The New Social Operating System.* Cambridge and London: The MIT Press.

Ross, A. (2016). *The Industries of the Future*. New York, London, Toronto, Sydney, New Delhi: Simon & Schuster.

Telliskivi (2016). *Creative City.* Retrieved April 30, 2016 from http://telliskivi.eu/en/loomelinnak/.

Terranova, T. (2004). *Network Culture. Politics for the Information Age*. New York and London: Pluto Press.

The Economist (2013). How did Estonia become a leader in technology? Retrieved April 30, 2016 from http://www.economist.com/blogs/economist-explains/2013/07/economist-explains-21?fsrc=scn/tw/te/bl/ed/howdidestoniabecomealeaderintechnology.

UNESCO (2009). *Measuring the economic contribution of cultural industries. A review and assessment of current methodological approaches*. Retrieved June 15, 2016 from http://www.uis.unesco.org/culture/Documents/FCS-handbook-1-economic-contribution-culture-en-web.pdf.

Vitale, C. (2014). *Networkologies. A Philosophy of Networks for a Hyperconnected Age – A Manifesto*. UK: Zero Books.

VRT (2016). *VRT Sandbox*. Retrieved January 15, 2017 from http://sandbox.vrt.be.

Nicole Gonser, Markus Grammel, Johann Gründl and Gisela Reiter
FHWien University of Applied Sciences of WKW, Austria

Diverse society, diverse perception: a case study of public service media in Austria

Abstract: Austria was one of the last countries in Europe to abandon the broadcasting monopoly and allow commercial media to enter the electronic media market. More than a decade after market liberalization and deregulation, the Austrian public service media provider Österreichischer Rundfunk (ORF) is still popular among Austrian audiences. At the same time, it faces problems that are similar to other European public service media, such as decreasing numbers of viewers in linear TV and challenges to expand online on-demand services. This paper draws on a quantitative telephone survey, an experiment and qualitative interviews in order to examine the present situation of ORF from the audience's perspective. By investigating how and why different groups of people (do not) use or appreciate ORF, a set of best practices, as well as potential threats for the future of public service media in Austria, are discussed.

Keywords: audience research, routines, habits, qualitative interviews, quantitative survey, Austria.

Introduction

Public service media (PSM) in Europe were established to act in the public interest, to create value for all citizens by providing goods and services of democratic, social or personal relevance. This includes diverse content such as the coverage of political or local events, even if it is not profitable (Harrison and Woods, 2001; Berg, Lowe and Lund, 2014). However, audiences increasingly appear to fragment for reasons of ever increasing media choices and a societal trend towards individualization due to the development of online tools and network practices (Katz, 1996; Napoli, 2011). The challenge of reaching diverse groups within society, particularly younger generations and underprivileged people, is regarded as one of the most critical obligations of any PSM enterprise. In line with all of this, PSM outlets across the continent are currently struggling to retain mass appeal and legitimacy. In countries where PSM are funded through the system of license fees, the data often indicate decreasing willingness to financially support

PSM. Without broad citizen support, the concept of PSM is losing ground (e.g., Bardoel and d'Haenens, 2008).

This paper explores the current situation of PSM and their relations with diverse audiences in Austria. The German-speaking country in Central Europe is considered an interesting case study due to its unique position. On the one hand, Österreichischer Rundfunk (ORF) is confronted with the same problems as other European PSM enterprises, such as criticism for receiving public subsidies. On the other hand, the late liberalization of the radio and broadcasting market, which was only completed in 2002, allowed ORF to remain the most important national radio and TV outlet up until now. The same applies to online services of ORF, which remain popular among the media users in Austria.

The current study focusses on the audience's perspective. The research question is: How and why do different (groups of) people use ORF or refrain from using PSM in Austria? The goal is to indicate how different groups in Austrian society perceive the performance of PSM and the way public service values are delivered. This paper examines people's evaluations of PSM quality and practices. In the study, specific features of the Austrian media landscape, i.e. historical, social, cultural and political circumstances, as well as potential models for the development of PSM are considered. The ideas presented here are likely to enhance the understanding of the ways in which PSM in other countries need to evolve in order to stay relevant for a large number of contemporary media users.

Public support in public service media – theoretical considerations and practical implications

Media are often described as shared cultural forums. They provide common ground for everyday talk, but also for the most pressing and important issues in society, and for how those issues should be discussed. The metaphor of television as campfires of modern societies reflects this notion. Especially in Europe, PSM have long been places where large audiences gathered in one place for specific period of time. With audiences becoming more individualized and fragmented, some fear for their role in sustaining social cohesion.

There are two main reasons for an increasing fragmentation of the audience (Napoli, 2011), namely the growing abundance of media choices and a broader socio-cultural trend towards individualization. In broadcasting media, due to cable and satellite technology, the number of available channels has grown enormously. Digitization has boosted this development, which culminated in a multiplication of media choices across different types of content on the Internet. More and more services are now available on demand. Some scholars observe this change with grave concern (Katz, 1996; Sunstein, 2001), but empirical findings reveal a more complex picture. People do not withdraw to isolated enclaves where they only choose media that meets their personal interests or supports their own views. However, it is true that former television strongholds, for example in the United States, have lost their reach significantly (Webster, 2005). Webster and Ksiazek (2012) show that the notion of drastic dismembering of society is not appropriate. Instead, people's media repertoires overlap, and these points of convergence have turned out to be the most popular media choices. The study indicates three reasons why popular offerings will remain, even in times where each individual has countless options to choose from. First then, according to the authors, not all media products are of the same quality. Audiences tend to choose and gather around offerings of higher quality, if the price does not hinder them. In addition to this, media consumption has a social component. Social desirability plays a role; media provide topics for conversation in everyday life. Conversations circling around media content attract others to this content, because they want to know what people are talking about. Finally, media are experience goods. Thus, people rely on recommendations and search algorithms to navigate through the abundance of choices, which usually promote popular media products (Webster and Ksiazek, 2012). Nevertheless, there is evidence that today's audiences have become more diverse. Younger generations avoid choosing traditional media such as television or radio. Meanwhile, older generations are rarely familiar with online-based media (European Commission, 2015: 7–19).

It might be argued here that such diverse audiences go in line with diverse theoretical approaches. There might be more or less suitable concepts to explicate PSM attention or avoidance among certain groups of people or in certain situations. One of the most prominent explanations for media choices is the uses and gratifications approach, whereby active users choose the offering that they think will give them the highest fulfilment of their needs. These sought gratifications are often condensed into lists, including motives such as information, entertainment, escape from the stress of daily life, or improving social interaction (Katz, Blumler and Gurevitch, 1973; Ruggiero, 2000). As levels of audience activity and involvement vary, the uses and gratifications approach does not seem to go far enough. Ritualized or habitual behaviour also plays an important role in people's attention towards media (Rubin, 1993; Rubin and Perse, 1987). Furthermore, people do not usually choose from all available options, they tend to rely on certain media repertoires as a result of their ongoing selectivity, experience and habits. Media repertoires are those media offerings used on a regular basis; they reduce the costs related to selective media exposure by narrowing down the offerings that are to be considered (Hasebrink and Popp, 2006; Kim, 2014; Taneja, Webster, Malthouse and Ksiazek, 2012). Further possible explanations for people's attention to media in general and PSM in particular might be schemata and decision heuristics that allow for fast and frugal media choices. For example, such decisions are based on mere recognition; people are more likely to resort to media choices, brands, or personnel they already know or recognize than to content they experience for the first time (Marewski, Galesic, Gigerenzer and Hartmann, 2009; Rumelhart, 1984). People's media attention might also be guided by the presumed obligation to stay informed; they may assess attention to news as their civic duty (Poindexter and McCombs, 2001).

While public support is crucial to the concept of PSM, academic concern is lacking. Arguments on this matter are usually based on either ratings or opinion polls, or a combination of these. Expectations towards PSM and their assessment are not adequately researched. In this regard reports and studies by regulatory authorities, such as Ofcom (2014) in the UK and PSM themselves as in the case of ARD in Germany (Reitze and Ridder, 2011) provide insights on the evaluation of PSM by the public. The Ofcom (2014) report shows that satisfaction with the performance of PSM in the UK remains high. For instance, the study indicates that 77 percent of British viewers consider themselves to be quite or very satisfied with the British Broadcasting Corporation (BBC) offerings. The report also claims that audiences appreciate online and on-demand services. While Ofcom's report focuses solely on PSM, the German long-term study *Massenkommunikation* (translates to mass communication) contrasts PSM to commercial television programs (Reitze and Ridder, 2011: 105–134). On the one hand, the results in Germany show that factuality, trustworthiness, and competence are attributes attached more often to PSM than to private media companies. On the other hand, the content provided by private media enjoys a casual, modern, and entertaining image. Nevertheless, people are more likely to depend on PSM for information, as 77 percent of Germans say they usually obtain information from PSM rather than commercial television enterprises.

Public service media in Austria

Austria, a small EU member state with approximately 8.5 million inhabitants, offers some peculiarities and insights that make its study worthwhile. Hallin and Mancini (2004), consider that media-political relations in Austria represent the democratic corporatist tradition, which is characterized – above all – by strong political parallelism and high journalistic professionalization. With neighboring Germany sharing the same language and similar culture, media outlets face huge competition from abroad (Künzler, Puppis and Steinmaurer, 2011; Puppis, 2009). PSM and commercial channels from Germany have been popular since the 1980s, whereas the first licenses for commercial media outlets in Austria were granted in 1995 for radio and 2002 for television.

Due to this, the Austrian ORF has historically held a strong position in the market, although audience shares have recently decreased. Its two main television channels – ORF eins and ORF 2 – reached 69 percent of the TV audience in 1991, while by 2014 these numbers have dropped to 49 percent (Medienforschung ORF, n.d.-b). Nevertheless, the market shares of ORF eins (11.8 percent in 2015) and ORF 2 (21.4 percent) among Austrian viewers are significantly higher than the market shares of any other channel (Medienforschung ORF, n.d.-c). In addition, ORF operates two special interest channels called ORF Sport +, which focuses on less popular sports events, and ORF III, which deals with culture and information. Moreover, there is a long-term cooperation with German and Swiss PSM to operate the transnational TV channel 3sat with various broadcasts from the three countries.

Besides various TV channels, ORF provides three nationwide radio channels: Ö1, Ö3 and FM4. Ö1 can be described as the most serious and information-oriented radio station on offer with a broad range of newscasts, reports, radio plays and classical music. Ö3 – a music-oriented format, which combines entertainment and news, is the most successful radio station in Austria. In the first half of 2015, its daily range was 44.5 percent among 14–49 year-old Austrians (Medienforschung ORF, n.d.-d). FM4 was established in 1994 and since then has followed the idea of giving a platform to "the growing alternative culture and way of living of the younger generation" (FM4, n.d.). Apart from the national radio channels, ORF runs nine regional radio channels (Ö2), one for each federal state of Austria, which are produced by nine regional newsrooms. The newsrooms also produce content for TV news coverage.

ORF has Austria's most frequently accessed news website orf.at. Half of the Austrian Internet population visit ORF's web services at least once a month (Medienforschung ORF, n.d.-a). Another service that has gained popularity in recent years is the so-called ORF TVthek, a video on demand service offering mainly catch-up television.

While the market shares of ORF and its position in the market are well documented, evaluations, usage patterns, or support for PSM from the audience's point of view of have not yet become the subject of systemic investigation (Gonser, 2011). The consideration of public support is usually only confined to discussing declining or steady ratings. ORF itself, as part of its quality assurance measures, conducts a regular survey as well as focus groups on the audience's satisfaction with its programs. However, these inquiries are mainly for internal use and therefore are not published in a scholarly way (ORF, n.d.; Schächter, 2014).

Methodology

This paper is mainly based on qualitative results of the research project "Public Value goes international"[1], which focussed on the audience's attitudes towards PSM in Austria by evaluating semi-structured qualitative interviews (N=48) conducted in the winter of 2014 and spring of 2015. In order to increase the depth of the analysis, interviewees were selected according to three demographic criteria (see: Table 1): sex (f=24; m=24); four age groups (in years) 18–29 (AG1), 30–49 (AG2), 50–69 (AG3) and 70+ (AG4) (n=12 per age group), and three levels of education Primary (P), Secondary (S) and Tertiary (T) (n=16 per educational level). The interviewees were individually coded to protect their anonymity using the # key, random Arabic numerals and the three demographic criteria: #1 to #48 (sex/age group/education level), for example #32 (f/AG3/T). The study used *Atlas.ti* to code and analyze the interviews (Friese, 2014).

Table 1: Participants in the interviews

		Level of education			
Age group	**Sex**	**Primary (P)**	**Secondary (S)**	**Tertiary (T)**	**Total**
AG1 (18–29 years)	Male (m)	#1	#17	#33	6
		#2	#18	#34	
	Female (f)	#3	#19	#35	6
		#4	#20	#36	
AG2 (30–49 years)	Male (m)	#5	#21	#37	6
		#6	#22	#38	
	Female (f)	#7	#23	#39	6
		#8	#24	#40	

1 The project "Public Value goes international" (2014–2016) brings together PSM researchers from Austria, Belgium, Finland and Germany to collaborate on audience- and content-related issues in several European countries. It receives funding by Vienna Municipal Department 23 for Economic Affairs, Labour and Statistics (MA23); further information: www.journalismusdreinull.at/en.

		Level of education			
Age group	**Sex**	**Primary (P)**	**Secondary (S)**	**Tertiary (T)**	**Total**
AG3 (50–69 years)	Male (m)	#9	#25	#41	6
		#10	#26	#42	
	Female (f)	#11	#27	#43	6
		#12	#28	#44	
AG4 (70+ years)	Male (m)	#13	#29	#45	6
		#14	#30	#46	
	Female (f)	#15	#31	#47	6
		#16	#32	#48	
Total		16	16	16	48

Source: Authors.

Nonetheless, this paper also draws on data from a previous research project[2], which included a quantitative telephone survey (N=1,000 across all ages) in the winter of 2009/2010 (Gonser, 2010; Latzl and Troxler, 2010) and an experimental study of 90 Austrian students in May 2011 (Neumüller and Gonser, 2013) for secondary analysis. Some of the survey items resemble the aforementioned German study *Massenkommunikation* (Reitze and Ridder, 2011; Breunig and Engel, 2015) and the British annual PSB report (Ofcom, 2014). In the experiment, three groups of students were shown the same TV news footage. In Group 1, the newscast did not display any TV channel logo; in Group 2, the logo of ORF appeared, and in Group 3 the logo of ORF's commercial competitor ATV was shown – from which the TV news footage originally came. The present study combines quantitative and qualitative research methods to observe objectives from different perspectives and with the benefits of every method. Thus, our results from the quantitative surveys are amplified by using qualitative data for deeper understanding.

Findings from quantitative studies

The quantitative data show that Austrian citizens highly agree that PSM are important for society and, to a somewhat lesser degree, that they have an impact on their daily life. For instance, when asked about the importance of ORF, 76 percent of the survey participants across all age groups (N = 1,000) agreed or fully agreed

2 The project, which took place from 2008 to 2012, concentrated on the specifics of the national broadcasting market. It was financially supported by the Austrian Research Promotion Agency (FFG) and the Vienna Municipal Department 27.

that ORF is important for individual citizens. The same question posed on the importance for society as a whole had the support of 81 percent of respondents. In addition to general tendencies, several differences between younger and older people were observed. For example, people over the age of 50 were more likely to emphasize the importance of PSM for society (84–94 percent) and for themselves (79–88 percent). At the same time, only 73 percent of respondents from the 20–29 year-olds age group perceived the importance of PSM for society, and 67 percent said ORF was important for themselves (see Figure 1).

Figure 1: Importance of public service broadcasting for the individual and for society as a whole

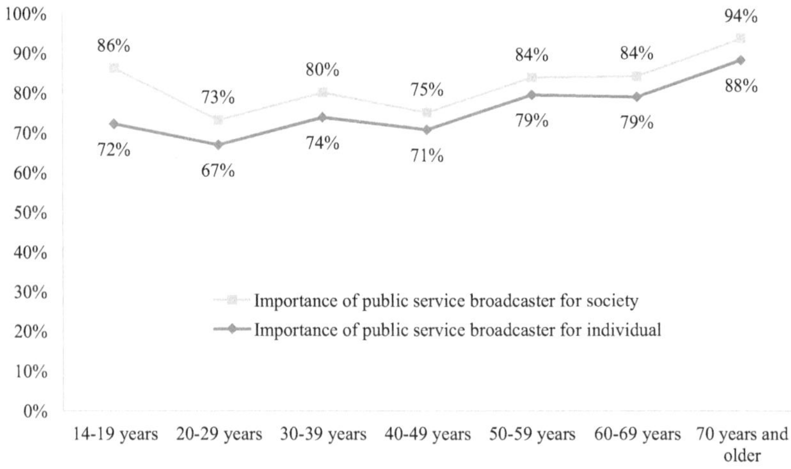

N = 1,000, data evaluated on the 5-items scale: 1 = "not important at all", 5 = "very important". The figure shows the percentage of interviewees who agreed and fully agreed. Source: Authors.

More specific attributions towards PSM and commercial media were also analyzed during the experiment in which 90 Austrian students were asked to evaluate TV news based on media outlets' images. Participants considered the same TV news story to be more matter-of-fact and better researched if it was branded as footage from ORF. Compared to the same material branded as a newscast by the private competitor ATV (where the news was broadcast originally), the ORF-labelled news story was perceived as more informative, serious and trustworthy. At the same time, the same news item was categorized as less modern and varied (Neumüller and Gonser, 2013). These assumptions confirmed the general perception of ORF as less modern, similarly entertaining and independent, but a more likeable, sophisticated, trustworthy and informative media outlet than its commercial competitors (see Figure 2). This resembled data gathered when studying the public perception of PSM in Germany (Reitze and Ridder, 2011).

Figure 2: Image of PSM programs (means for ORF eins and ORF 2) and of commercial programs (means from Puls 4 and ATV)

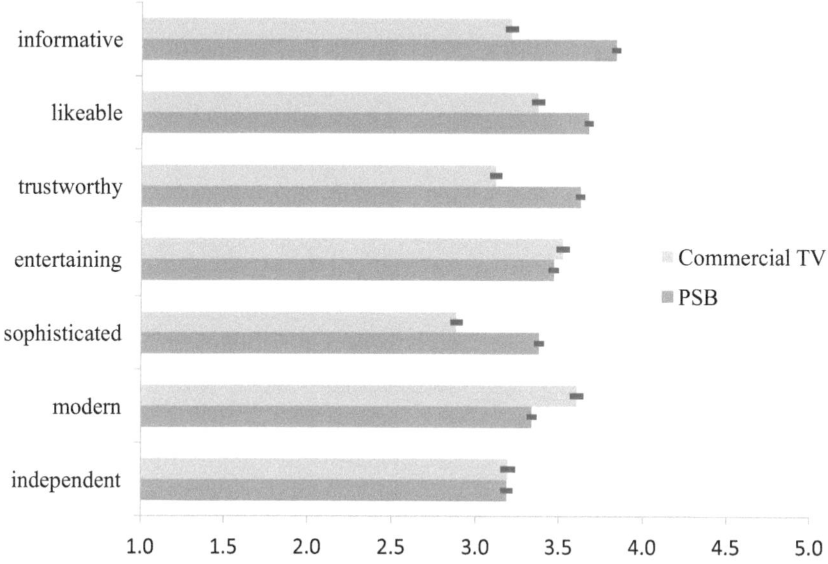

N = 1000. Data evaluated on the 5-items scale: 1 = "attribute does not apply at all", 5 = "attribute applies completely". Mean values and 95 percent CI are highlighted. Source: Authors.

In the telephone interviews, older people indicated they used ORF 2 more often than ORF eins, while the news website orf.at was used more often by representatives of younger generations[3]. The in-depth study of media use also revealed the way the two main TV channels were perceived. For instance, ORF 2 was seen as creating more value for society than ORF eins: 67 percent of respondents, compared to 59 percent for ORF eins, said that it offered high value to Austrian society. This might be due to the fact that the overall goal of ORF eins is to reach younger audiences with more entertainment-oriented and international productions (see Figures 3 and 4).

3 This survey was undertaken in the winter of 2009/2010, it is therefore safe to assume that the overall usage of orf.at has risen since then. Market research supports this assumption. In January 2010 orf.at registered 4.8 million unique clients; by May 2015 the number had increased to 8.8 million (ÖWA, n.d.-a, n.d.-b).

While both studies referred to above give insight into people's assessment and usage of PSM, they do not tell how the audiences reach their preferences and conclusions. This is why a qualitative in-depth approach was selected for the more recent inquiry.

Figure 3: Usage of ORF offerings

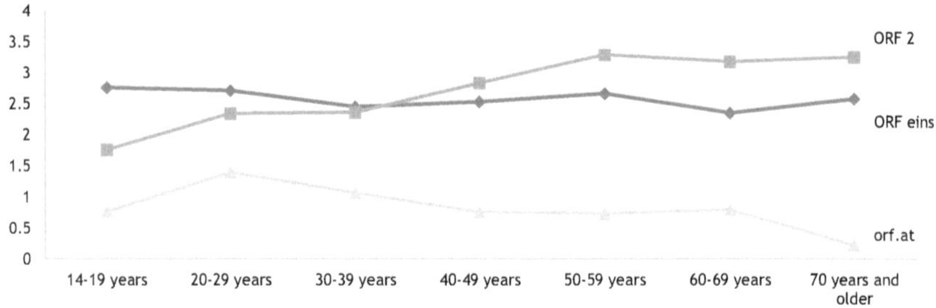

N = 1,000. Data evaluated on the 5-items scale 0 = "never", 4 = "on a daily basis". Means of answers by age groups. Source: Authors.

Figure 4: Assessment of main PSB programs' value for society

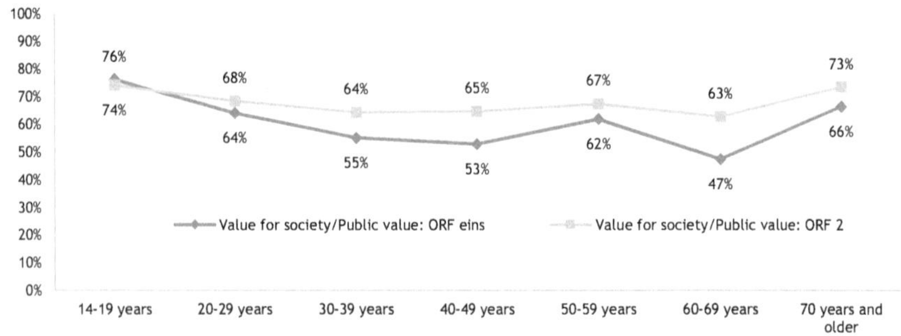

N = 1,000. Data evaluated on the 5-items scale 1 = "not at all high", 5 = "very high". Percentages of answers in the top 2 categories (high and very high). Source: Authors.

Findings from qualitative interviews

The interviews revealed a vivid and multi-faceted relationship between the Austrian PSM and their audience. Individual differences might have been found in routines and habits as well as in expected gratifications and schemata. Age and socialization seemed to influence both attitudes towards PSM in general and the actual ORF use. In particular, the use of linear and non-linear services drew a line between audience groups. Moreover, well-known media representatives such as anchor-men and -women appeared to exert influence on the way people think about and turn to PSM in their everyday lives.

Routines and habits

Certain routines and habits of PSM usage were indicated in every age group of respondents, concerning all of ORF's services, throughout the day. For instance, #30(m/AG4/S) pointed out that the radio is turned on when he is still in bed, whereas another interviewee gets his first update on the events of the day from the web:

> My day starts with orf.at, there I get most of the information that I need for the day. [#5, m/AG2/P]

A common practice among several interviewees was to visit the news website orf.at repeatedly during the day, for example:

> It starts in the morning; at noon, I take a second glimpse; in between, I have to work. In the evening, I am interested in how matters have developed. [#9, m/AG3/P]

Another interviewee, a self-confessed "a news junkie" gathers information predominantly online:

> I feel what I do is not healthy any more. I permanently browse platforms like *orf.at* (…) to learn what's happening. [#36, f/AG1/T]

While the radio is listened to mostly in the morning and online news are consumed all day long, Austria has a widespread tradition of watching the evening news on TV. This particularly holds true among older interviewees such as #42(m/AG3/T) who watches *Zeit im Bild*[4] and #45(m/AG4/T):

> In the evening I like to watch *Niederösterreich Heute* or *Wien Heute*[5], if my wife joins me. [#45, m/AG4/T]

For the older generations, sitting down at a certain time in front of the TV set is embedded in their daily routine. It can be seen as a consolidated and rather unalterable benchmark in their lives.

Linear TV use is a huge contrast to the preferences of some of the younger audience. The invariable practice of several respondents was to turn to the computer in order to stream. The content may be mainly produced by PSM for their TV

---

4 *Zeit im Bild* is ORF's main newscast.

5 *Niederösterreich Heute* and *Wien Heute* are two of ORF's regional newscasts.

channels but any notion of access and use other than streaming appears odd or out-dated to them: One of them explained that she and her boyfriend:

> [we] do not have a TV set any more. We only stream. If there's something we're interested in – if, for instance, a friend sends us a link (…) we stream it. That's our way of watching TV. [#20, f/AG1/S]

Non-linear streaming does not necessarily mean avoidance of content originally broadcast on linear TV. For instance, #39(f/AG2/T) said she watched the news online, mostly on orf.at or the TVthek, conferring the notion that streaming offers an alternative way of consuming TV. It gives users the freedom of choice when to watch on a range of devices. In addition, streaming enables users to be their own directors:

> Whenever I watch something that has originally been on TV, I mean content by ORF, 3Sat, Arte or the like, I use the app and watch it on demand because it allows me to take a break or jump to the next section. I prefer that. [#36, f/AG1/T]

Gratifications and schemata

As demonstrated above, linear and non-linear broadcast use is not limited to a particular age group. However, data gathered from the interviews imply that the young and middle-aged make (more) deliberate decisions on when and why they watch TV or listen to the radio. Interviewees correlate listening to broadcasts (radio or TV) to relaxing after an exhausting workday:

> I only turn to light entertainment when I am very tired, to fall asleep faster; thus, it should be relaxing. [#11, f/AG3/P]

> the TV is on only in the evening, to relax (…) I've become used to watching TV one hour before going to bed. [#38, m/AG2/T]

Apart from entertainment and relaxation, the desire for reliable information was another reason for using PSM, regardless of age. Interestingly, specific circumstances like upcoming elections or catastrophes might also attract listeners and viewers who do not turn to linear radio or TV normally as part of their everyday routines. One predominantly online user, talked about situations where she would prefer traditional TV news coverage:

> *Zeit im Bild* keeps you up-to-date. If there is an alarm message for instance, you immediately know why. [#4, f/AG1/P]

A radio listener referred making exceptions to her ordinary media routines if she is in need of specific information:

> I rarely listen to the radio, only if there is something of particular interest to me like traffic information on Ö3. [#12, f/AG3/P]

Fast and up-to-date news are the main arguments for the online service orf.at:

> It is obvious why I use the ORF homepage: I want to hear the news as fast as possible. The site is continually updated; if you only have a moment to spend, the ORF homepage is probably the best choice. [#22, m/AG2/S]

Nevertheless #45(m/AG4/T) appreciated that he could see at a glance what was happening in the world when accessing Austrian PSM's official website and he also indicated being interested in news and gathering pictures and headlines from orf.at.

Another motivation to turn to the offerings of ORF is follow-up conversation on media coverage. Some of the interview partners explicitly stated that they use media in order to be prepared for conversations with friends or customers at work, such #2(m/AG1/P) who hoped to find interesting news on orf.at in order to be ready to join the conversation if anyone brought up the issue:

> I'm a hairdresser and I need that sort of general knowledge to chat with my customers if they start talking about it. [#4, f/AG1/P]

Another reason is to act on personal recommendations:

> If a friend's talking about news you haven't heard yet, you're very likely to look it up. Or, if she sends you a video from the *TVThek*, you're likely to watch it. [#20, f/AG1/S]

Prominence and quality

The interviews provided evidence that specific PSM programmes and personnel have a crucial role in attracting the attention of audience groups that would otherwise be out of touch with PSM. In Austria, this seems to be the case with the ORF anchor-man, Armin Wolf, who is widely known and respected as a top journalist and he is successfully (privately) engaged in social media. Due to his reputation, people not only trust him when he presents the late-night news on TV, but also identify him as a credible source online like #39(f/AG2/T) who admitted to primarily reading his posts and gathering news from his status messages via Facebook and Twitter. There is also the suggestion that Mr. Wolf's engagement in social networks may inspire users to reconnect with PSM particularly if Facebook user's friends share his links or comments:

> Frequently, posts by Armin Wolf appear in my Facebook timeline because many of my friends like them, which occasionally makes me click on some statistics or other things he mentions. [#20, f/AG1/S]

The phenomenon of Armin Wolf and his followers can be seen as proof of trustworthiness of PSM and their staff.

In the interviews, representatives from all age groups called for PSM to be distinctive from commercial media and to offer higher quality. As a tendency, older interviewees were more likely to attribute these expected characteristics to PSM, such as #42(m/AG3/T)'s view that PSM have the duty to inform the public, which they more or less fulfil and #14(m/AG4/P) beliefs that ORF offers more high-quality programs than private TV and radio channels.

It is noteworthy that many of the expectations and positive evaluations uttered by the audience resemble some of the criteria of quality journalism. People expected PSM to tell the truth, to be independent from political or economic influences, to tell unbiased and well-researched stories, and to give a voice to the unheard. As well as this, at least to some degree, people also considered PSM to fulfil those expectations, which are key notions of reliable and relevant journalism (Kovach and Rosenstiel, 2007). This might be seen as an indicator that the Austrian audience still perceives ORF as an agency of quality journalism.

This might be seen as an indicator that the Austrian audience still perceives ORF as an agency of quality journalism.

License fees

The interviews unveil a paradox: despite heavy ORF usage, a very negative attitude towards paying regular charges for PSM was found among a remarkable number of respondents. Several interviews featured a lack of or inaccurate knowledge of how or which financial resources ORF receives and which services these resources maintain. Younger users were more likely to be reluctant to pay any fees in addition to fees for cable TV providers. On an access-based level, reasoning like that is fully comprehensible because, indeed, the cable provider connects the PSM services, together with an abundance of other channels, to viewers' homes. Isabel was unaware that none of her money goes from the cable service provider to ORF, while the PSM fees, which are mandatory for any Austrian household with a TV or radio, go into content creation, staff costs and the like.

Conclusions

The aim of this paper was to indicate the ways and reasons why diverse societal groups in Austria use or refrain from using PSM. The findings presented here are based on a multi-method design, including experimental, quantitative and qualitative studies from two consecutive research projects designed to measure the public perception of ORF. What can be learnt from quantitative and qualitative research is that Austrians attribute high importance to PSM, especially when asked about the contribution of ORF to the society as a whole. Remarkably, none of the participants reported that they totally refrain from using ORF, which is an indication that PSM outlets in Austria are (still) appealing to a large and diverse audience.

Considering the results of research on ORF, it is tempting to conclude that PSM in Austria are well suited to continue to provide popular offerings for large segments of the audience, even in these times of fragmented audiences. This is due to the fact that ORF is part of the daily routines and media habits of Austrians. The variety of services, ranging from linear radio and TV to non-linear online content, appeals to different lifestyles as well as individual tastes and time budgets. In addition to this, ORF delivers topics for follow-up conversation. Some people explicitly mentioned that they listen to public service radio or read public service news online in order to be able take part in everyday conversation. In Austria PSM is seen as a credible and high quality news provider. For example, the quantitative findings show that people associate positive adjectives, like informative and trustworthy, with ORF's news coverage. Apart from that, people trust media representatives, such as the ORF news anchor-man, Armin Wolf, as thoughtful and reliable sources of information. Finally, ORF is recommended, not only offline, but also online through social media. People's personal selection heuristics favour PSM content because of the popular media brand and attributed qualities.

The semi-structured interviews confirmed theoretical conceptions that the relationships of people with the media in general, and PSM in particular, are complex. They tend to include habitual usage patterns, active gratification seeking, and at times just taking what comes along. A beloved habit for many Austrians is to tune in to the radio in the morning. The desire to receive news early in the day is not restricted to the elderly audience, but can also be found among younger users. While some still listen to (online) radio in the morning, many turn on their phone as part of waking up. When doing so, many rely on ORF's news site orf.at to get an update on current events in the morning and later on during the day. Of course, ORF's services are not the only offerings used on different devices, but they remain constant in many people's media repertoires. In the course of a day, people choose different selections of all available offerings. While there is still space for selectivity and audience activity, people also "rely on habit and iteration in creating their media repertoires" (Taneja, Webster, Malthouse and Ksiazek, 2012: 964). Based on the analysis of the interviews, Webster and Ksiazek (2012: 51) statement that although "no two people will have identical media repertoires, the chances are they will have much in common" can be believed to be true in Austria as well. Indeed, ORF is frequently shared in many repertoires. Assuming that the evening news is included in two people's media repertoires, it is very likely that both tune in to ORF's newscast *Zeit im Bild*. When it comes to online news, the usage of orf.at turned out to be a common answer. A similar situation occurred concerning radio usage, as one of the national or regional ORF channels is very likely to be chosen. Respondents relying on social filtering and social media also mentioned that people share PSM content with them frequently.

Despite the manifold ways in which people are accessing and using PSM in Austria nowadays, the interviews also uncovered problematic developments that could undermine the importance of ORF. First, it is obvious that PSM – despite late liberalization of the national radio and TV market – are not the only media in Austrian citizens' media repertoires, and that not all PSM offerings can be found in everyone's repertoire. Particularly with younger users, commercial media use appears to be greater than PSM. Second, only a small number of interviewees expressed a general willingness to pay for ORF. This is more a hypothetical issue than an actual threat to the PSM's financing, as everyone who has a radio or TV set in Austria is compelled to pay licence fees. Still, the perceptible discontent must be interpreted as a sign of decreasing support for the concept of PSM and must be taken seriously.

As pointed out earlier, the audience has not yet fully recognized ORF's transition from public service broadcasting to public service media. For instance, orf.at is very popular, but many do not think of it as part of the license fees. Consequently, several participants were averse to license fees because they believe they are paying for services that they do not use at all. An advanced understanding of which content or services are funded through license fees appears to enhance the individual's willingness to pay. In the development of such an understanding, ORF may be advised not to leave the audience uninformed. There should be an expansion of information and communication with the public about the services and values provided in order to prove their digital competence. Due to the fact that broad citizen support is identified as crucial for the concept of PSM in general and the viability of national PSM in particular, the recommendation to improve and permanently update communication efforts may be put to PSM companies all over Europe. Drawing conclusions from the case of ORF, another recommendation should be directed towards national PSM regulators: although it seems reasonable that regulatory authorities ensure competition in the media market, they should not undermine PSM's capacity to move wherever the audiences are.

Allowing for innovation and flexibility is essential for PSM to offer services in different ways to remain relevant to (potentially) every citizen.

References

Bardoel, J., and L. d' Haenens (2008). Reinventing public service broadcasting in Europe. Prospects, promises and problems. *Media, Culture and Society*, vol. 30(3): 337–355.

Berg, C.E., G.F. Lowe, and A. B. Lund (2014). A market failure perspective on value creation in PSM. In: G.F. Lowe and F. Martin (eds.), *The value of public service media*. Göteborg: Nordicom, 105–126.

Breunig, C., and B. Engel (2015). Massenkommunikation 2015: Funktionen und Images der Medien im Vergleich [Mass communication 2015: Media's functions and images in comparison]. *Media Perspektiven*, 7: 323–341. Retrieved January 25, 2016 from http://www.ard-werbung.de/fileadmin/user_upload/media-perspektiven/pdf/2015/07082015_Breunig_Engel.pdf.

European Commission (2015). *Standard Eurobarometer 82. Media use in the European Union* (No. 2015.2370). Retrieved December 7, 2015 from http://ec.europa.eu/public_opinion/archives/eb/eb82/eb82_media_en.pdf.

FM4 (n.d.). *About Radio FM4*. Retrieved January 11, 2016 from http://fm4.orf.at/radio/stories/about.

Friese, S. (2014). *Qualitative data analysis with ATLAS.ti*. Thousand Oaks, CA: Sage.

Gonser, N. (2010). Public Value und die Rolle des Publikums: Zwischen Anspruch und Wirklichkeit [Public Value and the role of the audience. Between claim and reality]. *Medien Journal*, vol. 34(2): 40–50.

Gonser, N. (2011). *Integrativ und individuell: Unterschiedliche Ansprüche verschiedener Publikumsgruppen* [Integrative and individual. Different claims of different audiences]. *Texte*, 6: 20–23.

Hallin, D. C., and P. Mancini (2004). *Comparing media systems: Three models of media and politics*. Cambridge: Cambridge University Press.

Harrison, J., and L.M. Woods (2001). Defining European public service broadcasting. *European Journal of Communication*, vol. 16(4): 477–504.

Hasebrink, U., and J. Popp (2006). Media repertoires as a result of selective media use: A conceptual approach to the analysis of patterns of exposure. *Communications*, vol. 31(3): 369–387.

Katz, E. (1996). And deliver us from segmentation. *The ANNALS of the American Academy of Political and Social Science*, vol. 546(1): 22–33.

Katz, E., J.G. Blumler, and M. Gurevitch (1973). Uses and gratifications research. *The Public Opinion Quarterly*, vol. 37(4): 509–523.

Kim, S.J. (2014). A repertoire approach to cross-platform media use behavior. *New Media & Society*, vol. 7(15): 1–20.

Kovach, B., and T. Rosenstiel (2007). *The elements of journalism: What newspeople should know and the public should expect*. New York: Three Rivers.

Künzler, M., M. Puppis, and T. Steinmaurer (2011). Public Value in Kleinstaaten: Zielsetzungen, regulatorische Vorgaben und Strategien öffentlicher Rundfunkorganisationen in einer konvergenten Medienwelt [Public Value in small states. Defining goals, regulations and strategies of PSM in convergent media landscapes]. In: M. Karmasin, D. Süssenbacher, and N. Gonser (eds.), *Public Value: Theorie und Praxis im internationalen Vergleich* [Public Value: Theory and practical experience in comparison]. Wiesbaden: VS, 27–44.

Latzl, D.K., and R. Troxler (2010). Der Wert des öffentlich-rechtlichen Rundfunks für Jugendliche am Beispiel des ORF [The Value of PSB for young people as a case study of the ORF]. *Medien Journal*, vol. 34(2): 15–27.

Marewski, J.N., M. Galesic, G. Gigerenzer, and T. Hartmann (2009). Fast and frugal media choices. In: T. Hartmann (ed.), *Media choice: A theoretical and empirical overview*. New York: Routledge, 102–127.

Medienforschung ORF (n.d.-a). *ÖWA Plus: 4. Quartal 2014*. Retrieved December 17, 2015 from http://mediaresearch.orf.at/index2.htm?internet/internet_oewa%20plus.htm.

Medienforschung ORF (n.d.-b). *TV-Tagesreichweiten 1991–2014*. Retrieved December 17, 2015 from http://medienforschung.orf.at/c_fernsehen/console/console.htm?y=1&z=1.

Mediaforschung ORF (n.d.-c). *TV-Marktanteile 2014 nach Sendern*. Retrieved December 17, 2015 from http://mediaresearch.orf.at/c_fernsehen/console/console.htm?y=3&z=1.

Medienforschung ORF (n.d.-d) *Radio-Reichweiten, 1. Halbjahr 2015, Erwachsene 14–49, Mo-So*. Retrieved December 17, 2015 from http://mediaresearch.orf.at/c_radio/console/console.htm?y=1&z=2.

Napoli, P.M. (2011). *Audience evolution: New technologies and the transformation of media audiences*. New York: Columbia University Press.

Neumüller, M., and N. Gonser (2013). Alles anders? Unterscheidbarkeit als Kriterium für Public Value [Everything different? Variety as criteria for distinction of Public Value]. In: N. Gonser (ed.), *Die multimediale Zukunft des Qualitätsjournalismus* [The multimedia future of quality journalism]. Wiesbaden: Springer VS, 15–34.

Ofcom (2014). *PSB annual report 2014* (Research report). Retrieved June 30, 2015 from http://stakeholders.ofcom.org.uk/binaries/broadcast/reviews-investigations/psb-review/psb3/PSB_Annual_Report_2014.pdf.

ORF (n.d.). *Qualitätssicherungssystem* [Quality Assurance System]. Retrieved June 29, 2015 from http://zukunft.orf.at/show_content2.php?s2id=176.

ÖWA (n.d.-a). *ORF.at Network: Jänner 2010.* Retrieved July 8, 2015 from http://www.oewa.at/index.php?id=14477&style=details&siteid=18.

ÖWA (n.d.-b). *ORF.at Network: Mai 2015.* Retrieved July 8, 2015 from http://www.oewa.at/index.php?id=17069&style=details&siteid=18.

Poindexter, P.M., and M.E. McCombs (2001). Revisiting the civic duty to keep informed in the new media environment. *Journalism & Mass Communication Quarterly*, vol. 78(1): 113–126.

Puppis, M. (2009). Media regulation in small states. *International Communication Gazette*, vol. 71(1–2): 7–17.

Reitze, H., and C.M. Ridder (eds.) (2011). *Massenkommunikation VIII: Eine Langzeitstudie zur Mediennutzung und Medienbewertung 1964–2010* [Mass communication VIII: A long-term study for usage and evaluation of media]. Baden-Baden: Nomos.

Rubin, A.M. (1993). Audience activity and media use. *Communication Monographs*, vol. 60(1): 98–105.

Rubin, A.M., and E.M. Perse (1987). Audience activity and television news gratifications. *Communication Research*, vol. 14(1): 58–84.

Ruggiero, T.E. (2000). Uses and gratifications theory in the 21st century. *Mass Communication and Society*, vol. 3(1): 3–37.

Rumelhart, D.E. (1984). Schemata and the cognitive system. In: R.S. Wyer, and T.K. Srull (eds.), *Handbook of social cognition*. Mahwah: Erlbaum, 161–188.

Schächter, M. (2014). *Das Qualitätssicherungssystem des ORF im Jahr 2013: Gutachten zur Bewertung der Gesamtleistung* [Quality Assurance System of ORF in 2013: Survey of evaluation of the overall performance]. Retrieved June 29, 2015 from http://zukunft.orf.at/rte/upload/texte/2014/veroeffentlichung/orf_gutachten_2013.pdf.

Sunstein, C.R. (2001). *Republic.com*. Princeton, Oxford: Princeton University Press.

Taneja, H., J.G. Webster, E.C. Malthouse, and T.B. Ksiazek (2012). Media consumption across platforms: Identifying user-defined repertoires. *New Media & Society*, vol. 14(6): 951–968.

Webster, J.G. (2005). Beneath the veneer of fragmentation: Television audience polarization in a multichannel world. *Journal of Communication*, vol. 55(2): 366–382.

Webster, J.G., and T.B. Ksiazek (2012). The dynamics of audience fragmentation: Public attention in an age of digital media. *Journal of Communication*, vol. 62(1): 39–56.

Tiziano Bonini
Siena University, Italy

The participatory turn in public service media

Abstract: This paper discusses the current condition of public service media (PSM) as the network society and the emerging digital culture are changing the values traditionally embedded in the concept of PSM and the nature of media audiences. In doing so, the study takes the holistic view on several challenges that contemporary PSM have to face. Since its establishment, PSM have never been under as much pressure as with today's ongoing financial, economic and political crises, as well as other global socio-economic challenges. The paper argues that in order to understand the current necessary shifts in PSM one needs to take into account current PSM funding models, discussing both their advantages and weaknesses under the light of the changing media ecosystems. Finally, it addresses a need for participatory turn that advocates for a change in the way PSM have framed the audience's participation: from user-generated content to more structural participation.

Keywords: participatory turn, network society, user-generated content, structural participation, active audience, public service values.

Introduction

For most of the twentieth century, public service media (PSM) were institutions that were taken for granted; their services were regarded as guaranteed and essential components of European societies. On the other hand, at times, PSM considered themselves and their position of privilege with a sense of entitlement. But since the end of the 20th century, PSM have been called into question by both the liberalization of the telecommunications markets (Lowe and Berg, 2013) and by the emergence of the internet and digital culture (Lowe and Bardoel, 2007; Enli, 2008). The European Broadcasting Union (EBU, 2012) has recently put the emphasis on six core values for every PSM enterprise. This list includes universality of access, independence, excellence, innovation, diversity, and accountability; but these are hard values to maintain in an age of economic and political crisis and commercial and technological competition. Born (2005: 7), who studied change management and production culture in the case of BBC, once claimed that "each building block of the phrase 'public,' 'service' and 'broadcasting' has long been cast into doubt." Since their establishment, PSM have never been under as much pressure as with today's ongoing financial, economic and political crisis (Iosifidis, 2010). PSM is also challenged by neoliberal sentiments, convergence, internationalization and globalization, privatization and commercialization (Syvertsen, 2003). All of this creates a situation, in which the values and legitimacy of PSM is being questioned and called for adaptation to the new age.

Scholars have dared to declare that the end of PSM is drawing near. Hendy (2013: 2), in his recent work on public service, quotes scholars such as Tracey, "who believes that if the public service was once the single most important social, cultural and journalistic phenomenon of the twentieth century, it had definitively become a corpse on leave by the start of the twenty-first." But Hendy does not agree with Tracey in declaring PSM a walking dead institution. He rather claims that "its disappearence would represent a real and deep-seated crisis within liberal democracy" (Hendy, 2013: 3). Hendy argues that traditional values of PSM, such as freedom of commercial influence and pluralism have a role to play. In addition to a set of traditional values, he adds new social values, such as *mindfulness* "of the value to be found in collective experiences and in nurturing our collective potential" (Hendy, 2013: 3). This emphasis on the social benefits of PSM is a recent one; Bardoel and d'Haenens (2008: 343) claim that:

> Traditionally, the political function of PSB [public service broadcasting – Author] in relation to democracy, pluralism and public debate was emphasized, but more recently socio-cultural goals, such as serving social integration and cohesion, cultural bonding and bridging, have become more prominent.

Trappel (2014) believes that the ongoing process of change requires PSM to reconsider the value creation model: the more media firms concentrate on the creation of social value, alongside economic and business value, the better these firms will perform and succeed in the age of mass-self communication. Following Picard (2010: 61), Trappel proposes a reconceptualization of the values associated with PSM thus far, in favour of a greater emphasis on the social benefits that PSM can generate (2014: 132–141).

Recent debates make it clear that a transition from traditional values associated with PSM in the 20th century is underway, leading to a new series of values that are more suitable to the context of the network society, which places social benefits before economic ones. The process formally began in 2004, with the BBC's publication of the document *Building Public Value: Renewing the BBC for a Digital World*. Here, the BBC proposed increasing its public value by encouraging citizens to use, understand and enjoy digital information technologies; supporting active and informed citizenship; providing programmes that enrich lives and culture, included multimedia interactive resources and participatory storytelling projects. This transition to a new social role of PSM in the digital age is still in its early stages, but it has already found its way into the official documents, including

European ones. EBU (2014a) recently published the document *EBU Vision 2020. Connecting to a networked society*, in which this transition towards the social benefits of PSM is highly emphasized. According to EBU (2014a: 10): "The key is to open our organizations and connect with a networked society by continuously building trust and Return on Society."[1]

This paper offers an overview of the PSM's stressful condition in Europe and proposes a normative shift towards the participatory model of PSM. The hypothesis is that in a more networked and interactive media environment, the role of PSM audiences is transforming itself into a more open and participatory one. Audiences are always more used to not only to receiving content, but to produce, circulate and share content (Jenkins et al., 2013). A participatory turn is happening in the way audiences engage with media content and media companies. PSM values then, should follow this change and adapt to the changing ecosystem of media and the shifting habits of media consumption. The paper evidences that PSM companies in Europe are already discussing the issue of participation, but still they only associate audience participation to user-generated content. This paper argues that PSM's perception could benefit from a deeper PSM commitment in extending audience participation models and tools, which include letting people participate not only in the generation of content but also in the decisional process about PSM governance and funding. For this reason, an overview of all the existing PSM funding models will be given. In addition, the paper will emphasize the weaknesses and advantages of every model. Thirdly, the paper will advocate for a reform in the direction of a funding model able to make sense of the participatory turn currently happening in the way audiences engage with the media. To do so, consideration on "participatory turn" and for "structural participation," concepts initially developed by Carpentier (2011), will be provided.

Funding public service media and its impact on PSM perception

Lowe and Berg (2013) describe four modes of receipt for funding media: license fees, direct subsidy, subscription or pay-per-view, and advertising. Each of these

1 EBU uses the term Return-on-Society to describe the various positive effects PSM can have on society: "It is the social equivalent of the economic term return-on-investment (RoI), that measures the revenues weighed against a company's investments. Return-on-society is not yet well defined, but can encompass various dimensions. The proposal is to develop this concept and coin (an equivalent of) this term in order to make the case for PSM" (EBU, 2014a: 10).

models has different implications for the independence, reputation, cultural diversity and content quality of PSM (Syvertsen et al., 2014). On average, EBU members receive 60 percent of their financing from license fees, 29 percent from commercial income such as advertising, sponsoring, merchandising and programme sales, and 10 percent from non-license fee public funding (EBU 2014b). There are many differences among European countries. In Finland, Norway and Sweden, license fees account for more than 90 percent of their PSM's total income. In Germany, ARD and ZDF receive 83.5 percent of their income from license fees and 0.9 percent from public funds. In France, license fees cover 65 percent of the PSM income. In Italy, RAI relies on advertising for 31 percent of its income and on license fees for 60 percent. In the UK, license fees represent 70.4 percent of the total income of the BBC, and public funds 8 percent accordingly (EBU 2014b). Depending on advertising revenues means producing attractive consumers for ad investors. Lowe and Berg (2013: 91) highlight that:

> for a media firm that depends on advertising revenue, there is no economic benefit to producing content that appeals to people of limited interest to their advertiser base. Thus, the funding mode has impact on content in various ways, mainly indirect but, nonetheless, real.

The total level of PSM funding in the EBU area was €33.8 billion in 2012. This represents an increase of 1.3 percent over 5 years (2007–2012). However, if the effects of inflation were taken into account, then the 2012 total funding of PSM would be down 9.8 percent between 2007 and 2012 (EBU 2014a).

These figures, provided by the EBU, show that the trend during the last few years moves in one direction: towards budget cuts and revenue reduction, though proportions vary between countries. Commercial revenues of most EBU Members have been steadily falling since 2005. EBU (2014a: 69) research shows that:

> in 2007 advertising brought in 16.6% of the total income of EBU Members and was the second highest source of revenue. From 2007, it dropped gradually to reach 10.5% in 2012. Consequently, it has become the fourth source of income for PSM.

Direct subsidy also has service implications, as Lowe and Berg (2013: 91) claim:

> In many cases, this approach facilitates political involvement in deciding the kinds of content that are made or the angle taken. However, influence need not be direct to cause problems.

In recent years some European countries decided to replace the license fee with funding from the State budget. As Klimkiewicz (2015: 114) notes:

> although these changes were justified on the grounds of greater efficiency and thus dictated by mere technical incentives, it is clear that they reflected political choices, in some cases inspired by populist or economic premises.

An EBU (2014b: 12) study reports that:

> the Dutch government announced a 20% cut in the media budget by 2015, including a reduction of €127 million for national public service broadcasting. Hungary's MTV reported a 37% reduction in public funding income in 2010.

Hungary represents a striking case of direct government intervention in a PSM's editorial line. Since 2010, when the right-wing party of Fidesz took power, the Hungarian public service MTV has been heavily conditioned by political pressure. Using news content analysis, Bajomi-Lazar and Toth (2013) demonstrate how news reporting by the Hungarian PSM has shifted to unbalanced news coverage since the last government election.

The BBC faced a cut of 16 percent of its budget in 2010 and is expected to cut up to 600 jobs in news and radio by 2017 (Plunkett, 2014). In Spain, Bonet et al. (2014: 11) claim that:

> the serious financial crisis since 2008 was used by PP government to justify its decision in 2012 to reduce state contributions, such that RTVE accumulated a deficit of more than 300 million Euros between 2010 and 2013.

In 2009, in France, former President Sarkozy changed appointment mode, giving direct power to the President to nominate the CEO of France Televisions. The French reform of 2009 also ruled that all commercials were to be phased out by the end of 2011. The loss of €450 million from advertising in 2009 has been replaced with state revenue, making the French PSM more dependent on political decisions. In 2013, the Greek PSM was shut down under EU pressure to cut public sector jobs through an authoritarian action enforced by the Greek police. The most recent case of political pressure on a PSM happened in 2015 when the Polish government reformed the PSM and strengthened its political control over the public broadcasting companies Telewizja Polska (Polish Television) and Polskie Radio (Polish Radio). The commixture of politics and public service has repercussions on how citizens perceive the quality of information provided by the PSM.

Subscription funding also affects services. This approach can be organized according to a donation model, as in the United States. That model could be a realistic alternative to the license fee if, as Lowe and Berg (2013: 91) state, "an essential goal is to maintain arm's length from *both* the state and the market," but this option is not stable. The downturn in the general economy has impacted donations, both in the number of donors and the amount of each donation (Corporation for Public Broadcasting, 2012).

Therefore, the license fee still seems to be the best model for keeping PSM equidistant from both politics and the market (Nissen, 2006). This distance is vital in nurturing the reputation of PSM. If we compare data relative to citizens' trust of PSM (BBC, 2013b) with data regarding the effect of the license fee on PSM budgets (EBU, 2014b), we may observe that, in countries where PSM count on license fees for more than 70 percent of their revenue, citizens perceive PSM as being of higher quality (Table 1).

Table 1: Relationships between PSM dependence on license fees, PSM reputations and license fee rates

PSM/country	Proportion of funding from the license fee (in percent)	Proportion of respondents in each country rating the quality of the PSM TV channels as "very good" (in percent)	Household license fee rates (in Euros)	License fee evasion rate
BBC/UK	70.4	32	179	5.8
SRSweden	93	20	238	12
ARD-ZDF/ Germany	83.5	17	215	1*
RTP/Portugal	35.6	7	31.8	0.5**
FT/France	65.3	5	133	1***
TVE/Spain	0	6	0	0
RAI/Italy	60	4	113.5	27

*Household tax, ** License fee included in the electricity bill, *** Household tax.
Source: Based on data from EBU (2014b) and BBC (2013).

Table 1 shows how the reputation of PSM is generally higher where PSM depend mainly on their own fellow citizens' economic contribution. This correlation is not yet provable, because the quality of PSM content not only depends on the funding variable, but also on other economic, historical and political variables. More specific, independent studies in this direction are therefore needed, in order to truly demonstrate whether a strong correlation exists between the funding model of PSM and their reputations. Furthermore, the cross-sectional data in Table 1 considers too few countries (and does not evaluate radio stations) in order to show a general trend. Even if the license fee seems to be the model that guarantees the most editorial independence among PSM funding models adopted to date, it is a contribution that is not evenly supported by European citizens. Data for 2013/2014 (see Table 1) indicate that the evasion rate in the UK is close to 6 per-cent and 27 per cent do not pay the RAI license fee in Italy. With regard to the license fee, one of the most crucial challenges is the link between the provision of PSM content and services and reception via the television device has become obsolete. Debate over its reform revolves around three possibilities: 1) complete abolition; 2) extension to digital devices; 3) transformation into a compulsory "excise duty" collected from all households and citizens, which is currently being used in many European countries. Germany (Herzog and Karppinen, 2014) and Finland (Ala-Fossi, 2012) have already chosen the third option.

Overall, it is believed that the license fee still represents the best model for PSM funding, but we also feel it must be adapted to the changing ecosystem of media and the shifting habits of media consumption, on the basis of the participatory turn that is taking place in the world of traditional and digital media. But now we have to define what we mean by "participatory turn," in order to explain why a participatory turn in the values and in the funding models of PSM might con-tribute to the creation of more open and participatory PSM enterprise.

The participatory turn

John Reith's initial idea for public service broadcasting services, the forerunner of PSM, was based on the concept of inclusiveness and access to culture for all (Reith, 1924: 34, 64). Reith's model, which held up throughout the 1900s, until the liberalization of the telecommunications markets and the diffusion of the Internet, was a top-down system, where information, culture and entertainment were only decided by an inner circle of professionals who chose content and scheduled it for us. But in the age of the audience fragmentation (Napoli, 2011) and of social networks' digital platforms (van Dijck, 2013), as Hendy (2013: 107) notes,

> Who needs a whole industry of publicly funded professional broadcasters toiling away at pre-selecting material, producing programmes or creating schedules for us, when we can shoot our own films, record our own audio, write our own blogs and listen or watch or share among friends whatever we want whenever we want? (…) Public service broadcasting – originally conceived as a means of showing us a wider world and shap-ing us into more cultivated, more informed, clear-thinking humans – is losing whatever normative hold it once had.

The multiplication of media content products, the diffusion of low-cost commu-nication and editing software technology, the emergence of distribution platforms for personal content (from YouTube to SoundCloud), have all contributed to educating the public towards increased participation in producing media content.

As Gauntlett emphasizes (2011), our culture is shifting from the "sit back and be told" model of the twentieth century to a "making and doing" one. This shift was not missed by Murdock (2004: 7) who reveals that:

> Public service broadcasting has traditionally constructed its audiences primarily as listeners rather than speakers or performers, spectators rather than image-makers. Over the last two decades however this sense of exclusion has generated increasing demands from viewers and listeners for more participation in the making of screened culture and the organisation of public debate.

Today's citizens and users of PSM have many more tools than before for interacting with media, making their voice heard, circulating media content within their own networks and producing their own content. The contemporary network society we live in has produced a new configuration of mediated publics: the networked publics. Networked publics represent the missing link in Abercrombie and Longhurst's (1998) historical periodization. Ito (2008: 2) was one of the first to use the term:

> The term *networked publics* is an alternative to terms such as *audience* or *consumer*. Rather than assume that everyday media engagement is passive or consumptive, the term *publics* foregrounds a more engaged stance. Networked publics take this further; now publics are communicating more and more through complex networks that are bottom-up, top-down, as well as side-to-side. Publics can be reactors, (re)makers and (re)distributors, engaging in shared culture and knowledge through discourse and social exchange as well as through acts of media reception.

This concept was further developed by Boyd (2011: 41) who argues that networked publics are "publics that are restructured by networked technologies." What distinguishes networked publics from other types of publics is their underlying structure:

> Networked technologies reorganise how information flows and how people interact with information and each other. In essence, the architecture of networked publics differentiates them from more traditional notions of publics (Boyd 2011: 41).

Networked publics represent the type of public that has emerged from the network society and refer to any type of public that is organised in a network. Networked publics belong to the vast multitude of *produsers* (Bruns, 2008). Produsage refers to the type of user-led content creation that takes place in a variety of online environments. This concept blurs the boundaries between passive consumption and active production. However, the term *produser* emphasizes the productive aspect of the consumers/users, while the definition proposed by Bonini (2015) – networked listeners – highlights the connections among listeners.

As Mary Hockaday, the Head of the BBC Newsroom, explains public service broadcasters are "shifting to a new formulation: Inform, Educate and Connect," which means that they are:

> no longer just trying to draw people in, but also more confidently reaching out on social networks, and a full range of distribution platforms that work for audiences, and that some of our journalism is done in partnership with the wider world (Hockaday 2012: 7).

This new media ecosystem, created from a mix of broadcasting and networking (social media) cultures, has transformed how media content circulates. In this regard, Jenkins et al. (2013: 2) refer to *spreadable media* as all the media content that is put into circulation according to a hybrid model, which is a mix of top-down and bottom-up forces:

> This shift from diffusion to circulation signals a movement toward a more participatory model of culture, one which sees the public not as simply consumers of preconstituted messages, but as people who are shaping, reframing and remixing media content in ways which might not have been previously imagined. And they are doing so not as isolated individuals, but within larger communities and networks, which allow them to spread content well beyond their immediate geographic proximity.

This change in the nature of mediated publics has been noted also by a recent EBU (2014a) Vision 2020 document, in which the EBU (2014a: 11) claims that the focus of PSM should shift:

- from an emphasis on PSM as a 'deliverer' to a two-way approach that fosters dialogue and interaction;
- from 'one-to-many' to a more personalized approach that satisfies a wider range of needs for varied quality in a diversified society;
- from a closed, or fortress-like institution to one that is open and connected to networks of people, communities, cultural organizations and civic society.

The BBC has conducted audience research showing that only 23 percent currently remain passive, while 60 percent participate in easy ways on social media platforms (liking, sharing, posting short comments, etc.) and 17 percent are very active (EBU, 2014a).

PSM have always had difficulty in granting spaces for real participation to their own audiences, but things have changed a great deal over the last few years. The number of radio and television programs that call for greater audience participation is growing constantly (Jackson, 2010), from the pioneer *Video Nation* (1992), to the more recent Danish Radio programme *Blokken*, whose slogan was "You supply, we present" (Bechmann, 2011) and the BBC radio programme *The*

Listening Project (2012), which provides production tools and asks "people up and down the country to share an intimate conversation with a close friend or relative, to help to build a unique picture of our lives today" (BBC, 2013). For the BBC, Hutchinson (2014: 230) claims,

> these user-generated content projects facilitate an increased representation of its public, while building social capital amongst its participants.

The BBC has also created a special newsroom for dealing with user-generated content (UGC) and benefits from its existence, (Wardle and Williams, 2010).

A decade has passed since Jenkins (2006) anticipated the so-called "participatory turn" of the audience, but nowadays his vision is becoming even more real. Enli (2008) suggests the core values of PSM should evolve to "educate, entertain and participate." Enli (2008) claims that PSM used participation as a concept for gaining legitimacy and expanding their activity to digital platforms, but, as we will see in the next section, there are many different meanings of participation and so far PSM have focused more on a weak version of participation, while we believe a stronger one would enable PSM to better adapt to the changing ecosystem described here.

Conclusions

This brief overview shows that PSM scholars and PSM institutions now seem to be more convinced of the need to change the values of PSM in order to provide for greater citizen participation, which should translate into social benefits for citizens themselves. Everyone seems to agree on adding the dimension of participation to the classic Reithian triad. But what kind of participation? Until now, in the best-case situations, PSM have allowed citizens to participate in content production. Even when PSM have accepted working with user-produced content, the users themselves have always had very little decision-making power. Citizens not only have limited space for deciding how to use content they have generated, but they almost never have the possibility to participate in the editorial decisions of programs as well. As Jakubowicz (2010: 17) reminds us:

> Participatory programming can also mean public scrutiny of editorial policy and a broadcaster–audience dialogue about it. Public scrutiny is made possible, for example, by 'Open Newsroom,' a project of Aktuellt, a daily news programme of the Swedish public television SVT which publishes on its website film recordings of staff meetings and other discussions among journalists, only minutes after they occur.

Participation, according to Carpentier, not only deals with "participation in the production of media output (content-related participation)" but also in "media organizational decision-making (structural participation)" (2011: 68). Carpentier asserts that we can only truly call it participation if the citizens/producers are recognized as holding a certain amount of power in the decisions over what content should be broadcast, or even in the broadcaster's editorial and business choices. Carpentier argues the central keyword in recognizing real participative practices is "power": power to decide what to produce and how to publish it, and power to decide how the media organization should work. If PSM have recently opened up more to audience participation in content production, there is still almost no trace of them opening up to audience participation in their economic management and editorial decisions. As Jakubowicz (2010: 17) notes,

> Kleinsteuber (2008) called for meetings of the Administrative Councils of German PSB institutions to be held in public (and broadcast online), with all the documentation to be uploaded on the internet as a matter of routine,

but audiences still have no seats on any PSM company's board of directors, though audiences are their main stakeholders in many countries. In order to achieve the full participation of citizens who play an active role in the decisions made by public media companies, allowing a few editorial spaces and reworking the UGC is not enough. Full citizen participation in PSM should also include what Carpentier calls "structural participation," where citizens have a voice in the company's editorial choices. Deliberation and participation rights represent, according to Murdock (2004), core cultural rights, which PSM should nurture. If the PSM audience is made up of citizens, then PSM must guarantee their 'core cultural' rights.

For this reason we advocate a shift in the concept of citizens' participation, from a user-generated contents' model of participation to a more structural participation, in the form of a "citizen-generated" or, better, a "citizen-centred" PSM. The participatory turn favoured by the rise of the network society and the networked publics could open up new ways of citizens' participation to the governance and funding models of PSM, like, for example, civic crowdfunding. We advocate for new models of governance and funding PSM, in which citizens are not simply viewed as passive tax payers but active voters and decision-makers (Bonini and Pais, 2017). These models could be based on the integration of crowdfunding schemes into the license fee traditional model, encompassed within those forms of crowdfunding that aim for social impact, which Ridgway (2015) calls 'crowdfunding the commons' as well as within those forms of participatory budgeting that today are labelled as 'civic crowdfunding.' Employing crowdfunding into innovative funding models for the media is a new and emerging issue: even if practical applications of this idea still do not exist, crowdfunding as a new funding tool for media companies has already been discussed by some scholars, like Cagé

(2015), that has proposed to introduce crowdfunding into the funding schemes of not-for-profit media. New forms of license fee based on civic crowdfunding and in the concept of participatory budgeting could transfer some portions of decisional power into the hands of tax payers and make the PSM enterprises more dependent on citizens' decisions rather than on political ones.

Finally, allowing citizens to take part in decisional processes of PSM means extending the deliberative rights and the right to participation of all citizens/ listeners, as Williams (1976: 136) imagined almost forty years ago, when he advocated a truly democratic public communication system where:

> (…) all decisions about the actual allocation of resources should be publicly argued and open to challenge and review.

References

Abercrombie, N., and B. Longhurst (1998). *Audiences: A Sociological Theory of Performance and Imagination*. London: Sage.

Ala-Fossi, M. (2012). Social obsolescence of the TV fee and the financial crisis of Finnish public service media. *Journal of Media Business Studies* 9: 33–54.

Bajomi-Lazar, P., and B. Toth (2013). *Censorship and Manipulation within Hungarian public service broadcasters' news bulletins*. Center for Independent Journalism. Retrieved May 3, 2015 from http://www.cij.hu/en/censorship-and-manipulation-within-hungarian-public-service-broadcasters%E2%80%99-news-bulletins/.

Bardoel, J., and L. d'Haenens (2008). Reinventing public service broadcasting in Europe: prospects, promises and problems. *Media Culture & Society*, 30: 337–355.

BBC (2004). *Building Public Value: Renewing the BBC for a Digital World*. Retrieved May 24, 2016 from http://downloads.bbc.co.uk/aboutthebbc/policies/pdf/bpv.pdf.

BBC (2013). *Public and private broadcasters across the world – the race to the top*. Retrieved November 30, 2014 from http://downloads.bbc.co.uk/aboutthebbc/insidethebbc/howwework/reports/pdf/bbc_report_public_and_private_broadcasting_across_the_world.pdf.

Bechmann, A. (2011). User participation at the Danish Broadcasting Corporation 1998–2010. Changing patterns. In: N. Brugger (ed.), *Histories of Public Service Broadcasters on the Web*. New York: Peter Lang, 193–206.

Bonet, M., L. Arboledas, and J.A. Guimerà (2014). *Past Boundaries, Future Limitations: Spanish Public Broadcasting at Risk*. Paper presented at RIPE@2014 Conference, Tokio, August 27–29, 2014.

Bonini, T. (2015). The Listener as Producer: The Rise of the Networked Listener. In: T. Bonini, and B. Monclus (eds.), *Radio Audiences and Participation in the Age of Network Society*. London: Routledge, 1–35.

Bonini, T., and I. Pais (2017). Hacking Public Service Media Funding: A Scenario for Rethinking the License Fee as a Form of Civic Crowdfunding, *International Journal on Media Management*, 19:2: 123–143.

Born, G. (2005). *Uncertain Vision: Birt, Dyke and the Reinvention of the BBC*, London: Vintage.

Boyd, D. (2011). Social Network Sites as Networked Publics: Affordances, Dynamics, and Implications. In: Z. Papacharissi (ed.), *A Networked Self. Identity, Community, and Culture on Social Network Sites*. London: Routledge, 39–58.

Bruns, A. (2008). *Blogs, Wikipedia, Second Life and Beyond: From Production to Produsage*. New York: Peter Lang.

Cagé J. (2015). *Sauver les médias. Capitalisme, financement participatif et démocratie*. Paris: Seuil.

Carpentier, N. (2011). *Media and Participation*. Bristol: Intellect.

Corporation for Public Broadcasting (2012). *Alternative sources of funding for public broadcasting stations*. Washington, DC. Retrieved October 15, 2014 from http://cpb.org/aboutcpb/Alternative_Sources_of_Funding_for_Public_Broadcasting_Stations.pdf.

Debrett, M. (2010). *Reinventing Public Service Television for the Digital Future*. Bristol: Intellect.

EBU (2011). *Public Radio and new media platforms*. Geneva: European Broadcasting Union.

EBU (2012a). *Empowering Society. A Declaration on the Core Values of Public Service Media*. Geneva: European Broadcasting Union.

EBU (2012b). *Funding of Public Service Media 2011*. Geneva: European Broadcasting Union.

EBU (2012c). *EBU Viewpoint. PSM Funding*. Retrieved November 30, 2014 from http://www3.ebu.ch/files/live/sites/ebu/files/Knowledge/Publication%20Library/EBU-Viewpoint-PSM-Funding_EN.pdf.

EBU (2014a). *EBU Vision 2020. Connecting to a networked society*. Geneva: European Broadcasting Union.

EBU (2014b). *Funding of Public Service Media 2013*. Geneva: European Broadcasting Union.

Enli, G.S. (2008). Redefining public service broadcasting multi-platform participation. *Convergence: The International Journal of Research into New Media Technologies*, 14(1): 105–120.

Gauntlett, D. (2011). *Making is Connecting.* Cambridge: Polity Press.

Hallin, D., and P. Mancini (2004). *Comparing Media Systems: Three Models of Media and Politics.* Cambridge: Cambridge University Press.

Hendy, D. (2013). *Public Service Broadcasting.* London: Palgrave Mcmillan.

Herzog, C., and K. Karppinen (2014). Policy streams and public service media funding reforms in Germany and Finland. *European Journal of Communication* 29(4): 416–432.

Hockaday, M. (2012). *BBC News: Why Good Journalism Matters in the Digital Age.* Talk at the London School of Economics. London, October 9, 2012.

Hutchinson, J. (2014). Extending the Public Service Remit through ABC Pool. In: G.F. Lowe and F. Martin (eds.), *The Value of Public Service Media.* Göteborg: Nordicom, 223–243.

Iosifidis, P. (ed.) (2010). *Reinventing public service communication: European broadcasters and beyond.* London: Palgrave Macmillan.

Ito, M. (2008). Introduction. In: K. Varnelis (ed.), *Networked Publics.* Cambridge MA: MIT Press, 1–14.

Jackson, L. (2010). *Harnessing collaborative innovation for the evolution of public service media.* Paper presented at RIPE@2010 Conference, London, September 8–11, 2010.

Jakubowicz, K. (2010). PSB 3.0. Reinventing European PSB. In: Iosifidis, P. (ed.), *Reinventing public service communication: European broadcasters and beyond.* London: Palgrave Macmillan, 9–22.

Jenkins, H. (2006). *Fans, bloggers, and gamers: Exploring participatory culture.* New York: NYU Press.

Jenkins, H., S. Ford, and J. Green (2013). *Spreadable media: Creating value and meaning in a networked culture.* New York: NYU Press.

Kleinsteuber, H.J. (2008). *Participation in the Management of Public Service Media. Broadcasting Councils in Germany: Making them Fit for the Future.* Paper presented at RIPE@2008 Conference, Mainz, October 8–11, 2008.

Klimkiewicz, B. (2015). Between Autonomy and Dependency. Funding Mechanisms of Public Service Media in Selected European Countries. In: K. Arriaza Ibarra, E. Nowak, and R. Kuhn (eds.), *Public Service Media in Europe. A Comparative Approach.* London: Routledge, 111–125.

Lowe, G.F., and J. Bardoel (eds.) (2007). *From public service broadcasting to public service media, RIPE@2007.* Göteborg: Nordicom.

Lowe, G.F., and C.E. Berg (2013). The Funding of Public Service Media: A Matter of Value and Values. *The International Journal on Media Management*, 15: 77–97.

Murdock, G. (2004). *Building the digital commons: Public broadcasting in the age of the Internet. The 2004 Spry Memorial Lecture, 3–7.* Retrieved October 20, 2014 from https://pantherfile.uwm.edu/type/www/116/Theory_OtherTexts/Theory/Murdock_BuildingDigitalCommons.pdf.

Napoli, P.M. (2011). *Audience Evolution: New Technologies and the Transformation of Media Audiences.* New York: Columbia University Press.

Nissen, C.S. (2006). *Public service media in the information society. Report prepared for the Council of Europe's Group of Specialists on Public Service Broadcasting in the Information Society (MC-S-PSB).* Strasbourg: Council of Europe.

Picard, R.G. (2010). *Value Creation and the Future of News Organization. Why and How Journalism Must Change to Remain Relevant in the Twenty-First Century.* Barcelona: Formalpress.

Plunkett, J. (2014). BBC expected to cut up to 600 jobs in news and radio, *The Guardian*, June 3, 2014. Retrieved June 2, 2015 from http://www.theguardian.com/media/2014/jun/03/bbc-cut-600-jobs-news-radio-james-harding.

Reith, B.J.C.W. (1924). *Broadcast over Britain.* London: Hodder and Stoughton limited.

Ridgway, R. (2015). Crowdfunding the Commons. In: G. Lovink, N. Tkacz, and P. De Vries (eds.), *Moneylab Reader: an intervention in digital economy*. Amsterdam: INC Institute of Network Cultures, 281–295.

Syvertsen, T. (2003). Challenges to Public Television in the Era of Convergence and Commercialization. *Television & New Media*, 4(2): 155–75.

Syvertsen, T., G. Enli, O. J. Mjøs, and H. Moe (2014). *The Media Welfare State. Nordic Media in the Digital Era.* Ann Arbor: The University of Michigan Press.

Trappel, J. (2014). What media value? Theorising on social values and testing in ten countries. In: G.F. Lowe, and F. Martin (eds.), *The Value of Public Service Media*. Göteborg: Nordicom, 127–144.

Van Dijck, J. (2013). *The culture of connectivity: A critical history of social media.* Oxford University Press.

Wardle, C., and A. Williams (2010). Beyond user-generated content: a production study examining the ways in which UGC is used at the BBC. *Media, Culture & Society*, 32(5): 781–799.

Williams R. (1976). *Communications.* London: Penguin.

Jonathon Hutchinson
University of Sydney, Australia

Intermediaries exercising influence through algorithms within public service media

Abstract: Media and communication systems have globally shifted beyond a mass media arrangement to promote increased user practices associated with social media. Social media activities, particularly in the public service media arena, have historically focussed on the potential of increased citizen participation. A body of work has also emerged to suggest social media and its associated user-generated content practice is merely tokenistic participation. However, contemporary innovative public service media (PSM) practice now engages algorithm culture through social media for user participation, bringing with it new research questions. Algorithm culture is the design of automated computational systems that incorporates large data sets based on user behaviour to inform collaborative cultural production practices. A salient question for policy makers and PSM leaders is how do they approach algorithm culture to address the remit of PSM in contemporary digital mediascapes. This chapter provides insights of cultural intermediaries as key co-creative agents of PSM algorithms and highlights the significance of influential social media users to promote maximalist participation.

Keywords: public service media, algorithmic culture, social media, cultural intermediation, microinfluencer.

Introduction

Referring to the impacts of printing and distribution technologies on the newspaper industry, Williams (1989a) describes the significance of technological changes for cultural institutions in terms of how technology can, in fact, limit diversity. His argument is built on the emerging and constraining tight economic pressures of the failing revenue models from classified advertising, and suggests that because of advanced printing and distribution technologies, newspapers were forced to focus their readership towards higher income groups:

> The technology which had promised both extension and diversity had, in these circumstances, produced a remarkable and specific kind of extension (what came to be called the 'mass' public) and, by comparison with its own earlier stages, an actually reduced diversity (Williams, 1989b: 213).

Through growing economic and social pressures, the newspaper industry as a particular type of cultural institution had fallen victim to its own technological developments of printing and distribution. In order to overcome these pressures, newspapers had to cater to a particular wealthier aspect of its audience, thereby reducing its public reach and limiting its diversity of voice within its content creation.

Fast forward three decades and our contemporary media environment is moving closer to what is considered an 'algorithmic culture,' which echoes the limiting publicness and cultural aspects of the newspaper industry's technological developments. Algorithmic culture is one which sees "the sorting, classifying and hierarchizing of people, places, objects, and ideas – increasingly to computational processes" (Striphas, 2015: 395). In the case of media organizations engaging in algorithmic culture, this usually results in a tailored content experience based on the user's past content consumption, or user specific playlists. Striphas (2015) astutely points out in his work on defining the current approach towards cultural production and distribution within an algorithmic culture the significance of the relationship between information, crowd and algorithm. This relationship between the key characteristics of an algorithm culture is increasingly prominent in mass media across networked communication systems, that deliver personalised, and thereby popular, media experiences to niche markets. This type of content delivery is most obvious in video on demand television systems such as Netflix, YouTube's suggested video feature, and iTunes's 'For You' selected music feature. However, as Striphas (2015) points out, culture, and the media systems that create, distribute and perpetuate an algorithmic culture are at risk of limiting *public* culture in favour of a mono-cultural reappropriation. Further, if PSM engages in the automation of content production and procurement, does it risk skewing its role as a facilitator of relevant public issues within the public sphere?

It is at this intersection of automated cultural production and a media system in the midst of incredible technological advances through personalisation and algorithmic delivery of specific and niche content, that public service media (PSM) becomes increasingly crucial. If we are indeed at risk of perpetuating elitist culture through our media system, due to the convenience and speed of an algorithmic culture, the role of a cultural institution, such as a PSM organization, is crucial in providing a cultural benchmark, primarily through its Reithian principles. PSM is ideally located in the media and cultural spheres as an organization that is based on Reithian principles such as "the application of the principles of universality of availability, universality of appeal, provision for minorities, education of the public, distance from vested interests, quality programming standards, program maker independence, fostering of the public sphere" (Cunningham, 2013: 62). The Reithian principles, which are often contested in contemporary media environments (Brevini, 2013), once again become increasingly significant as an antidote towards an elitist driven and automated culture that is generated by an algorithmic culture.

This chapter argues that one of PSM's crucial roles within a digital mediascape is to maintain its function as a cultural facilitator that engages with cutting edge computational algorithmic culture, while also maintaining its core Reithian principles. The chapter demonstrates this arrangement through the lens of co-creation, facilitated through cultural intermediation, which enables content production through a *étalonnage*[1] of interactions between professionally trained media producers and co-creative audiences. Cultural intermediation in this sense refers to the individuals that enable co-creation, for example social media producers, and a production system that includes cultural translation, negotiation and expertise transfer. The chapter argues that in a digital media ecosystem that seeks to produce and distribute automated culture, PSM should be engaging in these technologies to avoid cultural production that ignores the depth, or 'publicness,' of culture. At the core of this argument is the notion that the affordances of social media and its digital ecosystem provide an opportunity for PSM to showcase its relevance through its Reithian principles.

Positioning this argument within the influence economy that is associated with Multichannel Networks (MCNs) and their cultural intermediaries, this chapter draws on the Australian context by exploring one of its public service media organizations, The Australian Broadcasting Corporation (ABC). It highlights how PSM that engages with social media can collaborate with users, specifically 'super-users,' to engage broad audiences who both produce and consume culture. The chapter uses research data from one participatory scripted television comedy programme, *#7DaysLater* to highlight how cultural intermediaries operationalize collaborative co-creation of cultural products. Finally, the chapter argues that PSM, under the guise of a distinctive innovation institution (Cunningham, 2013), should be focussing on how cultural intermediaries should be engaging in a particular role of online facilitation. Cultural intermediaries not only engage the audience and encourage them to participate in a co-creative environment, but

1 The use of the term *étalonnage* best describes the process of parlance between producers and consumers of content within digital media environments. The content production/consumption model is not straightforward, nor is it one-way: it is often a contested and continually negotiated process to ensure all stakeholder groups are satisfied with outcome of the process.

are also responsible for generating new public issues through its strategic use of social media and the incorporation of cultural intermediaries.

Emerging issues for public service media in a digital mediascape

Public service media "has been tasked to serve the societal and cultural needs of each member nation and to promote democracy and participation within the national geographical boundaries" (Głowacki, 2015: 26). This, of course, is built upon PSM's origins of public service broadcasting (PSB) which emerged from the early British model of the British Broadcasting Company (BBC – which later shifts to the British Broadcasting Corporation). The objective of PSB "was to inform, educate and entertain with total independence from political power and commercial pressure" (Tremblay, 2016: 194), suggesting its *raison d'être* is to serve the public for its educational, cultural and societal needs. The thematic shift from PSB and towards PSM is taken as "common parlance as services are extended across 'new' media platforms and experiments undertaken into new interactive content forms" (Debrett, 2015: 557). Inherently, the trajectory of PSM is to continue to provide for the democratic, social and cultural needs of society (Brevini, 2013), yet extend these services into the digital environment.

European Broadcasting Union (EBU) in its Vision2020 strategy for PSM notes,

> Once, PSM were taken for granted; their services were regarded as 'guaranteed and essential' components of European societies (EBU, 2014: 5).

In this statement, at least in the western European context, PSM has always been understood as an essential component of the national, societal and cultural fabric of a nation. However, PSM has also been the target of much public criticism in recent times, especially in how it maintains its relevance in an over-saturated and digital media landscape. Barnett (2015) reminds us that PSM is increasingly under attack because of conservative governments, introspective and disorganised left political parties, hostile media environments, and substantially reduced funding arrangements. Tremblay (2016: 192) also observes the mounting pressure by governments on PSM in its "systematic reduction" in the field of media and communication, which he notes as a "gradual and calculated suffocation of public service media." At the same time, most PSM institutions are subject to Public Value Tests, or in the case of Germany the *Drei-Stufen-Test*, as a somewhat ambitious attempt to ensure PSM operations are indeed in line with that of its nation's citizens. Collectively, these issues demonstrate how PSM is under fire as an institution in an offline environment, which is the caveat for the mounting pressure for PSM to tentatively progress into the digital environment.

The public debates surrounding the relevance of PSM in the online or digital spaces have focused on a few important areas. Seemingly, PSM in digital media-scapes has been supported through arguments that note it should provide new multiplatform services beyond television and radio (Steemers, 2016), it is a tool for online citizenship and civic engagement (Debrett, 2015), or even as a locale for 'distinctive' media system innovation (Cunningham, 2015). These arguments build upon the recent scholarly contributions that bolster the value of PSM beyond the market failure argument (Edelvold, Lowe and Lund, 2014), debunk the so-called 'digital argument' (Donders and Bulck, 2014), or as a facilitator of user co-creation (Hutchinson, 2013). None of these arguments have entirely bolstered the relevance of PSM in the online environment, which is best demonstrated through regional re-thinking of the PSM strategy. Indeed the EBU are calling for action to make PSM indispensable (EBU, 2014) with an emphasis towards digital media. The UK government are suggesting digital media reform to its Charter, especially through universality, given that its current version is set to expire in late 2016 (DCMS, 2015). While in the Australian context, the ABC has its focus clearly on the production and distribution of digital content as it further develops its catch-up service, iView, to be more of a 'digital first' over terrestrial broadcast model (ABC, 2014; Gow, 2015).

The strategic and policy emphasis on digital technologies, coupled with the advent of incredibly sophisticated digital media technologies, especially social media, suggests digital PSM becomes increasingly significant as an apparatus for user, citizen and public engagement and participation. Although with participation as a key area of interest for PSM scholars, some have noted the marginalization of participation of users within PSM products and services. Głowacki and Jackson (2014) observed that increased participation with PSM through digital technologies is moot, highlighting that websites are often 'bolt-on' extras for marketing purposes and not core platforms utilized for content production and distribution. Jakubowicz (2014: 229) notes the decline of user-generated content (UGC) in PSM, suggesting that the use of UGC "seems to remain in most cases [as] marginal forms, either designed to obtain input (…) that professional journalists use in producing their programmes, under their exclusive control, or web pages (…) serving as a display case for UGC." In this light, increased participation within PSM has, in many cases, been used as a symbolic process to align the remit of PSM with digital citizen engagement. In this body of literature there is a point of departure to explore the shifting digital media landscape surrounding PSM, specifically the impact of algorithmic culture.

While many of these scholars mount compelling arguments for both the relevance of PSM, and how PSM audience participation through digital technologies has gone out of style, I argue that none have addressed the emerging issues surrounding the impact of algorithms. Algorithms are increasingly obvious in how media industries are distributing content, but they are also impacting on how content is being shaped and produced for subsequent audiences. A common example of this type of behaviour is best seen in publications like Buzzfeed or Vice Magazine, which collect data on the consumption habits of their media publications as a means to inform how future content is produced. This is not a new strategy in media production, but when conducted on the scale as seen through social media consumption, the potential for impact on the public sphere is potentially enormous. As a key media production house, PSM must be aware of how they too operate in the algorithmic space and their consequential impact on public issues. Burgess and Matamoros (2016: 79) note the significance of social media and public issues:

> Social media play a prominent role in mediating issues of public concern, not only providing the stage on which public debates play out, but also shaping their topics and dynamics.

Therefore, if algorithms shape how public issues emerge, and public issues impact on how future debates are shaped and discussed, PSM becomes a crucial agency to be actively participating and shaping cultural production through social media with its citizens.

Algorithmic culture and public service media

Before exploring algorithmic culture and its impact on PSM, it is crucial to understand what algorithms are, how they shape communication in digital media environments, and how PSM can engage cultural intermediaries and algorithms in this space. Gillespie notes two significant characteristics of computational algorithms. First an algorithm is "merely the steps for aggregating those assigned values efficiently, or delivering the results rapidly, or identifying the strongest relationships according to some operationalized notion of 'strong'" (Gillespie, 2014, np.). Second, he notes that algorithms "are "trained" on a corpus of known data" which builds on certified data either by "designers or past user practices." In the digital media production environment, users and audiences see these strong and trained approaches play out in the simplest of interfaces that present them with a selection of content: usually programmed by producers based on an informed corpus of data of past user practices. For example, algorithms are at play on the Netflix platform that presents a selection of 'popular' television content as a 'suggestion for you'. This type of practice is increasingly common across digital media properties of both commercial and non-commercial media organizations. In the Australian context of the ABC, this is most obvious through the ABC Radio mobile phone application and the 'Your View' section of the catch-up television smart phone application, iView. These examples indicate that algorithms are very much at play in the production of PSM content. However, the more interesting area to explore in this form of PSM content is how public culture is being produced around, by and through algorithms.

Williams (1989b) notes that culture is specific to each society based on finding common meanings and direction. Culture is very much present within a networked society, which Castells notes is the connection of "major social, technological, economic, and cultural transformations (...) to give rise to a new form of society, the network society" (Castells, 2007: xvii). What Castells so astutely highlights is the emergence of a new culture that is based around the multimodal, horizontal communication network: a cultural transformation that aligns our online world with our offline. So, in a new society that is encountering global cultural transformations and is diffused between on and offline existences, the ability to find common meanings and directions becomes increasingly difficult. An opportunity exists within this space for PSM to contribute to a global conversation across the network society by sharing and translating a national society's common meaning and direction among other nation states engaging with PSM. However, if algorithms are at play within our PSM's content procurement and production processes, does PSM stand to risk skewing the development of public issues and how those issues are further shaped and discussed within the public sphere?

This concern of skewing public issues is at the heart of an algorithmic culture. Striphas (2015: 395) carefully warns on algorithmic culture:

> offloading of cultural work onto computers, databases and other types of digital technologies has prompted a reshuffling of some of the words most closely associated with *culture*, giving rise to new senses of the term that may be experientially available but have yet to be well named, documented or recorded.

So, while culture within a network society is generated at a rapid rate, from a diverse group of individuals within multicultural backgrounds, attempting to make this data sortable and storeable (Andrejevic, 2007) for simple retrievability is entirely problematic. If we adhere to Striphas' warning, new and potentially incorrect meanings, issues and debates could emerge as seemingly significant to the participation and democratization within the public sphere. Further, these sorts of activities and approaches towards the production of public issues through algorithms could echo the limitation in access to information previously argued as the 'filter bubble' (Pariser, 2011), which suggests "culture is being reimagined as more of a sedentary locus than a trajectory of human development" (Hallinan and Striphas, 2014: 6). While PSM engage in algorithmic culture within the network society, they may indeed be at risk of disseminating inaccurate or insignificant information, or omitting the information entirely. Regardless of PSM's remit to engage in digital media technologies and to continually improve user interaction and engagement, algorithmic culture is potentially problematic.

Despite the potential issue of incorrect or insufficient information, PSM engaging with algorithmic culture can also address the recent concerns of universality (DCMS, 2015). For example, users who are interested in particular issues surrounding specific content, may be unaware of how that interest could translate to other areas such as political activism or civic participation. Using an algorithm to highlight additional content for users is a particularly useful and strategic method that PSM organizations could engage to increase citizen awareness of contemporary issues within the public sphere. The problem with generating public interest through algorithms however, is designing, developing and implementing the correct algorithm that will include citizens, and avoids perpetuating additional levels of 'othering.' As Gillespie highlighted earlier, algorithms are developed on a corpus of known data based on past user experiences. Through the generation of data that is based on past user experience PSM are presented with a unique opportunity to build upon their Reithian principles through algorithmic culture. It is possible to generate targeted, authentic and appropriate information through social media practices, which will enable PSM to reengage as key cultural institutions that co-create, archive, publish and distribute core cultural texts that describe our society, for all our society.

However, while focussing attention on the role of PSM in information collection and generation within a social media environment, it is crucial to rethink the relationship of PSM and convergence culture to reposition the PSM approach from being user-centric entirely, and more towards a user-*focused* model. While much of the earlier convergence culture research demonstrated the significance and impact of co-creation with PSM (see for example Flew et al., 2008; Wilson, Hutchinson and Shea, 2010), there has been a broad pushback that rejects the audience as co-creators altogether. As media organizations moved away from proprietary social media platforms in favour of well-established social media spaces, for example Facebook and Twitter, the focus on the audience has shifted away from them as co-creators (user-centric), and more towards an actively listening audience (user-focused). However, recent scholarship demonstrates that the audience are located somewhere in between these two dichotomies. This is especially the case with the increase of younger audiences interacting with PSM (Van Dijck and Poell, 2015). However, Vanhaeght and Donders (2016: 303) note that young people's participation in PSM is ultimately trumped by the media professional, prompting them to ask, "If youth perspectives were of so little value to the production process, why enable participation in the first place?" This timely observation is accurate about user-participation with media organizations broadly: they are interested in audience inclusion, yet are still developing an appropriate model. What these two academic sources inadvertently expose within PSM and media organizations broadly is that they fail to identify the significance of 'influence' of these highly active social media users. It is especially important to analyze this in the algorithmic environment: incorporating young people's perspective as a form of past user experience to develop suitable PSM content algorithms. These users can be referred to as PSM cultural intermediaries.

Public service media, cultural intermediaries and influence

Carpentier (2009) has problematized participation which is particularly useful for PSM. Through an approach of minimalist and maximalist participation, Carpentier (2009: 409) describes how participation can be aligned within societal fields. In the minimalist model, participation "is confined to the process of representation" to suggest those who are represented are the only individuals participating. Maximalist participation is a "balanced combination of representation and participation", which has a sufficiently significant impact on decision-making that is genuinely representative of an entire population. In the PSM algorithmic culture arrangement described in this paper, maximalist participation is significant for cultural decision-making that incorporates the perspectives of all citizens. The problem PSM face in attempting to incorporate maximalist participation through algorithms is how to engage citizens in the discussion, which cultural perspectives to include, and how to provide a democratic and participatory environment. This location of cultural calibration is an ideal space for cultural intermediaries to operate within to assist in knowledge, cultural and expertise transfer.

Cultural intermediaries were first mentioned by Bourdieu (1984) to describe the taste agents located between high and low cultural goods. He notes they are especially well equipped to translate the nuances of cultural texts to groups of individuals from different cultural backgrounds, that is, differing social-economic demographics. Since then the term has been aligned with individuals who are cultural market agents (Negus, 2002), contemporary taste agents that incorporate market knowledge (Maguire and Matthews, 2014) and authoritative co-creative taste agents who efficiently operate within media organizations for collaborative cultural production (Hutchinson, 2016). I have also previously argued the role of the cultural intermediary aligns with the operation of PSM through governance (Hutchinson, 2013), participatory culture and co-creation (Hutchinson, 2015), and locative and archival processes (Hutchinson, 2016). In this chapter, I develop this understanding of the cultural intermediary in the context of algorithmic culture, through the lens of the latest iteration of cultural intermediaries: microinfluencers (Abidin, 2015). To do so, I will explore the role of microinfluencers through the emerging phenomenon of Multichannel Networks.

Multichannel Networks (MCNs) are the intermediary agencies that exist between brands and social media influencers, or microinfluencers. For example, the UK based Gleam Futures are talent agents operating in an influential "social talent" economy with " individuals who have built considerable audience & influence on social media channels" (GleamFutures, 2016). This agency's role is to manage those popular social media producers who have amassed large amounts of followers, and to support them to influence their followers with commercial products. While this model is moot for PSM because of the commercial application, the framework remains significant in order to think through how influence is becoming its own economy within social media. Furthermore, emerging cultural intermediaries operating as microinfluencers act as conduits between social media users and organizations.

In the context of PSM, microinfluencers are useful in two capacities. First, they are essential distribution platforms that promote content through their large follower audiences. As a content distributor, they not only distribute official PSM content, they are also responsible for disseminating specific and unique public issues that are absolutely relevant to the public sphere. In this capacity, microinfluencers are key agents to facilitate public democratic and participatory conversation across social media channels. Second, microinfluencers also transfer the issues amongst the users, typically younger audiences in this environment, back into the PSM organization. This type of iterative feedback loop afforded through social media technologies enables producers to create cultural goods that align with Carpentier's maximalist participation model that display "professional quality and social relevance" (Carpentier, 2009: 408). In this communication model, socially relevant information, in the form of co-created content, is transferred from the PSM through cultural intermediaries to their audiences, and then back again from the users to the PSM organization.

Further to the maximalist participation argument, this is crucial for developing a suitable and appropriate algorithmic culture. As organizations build content production and distribution strategies around an algorithm culture, incorporating this type of existing user experience is crucial for the design, development and implementation of such technologies. This not only produces data on how audiences are accessing content and the content they are consuming, it also invites users for their input on socially relevant and public issues. Public service media organizations are digitally calibrating with their citizens by incorporating user input made possible by the cultural intermediary.

The following section draws on research that clearly demonstrates how cultural intermediaries operate within PSM across social media channels as information and user experience conduits. This research also demonstrates the key concepts highlighted in the previous two sections that demonstrates how PSM operates within the contemporary digital mediascape, and how cultural intermediaries are centrally located for both 'communication ins' and 'communication outs.'

#7DaysLater, participatory media and public service media

The Australian Broadcasting Corporation (ABC) is one of Australia's public service broadcasters, along with the Special Broadcasting Service (SBS), that rely on government funding to operate. Unlike other countries with PSM, the ABC operates in a unique environment, where two broadcasting provisions enable market based programming to operate alongside non-commercial programming. Australia, therefore, has two broadcasting licences, one commercial and one non-commercial. A dual licencing system also means the ABC is entirely reliant on the government to fund its operation. Although the ABC does have a commercial arm including retail, selling archival content for reuse, and the sale of productions to outside distribution retailers, the majority of its funding is provided by the Australian government.

Recently, ABC Television commissioned a group of popular YouTube producers, or microinfluencers, to produce a series of scripted comedy television under the programme title, *#7DaysLater*. *#7DaysLater* was a series of seven, six-minute programmes with a unique and entirely experimental production methodology. Its production methodology was ambitious in "(...) taking comedy to the scary arena of interactive storytelling where the audience gets to write the brief via social media for each weekly episode that will air just seven days later on ABC2" (ABC, 2013). The typical production methodology began on Monday morning with a Google Hangout to source broad ideas from the participating audience. The following phase was to take those curated ideas to the popular Morning Show on the national youth radio network, Triple J, to source additional audience input on plot ideas, characters, or script writing. The production would be scripted by Tuesday with shooting on Wednesday and Thursday. Postproduction was on Friday through to Sunday, with the episode going to air the following Monday evening. During the production process, the audience was invited to continue to contribute via multiple social media channels, including Facebook, Twitter, Instagram and YouTube. The season produced seven programmes that were reasonably well accepted in television viewership, however, the programme yielded enormous interaction across social media channels.

I have previously described the data collection process and methodology for this research project (see Hutchinson, 2015), and this will not be discussed in this book chapter. Instead, this work will explore the cultural intermediaries as they emerged in the Twitter conversation around the *@7DaysLater* Twitter username. Figure 1 below demonstrates how the Twitter conversation was mapped. Through a series of social network analysis (SNA) algorithms, the more significant nodes are located near the centre of the graph, while the larger nodes indicate more connected nodes. In other words, the more significant nodes that are communicating with large networks are the larger, centrally located nodes. If these nodes are topics, they are popular conversations among the networks. However if they are users, they represent the microinfluencers described above.

Figure 1: The entire Twitter conversation associated with the @7DaysLater Twitter handle

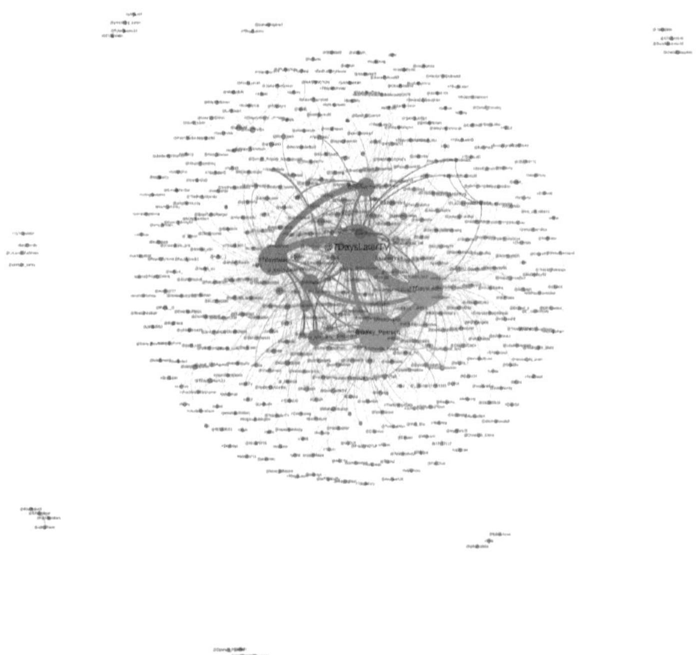

Source: Originally published in Hutchinson (2015).

Table 1 represents the zoomed in version of the conversation and highlights the concentration of the more significant nodes in the centre of the network graph. In this table we see the top 10 users within the *@7DaysLater* conversation.

Table 1: Top 10 Twitter users associated with the @7DaysLater conversation

Users
1. @7DaysLaterTV
2. @Daley_Pearson
3. @HarrisonTheFan
4. @MWhalan
5. @henry_and_aaron
6. @bajopants
7. @ABC2
8. @WASHINGTONx
9. @JordanRasko
10. @tomandalex

Source: Originally published in Hutchinson (2015).

If the *@7DaysLater* handle is extracted because it will be the most significant connection between all of the programme's conversations, along with the leading fan users of @HarrisonTheFan and @MWhalan, because they are super user fans of the show, we are left with seven microinfluencers. Each one of these Twitter microinfluencers are associated with the production of the programme and each user brings with them a large group of existing audience members. For example, @henry_and_aaron are a comedy duo that align with the description of YouTube producers with high influence capital because of their social talent expertise. Their Twitter account notes them as "an Australian comedy duo who create various on-line videos and viral content" (Inglis and McCann, 2016), and their YouTube page has approximately 10,500 followers. Their videos consistently attract large viewing numbers, ranging from around 2,000 views to their top video with just under 20 million views. These two YouTube content producers align with the description of the microinfluencer highlighted above. During the filming of *#7DaysLater*, they were brought in as guest stars, and this was also integrated into their own personal social media platforms. Many of the top Twitter users in Table 1 were also utilized in this capacity, which is a grounded example of Castell's network society being operationalized within PSM. In other words, the producers of the programme were engaging in the networks of the networks during the filming of the programme.

#7DaysLater is an exceptional example of how the cultural intermediary is being utilized as a genuine maximalist participatory agent. From Figure 1, it is clear to see how several key Twitter users that are associated with the conversation are distributing both content, along with conversational triggers. Although this is occurring within a scripted comedy television project, this is an incredibly important framework that highlights how PSM should be engaging in the digital media landscape. Beyond distributing content to larger networks of social media users, these cultural intermediaries are also translating significant talking points from the fans of the show back into the production of the programme. This was best demonstrated through one of the key Twitter users Nick Boshier, who was also heavily involved in the production of *#7DaysLater*. Boshier is also responsible for another very successful Australian comedy duo, *The Bondi Hipsters*, whose unique comedy style was also very prominent in the programme. Through Boshier's involvement, his social talent was obvious in the content production as he was acting as a taste agent who would translate cutting edge cultural tastes into ABC institutionalized television comedy.

Each of the microinfluencers associated with *#7DaysLater* demonstrate high social talent, which, as described before, aligns with influence as a social media currency. With high influence capital, microinfluencers are able to embody the cultural intermediary role of taste translator to translate cultural taste between PSM organizations and vast groups of social media users. Although the example given above is based in scripted comedy television, the framework *#7DaysLater* developed is exemplary on how contemporary PSM can engage citizens within the digital mediascape. In this role, PSM cultural intermediaries are best placed to understand how culture is functioning within society (listening), while also distributing key public issues (talking). They assist in developing maximalist participatory models, while also introducing existing user patterns to help develop PSM algorithmic culture.

Conclusions

This chapter has highlighted the contemporary digital media landscape in which PSM operates. Through the combination of social media, an influence economy, and cultural intermediaries, there is a new cultural calibration model occurring between cutting edge cultural activities and cultural institutions, such as PSM. This enables the PSM organization to understand what cultural practices are relevant beyond their existing programming, while also presenting them with an opportunity to disseminate the public issues that should be discussed within the public sphere. Combining this approach with contemporary digital media processes, PSM has begun engaging with the emergent algorithmic culture that sees the personalized cultural products delivered to individual consumers, while also providing an avenue for users to provide their input into the institution. The danger that has emerged with this automated process is the potential of either operating with incorrect information, or omitting socially relevant information altogether. This chapter has argued that the inclusion of cultural intermediaries as key cultural, knowledge and technology agents enables the correct design, development and implementation of an appropriate and socially relevant algorithmic culture.

Further to this argument, PSM operating with algorithmic culture to enable maximalist participation through professional and socially relevant content is an example of Cunningham's (2013) distinctive innovation model. The *#7DaysLater* case study clearly demonstrates how this model is working to satisfy both the audience and the media organization, and is an exemplar of how other media organizations could be operating in this space. The cultural intermediation model coupled with an algorithm culture could easily transfer from the PSM sector to the broader digital media sector seamlessly, bolstering the significance of PSM within the contemporary media environment. While in the PSM model, the goal is to engage users within a maximalist participation sense, within the commercial broadcasting sector, this cultural intermediation algorithm model could be reappropriated to enable these organizations to engage in content production that is authentically market driven.

The cultural intermediation algorithm culture that has emerged from PSM is an outcome that is crucial to its legislated remit in order to engage its citizens across digital media technologies to promote increased participation and citizen democracy. This is typical of the sort of innovation that we have come to expect from PSM, and following Cunningham's call for this innovation to be recognized as a distinctive role for PSM, the algorithmic participation model is a crucial function that is to be highlighted for media policy makers. For policy makers and PSM leaders alike, a cultural intermediation algorithm model is demonstrable of how PSM remains relevant within a network society, and places them at the fore of innovative practices. Most importantly, it demonstrates that it is possible for PSM to engage with its citizens across new and emerging communication technologies and ensure it maintains authenticity, value and publicness.

References

ABC (2013). *#7DaysLater*. Retrieved June 13, 2015 from http://www.abc.net.au/tv/programs/7dayslater/.

ABC (2014). *Strategic Plan 2013–16*. Retrieved August 28, 2015 from http://about.abc.net.au/wp-content/uploads/2013/08/ABCStrategicPLN2013-16FULLNEWS.pdf.

Abidin, C. (2015). Micromicrocelebrity: Branding Babies on the Internet. *M/C Journal,* 18(5): (n.p.).

Andrejevic, M. (2007). Surveillance in the Digital Enclosure. *The Communication Review,* 10 (4): 295–317.

Bourdieu, P. (1984). *A Social Critique of the Judgement of Taste* (1st ed.). London: Routledge.

Brevini, B. (2013). *Public Service Broadcasting Online: A Comparative European Policy Study of PSB 2.0*. London: Palgrave Macmillan.

Burgess, J., and A. Matamoros-Fernández (2016). Mapping sociocultural controversies across digital media platforms: One week of #gamergate on Twitter, YouTube and Tumblr. *Communication, Research & Practice,* 2(1): 79–96.

Carpentier, N. (2009). Participation Is Not Enough: The Conditions of Possibility of Mediated Participatory Practices. *European Journal of Communication,* 24(4): 407–420.

Castells, M. (2007). *The Rise of the Network Society* (2nd ed.). Oxford: Blackwell Publishers Ltd.

Cunningham, S. (2013). *Hidden Innovation: Policy, Industry and the Creative Sector*. Brisbane: University of Queensland Press.

Cunningham, S. (2015). Repositioning the Innovation Rationale for Public Service Media. *International Journal of Digital Television,* 6(2): 203–220.

DCMS (2015). *BBC Charter Review: Public Consultation*. Retrieved March 19, 2015 from https://www.gov.uk/government/uploads/system/uploads/attachment_data/file/445704/BBC_Charter_Review_Consultation_WEB.pdf.

Debrett, M. (2015). "Tools for Citizenship?" Public Service Media as a Site for Civic Engagement: An Australian Case Study. *Television and New Media,* 16(6): 557–575.

Dijck, J. v., and T. Poell (2015). Making Public Television Social? Public Service Broadcasting and the Challenges of Social Media. *Television and New Media,* 16(2): 148–164.

Donders, K., and H. Van den Bulck (2014). The 'Digital Argument' in Public Service Media Debates. An Analysis of Conflicting Values in Flemish Management

Contract Negotiations for VRT. In: G.F. Lowe, and F. Martin (eds.), *The Value of Public Service Media*. Göteborg: Nordicom, 145–164.

EBU (2014). *Vision2020. Connecting to a Networked Society*. Retrieved July 9, 2015 from http://www3.ebu.ch/files/live/sites/ebu/files/Publications/EBU-Vision2020-Networked-Society_EN.pdf.

Edelvold, C., G.F. Lowe, and A.B. Lund (2014). A Market Failure Perspective on Value Creation in PSM. In: G.F. Lowe, and F. Martin (eds.), *The Value of Public Service Media*. Göteborg: Nordicom, 105–126.

Flew, T., S. Cunningham, A. Bruns, and J. Wilson (2008). *Social Innovation, User Generated Content and the Future of the ABC and SBS as Public Service Media*. Retrieved August 10, 2013 from http://eprints.qut.edu.au/16948/.

Gillespie, T. (2014). Algorithm [draft] [#digitalkeywords]. Retrieved March 16, 2016 from http://culturedigitally.org/2014/06/algorithm-draft-digitalkeyword/.

GleamFutures (2016). *Gleam Futures Managers Social Talent*. Retrieved April 7, 2016 from http://www.gleamfutures.com/.

Głowacki, M., and L. Jackson (2014). Towards a Twenty-first Century Public Media: Conclusions. In: M. Głowacki, and L. Jackson (eds.), *Public Media Management for the Twenty-first Century: Creativity, Innovation, and Interaction*. London, New York: Routledge, 271–288.

Głowacki, M. (2015). Governance of Public Service Media in Poland: The Role of the Public. *Media and Communication,* 3(4): 26–34.

Gow, J. (2015). *Stop Laughing! This is Serious: Media Convergence, Funding Cuts, and Television Comedy at the Australian Broadcastign Corporation*. (Media and Communication Honours), University of Sydney, Sydney.

Hallinan, B., and T. Striphas (2014). Recommended for you: The Netflix Prize and the production of algorithmic culture. *New Media & Society,* 18(1): 117–137.

Hutchinson, J. (2013). Extending the Public Service Remit through ABC Pool. In: G.F. Lowe, and F. Martin (eds.), *The Value of Public Service Media*. Göteborg: Nordicom, 223–244.

Hutchinson, J. (2015). From Fringe to Formalisation: An Experiment in Fostering Interactive Public Service Media. *Media International Australia,* 155: 5–15.

Hutchinson, J. (2016). Moving convergence culture towards cultural intermediation: social media and cultural inclusion. *Continuum*, 30(2): 158–170.

Inglis, H., and A. McCann (2016). *Henry & Aaron*. Retrieved March 13, 2015 from https://twitter.com/henry_and_aaron.

Jakubowicz, K. (2014). Managing Spontaneity: User-Generated Content in the Media Ecology. In: M. Głowacki, and L. Jackson (eds.), *Public Media Management for the Twenty-First Century: Creativity, Innovation, and Interaction*. London, New York: Routledge, 216–233.

Maguire, J.S., and J. Matthews (2014). Introduction: Thinking with Cultural Intermediaries. In: J.S. Maguire, and J. Matthews (eds.), *The Cultural Intermediaries Reader*. London: SAGE Publications Ltd, 1–12.

Negus, K. (2002). The work of cultural intermediaries and the enduring distance between production and consumption. *Cultural Studies,* 16(4): 501–515.

Pariser, E. (2011). *The Filter Bubble: What the internet is hiding from you*. New York: Penguin Press.

Steemers, J. (2016). Blurred Lines: Public Service Media and the State. In: T. Flew, P. Iosifidis, and J. Steemers (eds.), *Global Media and National Policies: The return of the state*. UK: Palgrave Macmillan, 139–155.

Striphas, T. (2015). Algorithmic culture. *European Journal of Cultural Studies,* 18(4–5): 395–412.

Tremblay, G. (2016). Public Service Media in the Age of Digital Networks. *Canadian Journal of Communication,* 41(2016): 191–206.

Vanhaeght, A.-S., and K. Donders (2016). Moving Beyond Borders of Top-Down Broadcasting: An analysis of young users' participation in public service media *Television and New Media,* 17(4): 291–307.

Williams, R. (1989a). Communications, Technologies and Social Institutions *What I came to say*. London: Hutchinson Radius.

Williams, R. (1989b). *Resources of Hope: Culture, Democracy, Socialism*. London: Verso.

Wilson, C. K., J. Hutchinson, J., and P. Shea (2010). Public Service Broadcasting, Creative Industries and Innovation Infrastructure: The Case of ABC's Pool. *Australian Journal of Communication,* 37(3): 15–32.

Lizzie Jackson
London South Bank University, United Kingdom

The potential of machine mediation in the maintenance of public service media

Abstract: This production study argues predictive analytics (PA) and behavioural targeting (BT) will be useful for public service media (PSM). Whereas PA is the offering of digital content based on personal data, previous browsing behaviours, and user preferences, BT is the nuanced matching of content to audience segments. The topic is of critical importance for leaders of PSM, for media regulators and for audiences. The study draws on network and new media theory to provide context. The rationale for the study is the urgent need for PSM to begin using advanced digital production processes as mediation by machine is giving commercial digital firms a market advantage. An alternative PSM approach would benefit the quality of the public sphere. The use of predictive analytics and behavioural targeting is considered in four cases: the websites of *The Guardian* and the BBC in the UK, and *The Washington Post* and CNN in the USA.

Keywords: public service media, audience analysis, predictive analytics, behavioural targeting, big data, privacy.

Introduction

This production study on the distribution of digital media via computer networks explores predictive analytics (PA) and behavioural targeting (BT) also referred to as behavioural advertising; the automated 'matching' of content to audiences. Network Theory informs us that mediation by machine is an inherent aspect of the diffusion of content via computer networks and indicative of the recombinatory nature of digital media. PA is the collection and analysis of large reservoirs of personal and usage data (big data) by complex algorithms, often on an industrial scale. When sequentially coupled with BT – the matching of content to audience segments against previously indicated interests – 'natural' online browsing patterns are disrupted. It is argued that such mediation by machine is more than mere marketing, it is a way of delivering content to specific audiences. The large-scale adoption of predictive analytics and behavioural targeting by digitally adept commercial firms such as Facebook, YouTube, Amazon Prime and Netflix has given them a market advantage and commodifies audiences. Machine mediation can result in a 'filter bubble' or disruptive narrowing of information sources that becomes critical in the case of news services (Silverstone, 2007; Pariser, 2012). The topic is of the utmost importance for public service media (PSM) being concerned with the quality of the public sphere, and also for media regulators and audiences. The rationale for this study is to assist PSM to adjust focus from the currently dominant delivery paradigms of television and radio.

In order to find out how broadcasters and newspapers are beginning to use PA and BT, content analysis of four case studies are provided: the websites of *The Guardian* and the BBC in the UK, and *The Washington Post* and CNN in the USA. The sample group offers a level of international context and a range of orientation between public service and commercial activities. The Home and main section pages of the news sections of each websites was examined along with the website's Terms and Conditions, and Privacy Policy. The data was collected April–June 2015 and updated in January 2017 with a review of the privacy policies.

The growth of automated analysis and delivery

In the 'pure broadcast' era audience analysis largely related to the reach and popularity of television and radio programming. In the 1990s, broadcasters launched websites to accompany news channels and these began to offer the ability to examine audience consumption patterns in a more granular way through (for example) page 'views,' user retention (dwell time), website entry and exit routes and 'click-throughs' (browsing to other content). The audience analysis systems of broadcasting and Web-based media remained separate. The distribution of both broadcast *and* Web programming via internet protocols to SMART televisions, mobile devices and computers can extend this wider audience analysis to include broadcast content.

Automated mediation tools make it possible for YouTube, Netflix and Amazon Prime to understand how, when and where to deliver content to suit individual subscribers. These 'internet-born' companies have both the technical knowhow and departments of data scientists able to develop sophisticated algorithms that match people to content they might like. In the case of Amazon, the user data may already be available from previous transactions. In the 'Dot-com Boom' of the 1990's, the online retailer was able to amass tremendous amounts of data on consumers' buying preferences (Provost and Fawcett, 2013: 319). They also collected customer reviews and saw this as something that could give the company a critical commercial advantage. Skeggs and Yuill's 2013–2016 study 'Values and Value' looks at "what happens when economic value is accumulated from spheres previously considered non-economic, and the distortions and alterations in both economic and non-economic values this process creates" (Skeggs and Yuill, 2017).

The researchers find "Facebook makes considerable economic gain from commodifying friendship through the algorithmic conversion of 'likes' into advertising sales" (ibid); a new form of capital they term 'emotional capitalism.'

Global giants have the finance to speculatively expand and are now turning their attention to becoming suppliers of high quality media informed by audience feedback: "Amazon.com launched fourteen pilot programmes for its streaming video service and used customer feedback on it to help it select the five it ultimately produced" (Davenport, 2014: 49). Amazon, Netflix, YouTube and others are turning themselves into media producers by commissioning rich linear media for live-streamed and on-demand distribution and this is creating an increasingly challenging climate for public service media. The understanding and use of dynamic real-time audience analysis and distribution systems such as PA and BT are essential to compete with such commercial media (Davenport, 2014; Brynjolfsson and McAffe, 2014).

It is important at this point to ensure a shared understanding of concepts and terms. The internet is framed by Manovich (2013) as a 'meta-medium' comprised of computer code and concerned with the diffusion of content within networks of computer networks. In computer science diffusion refers to the movement of objects (such as a video or image file) through computer networks. Jenkins and others refer to the spreading of media by forwarding, recommending and so on as being an intrinsic element of participatory culture (Jenkins et al., 2013). Audiences are able to browse through Web-based recombinatory content via SMART televisions, mobile devices and computers in consumption patterns that resemble the flocking or swarming of birds and insects depending on what is of interest at any given moment (Gloor, 2006; Miller, 2010). Web-based media is a highly fluid media landscape referred to as a 'mediascape' by Głowacki and Jackson (2014) to point out the intrinsic difference from the linear distribution patterns of broadcast media.

Network theory illustrates computer networks are relational, they depend on hyper-connectivity and on being able to pass files, messages, and commands around routes that have been identified as being useful. This spreading of material through networks is called 'diffusion,' a term widely used in computer science. Web-based delivery offers multi-directional, multi-platform, distribution and consumption. Web-delivered media is served from computer 'servers' to receiving computers and viewed via 'web browsers' using internet protocols. Browsers are user-interfaces designed for the easy viewing of content. Instagram, Vimeo, Spotify, Netflix and so on run on what industry producers term 'platforms.' Platforms are driven by sophisticated databases capable of storing and retrieving large amount of 'big data' at very high speeds. Big data refers to a variety of data, as

Davenport explains "Some have defined big data in terms of three Vs (volume, variety, and velocity)" (2014: 7). The data we are concerned with here is audience browsing behaviour and personal information. Databases and their associated algorithms also offer the comparison, storage and retrieval of material to suit pre-defined preferences; a matching and responding exercise. To make these calls and responses faster, databases use algorithms. An algorithm is "a set of steps that are followed in order to solve a mathematical problem or to complete a computer process" (Merriam-Webster.com, 2016). Databases can communicate between platforms (SMART TVs, tablet computers, laptops, and mobile phones) as long as they are all using computer code. This gives 'Inter-operabililty', the ability to view the same video file, photograph, or word document on different receiving devices.

I argue PSM needs to become involved in the development of machine mediation works for several reasons. First, in order to provide a counter to what Pariser calls 'The Filter Bubble' (Pariser, 2012). Both Cushion (2012) and Iyengar and Kinder (2010) argue that audiences who are served only closely related content or 'same opinion' commentary may not receive a sufficiently broad selection of news resulting in an ever-reducing understanding of our world. Secondly, techniques such as PA and BT offer a means to ensure all audiences are made aware of the availability of public service content in a more sophisticated way than merely offering content 'on demand.' Audiences can indicate preferred reception devices and other access parameters to suit their competencies, age, location and so on. Third the lack of any balancing presence of PSM in debates relating to the future use of PA and BT might have implications for the mediascape going forward. Lastly, PA could be merely framed as 'Audience Analysis 2.0' however it is much more than that as it is also enmeshed in the fabric of the delivery of Web-based media across a variety of different delivery platforms. BT could be thought of as mere marketing, but again, it can be seen as a highly sophisticated way to nuance content delivery to specific audiences. Machine mediation is therefore of high importance to PSM as it creates a fresh model of content distribution.

Any lack of understanding of how Web-based media is delivered, and how machine mediation works, results in commercial media having an advantage. There is currently a critical imbalance of power between PSM and commercial media that is resulting in the growing commodification of audiences (Castells, 2009; Graham and De Sabbata, 2013; Freedman, 2014). In addition there are rising concerns worldwide relating to the misuse of personal data noted by Ess (2009) and Silverstone (2007). New European legislation in connection with the use of personal data will take effect in 2018 (European Commission, 2016).

An overview of how PA and BT works begins the chapter. This is followed by a short review of potential uses and abuses. An explanation of the international self-regulatory frameworks is then followed by a look at the four case studies, each of which is a provider or aggregator of news. Each is making the transition from being a 'traditional' media provider (broadcasting or newspapers) to a media landscape increasingly dominated by computer networks.

Defining machine mediation

Theories connected with 'New Media' show us how Web-delivered content is recombinatory (Bolter and Grusin, 2000; Lievrouw and Livingstone, 2002). Computer network theory assists us to see an emerging media landscape of multi-directional flows of material (Tanenbaum and Weatherall, 2014) that can be viewed on many different receiving devices. Networked media is a highly adaptive medium with a varying level of fluidity (Głowacki and Jackson, 2016) that 'solidifies' at times to enable reification, the making of meaning out of a thing (Vitale, 2014: 19). For example, moments of stasis can be found in the latest edition of a website home page. Computer science also gives us the notion of 'diffusion,' the spreading of material through networks of networks, a term also used by biologists to describe states of liquidity. Increasingly, the mediation of such flows of Web-based content is being automated. Text, images, video, other such media and social commentary is being diffused through networks using algorithms able to draw from large media stores in databases. It is impossible to do such processing by human hand; PA and BT are two examples of mediation by machine.

Siegel's definition of predictive analytics is "Technology that learns from experience (data) to predict the future behaviour of individuals in order to drive better decisions" (Siegel, 2013: 11). For Web-based media this is the analysis of both previous browsing behaviours and personal data. PA can be augmented by behavioural targeting, which is the segmentation of audiences into targetable groups. BT can be seen as a process that takes place after a user's browsing patterns and personal information have been analyzed. According to the Internet Advertising Bureau (a standards body promoting self-regulation for the advertising industry) BT is comprised of *contextual advertising* and *demographic advertising*:

> contextual advertising is where advertisements are served within a chosen 'context' by the selection of a website focused on a particular topic. An example is when a user is shown an advertisement for tennis rackets solely because he/she is visiting a tennis-related website. Behavioural advertising is also different to demographic advertising where advertisements are served based upon specific information provided by the user (e.g. gender, age, location) (Internet Advertising Bureau, 2009: 13).

An *advertising server* is a company that specializes in creating the technology that delivers advertising (banners for example) to the relevant page on a website. An *advertising network* is a firm that connects web-based businesses, content creators and advertisers. An *advertising exchange* acts as an open broker facilitating the buying and selling of advertising. A *data aggregator* is a firm aggregating information from many sources that might interest audience segments that have indicated a propensity for a marketable commodity or service.

Inter-operability between linked databases and content management systems offers the automated triangulation of member accounts, content files (video/audio/text/animation/photo and so on), plus – increasingly – geo-locate data. All this can be used to direct selections of media to different media platforms. At best this results in more meaningful selections of information, at its worst we may no longer be sharing the same public sphere but be experiencing a constructed reality. At the very worst, we may not even know this is happening because "In cyberspace we are constantly surrounded by relational databases, often without even realizing it" (MacCormick, 2012: 147). This brings us on to the need to address the potential benefits and drawbacks of machine mediation.

Uses and abuses

The Web-based media landscape is a meta-medium; composed of meta-tagged files that can be recombined to create both existing and new forms of media (Manovich, 2013). Organizations that understand and have capacity to produce such media are able to exploit the interconnected nature of networks to produce economic and societal value plus other newer forms of capital such as that relating to the previously noted 'emotional capitalism' identified by Skeggs, Yuill and Zschomler (2016). Televisions, computer tablets, and mobile phones are now capable of receiving web-based content. Marketing messages and purchasing opportunities can be inserted into browsing sessions, based on predicted interests. Young people get most of their news via social media (BBC News, 15 June, 2016) therefore we argue a very strong PSM presence online has become critical. For PSM this is irrelevant if you currently have little or no Web-based services.

The BBC launched online services in 1997 and this has more recently expanded to a broadcast channel (BBC3) in 2015 in order to cater for the media preferences of 16–35 year-old audiences. They are beginning to explore the automation of mediation, as a practical necessity. Their User Generated Content (UGC) Hub launched in 2005 and the journalists staffing the UGC intake desk use – mostly manual – matching to verify such content before it is used to substantiate or augment more conventional news stories (Meier, 2015:135). The volume of UGC received by the intake desk is high. There's a section on the BBC's news app for mobile phones ('My News') that responds to previously chosen interests an indication of the use of dynamic audience analytics. The BBC's News Lab is also experimenting with text-to-speech and artificial intelligence with a trial News Bot for BBC World and BBC Mundo. The bot will enable the sharing of news stories with others, plus suggest a new batch of links at the same time. One of the developers of the service, Labber Lei He says the BBC wants to keep the service simple and transparent in order to counter "concern over black box algorithms and biased distribution platforms, so we wanted to give users clear, simple commands to control the news they receive" (BBC News Labs, 2017). The BBC is also experimenting with new services that use cookies and other Web-based audience engagement processes to enable interactive and social platforms (http://www.bbc.co.uk/taster/).

The Japanese public service broadcaster, NHK, has recently been developing an earthquake and tsunami alert and response service for the public that aggregates sources of big data connected with such events. These trials have been successful and the service is likely to expand. The Canadian Broadcasting Company (CBC) has been adjusting its newsroom to enable the automated ingest, retrieval and delivery of news to multiple devices. The Head of CBC News Strategy, Andrew Cochran, envisions 'a river of content' that can be automatically sifted and received by any device to suit the requirements of CBC and the public (Cochran, 2016).

Machine mediation has other uses that audience analysis; it can produce new forms of expression such as data journalism. Hurrell and Leimdorfer (2015) define data journalism as broadly covering projects that use data to do one or more of the following:

1. Enable a reader to discover information that is personally relevant,
2. Reveal a story that is remarkable and previously unknown,
3. Help the reader to better understand a complex issue.

The researchers argue that data journalism has some longevity; the BBC has been offering simple tools for audiences to use (for example to interrogate finance and weather data) for over ten years. Simon Rogers who pioneered the development of data journalism when he was at *The Guardian* believes the concept is even older citing Florence Nightingale's use of graphical data to articulate mortality rates in the army from 1858. Data journalism "incorporates such a wide range now of styles – from visualization to long-form articles. The key thing they have in common is that they are based on numbers and statistics – and that they should aim to get a 'story' from that data" (Rogers, 2015:5). Rogers believes good data journalism is connected to drawing on diverse sources, a perspective supported by a range of scholars (Silverstone, 2007; Pariser, 2012; Freedman, 2014).

I now explore the characteristics connected with machine mediation that may have potential negative outcomes. One aspect referred to earlier is the narrowing of news caused by the 'filter bubble' offering restricted news sources based on your previous choices or opinions you concur with versus the challenging and the surprising. The matching that computers are able to do is becoming less crude; one of the essential characteristics of computers is they are able to 'learn,' sometimes referred to as 'machine learning.' Machine learning has been most prominently demonstrated by IBM's super-computer Watson that, in 2011, challenged a US game show Jeopardy! to a game of chess (BBC, 2011). Watson performed better as time went on, as the machine began to guess the probability of the game more accurately. According to McKinsey "machine learning is nothing like learning in the human sense (yet). But what it already does extraordinarily well—and will get better at—is relentlessly chewing through any amount of data and every combination of variables" (McKinsey, 2015: 2).

PA and BT are likely to assist producers to deliver content in a more nuanced way, as has been argued, however there is still a need for human intervention, for example in making editorial judgements connected with prior knowledge, cultural nuances, and so on. It is also still necessary to programme the 'learning machines' in order to have an acceptable level of consistency, repeatability, and objectiveness (Provost and Fawcett, 2013: 26). Facebook has recently been concerned with how to manage the injection of 'Fake News' items into its services (Solon and Wong: 16 December, 2016) and this has resulted in the forwarding of potential fake news to external – manual – fact-checking organizations such as Factcheck.org.

One of the key issues relating to the use of machine mediation is that there are fewer non-commercial platforms serving quality news using dynamic database-driven networked systems. Young people use social media platforms to learn about their world and the lack of balanced arrays of news is worrying. Silverstone (2007) and Cushion (2012) argue that being in possession of the facts as they are known from a sufficiently diverse range of sources is key to the preservation of deliberative democracy. Alex Pentland, a prominent data scientist also expressed his concern at a lecture hosted by the UK news aggregator *The Guardian* in January 2015:

> (…) the formation of social media echo chambers, in which a very limited number of viewpoints are given precedence and perpetually reiterated on sites such as Twitter. Pentland says that so many voices are given a platform that users become unable to assess the value of each and end up following a tiny number (Williams, 2015).

Objectivity and ensuring the quality of news has long been the province of PSM, and particularly so in a news environment. Any absence of a public service presence able to act as a balancing agent will be keenly felt in the future. PSM is currently less likely to have the infrastructure to manage such complex data gathering. The kinds of people needed to run big data initiatives (i.e. data scientists) are also different from conventional audience analysts "They are more facile with data, more experimental, and more product focused" (Davenport, 2014: 15). Many PSM firms are concentrating on making the transition from being 'pure broadcasters' to producing content on several platforms. However, the decision not to explore data management techniques would be foolish as machine mediation offers a powerful and sophisticated distribution tool. Let's now turn to review the self-regulatory frameworks for PA and BT that are in place in North America and Europe.

The self-regulatory frameworks

PSM has historically had a critical voice within debates connected with the development of policy and practice relating to media and communications. I argue that PSM should continue to have a presence is such discussions. There is also an opportunity to perform an important public awareness function, but until that happens national and regional advertising standards organizations are providing information and educational material for the public alongside acting as quasi-regulators, however such material is unlikely to reach the attention of young people (high users of web-based media) and other potentially vulnerable groups.

The European Interactive Digital Advertising Alliance (EDAA) provides an educational website giving information on how behavioural advertising works and an overview of European standards to assist consumers.[1] Seven key principles have emerged, of which four are noted here. First, there should be transparency in how automated tracking is used by media firms. Secondly, users should have choice and control of their own data, which should also be stored securely. Third, the monitoring and segmentation of audiences should have limitations, for example in connection with children's browsing behaviours. Lastly the EDAA recommends that education be provided for consumers about behavioural advertising and the European self-regulatory Framework.

In the USA the Digital Advertising Alliance (DAA), an independent non-profit organization representing American advertising and marketing associations, offers another similar self-regulatory Framework. Like their European counterpart,

1 *Your Online Choices. A Guide to Online Behavioural Advertising.* Retrieved March 8, 2016 from http://www.youronlinechoices.com/uk/about-behavioural-advertising.

the DAA has produced a set of principles connected with the transparency of 'interest-based' advertising. They encourage media firms to inform consumers about the practices and processes being used such as how to opt out. The DAA has also developed principles for mobile advertising (2013) in response to the growing use of PA relating to mobile devices. This includes the use of "cross-app data, precise location data and personal directory data." Enforcement of these standards began in 2015 (Digital Advertising Alliance, 2015).

Advertising Standards Canada (Adstandards.com, 2016) offers links to further information and an online tool that makes it easy for the public to opt out of tracking programmes. They also provide a 'TM Ad Choices' icon that is also becoming widely used in North America and Europe. The icon indicates companies who comply with recommendations on transparency and control over interest-based ads.

In order to illustrate how other news outlets are experimenting with machine mediation we now look at the four case studies, the BBC, *The Guardian*, CNN, and *The Washington Post.*

The mechanical mediation of news in the case studies

A comparative review of the use of PA and BT in news content was undertaken in the cases of *The Guardian* and the BBC in the UK, and *The Washington Post* and CNN in the USA. The Home and main section pages of each of the websites, the Terms and Conditions, and the Privacy Policies were all analyzed. The content analysis took place between April to June 2015 and the Privacy Policies for each website were examined again in January 2017. Overall, there is an increasing range of personal data being collected, this may be due to an expansion in the services these companies are offering resulting in the need for a wider range of personal data, for example, game play and game scores. There is also an increase in the embedding of third party services such as social media channels, inevitably accompanied by disclaimers and alerts advising users to check the privacy policies of these third party providers. The more commercially-oriented firms such as *The Washington Post* and CNN are making greater use of audience data analytics than the more public-oriented enterprises the BBC and *The Guardian*. The BBC appears not to be updating its Privacy Policy as comprehensively as *The Guardian*, *The Washington Post* and CNN who all updated their documentation in 2016. The BBC's web page on Cookies mentions a 'recent' (2012) European law connected with the use of Cookies.

Table 1 illustrates the overall range of personal information that is being collected.

Table 1: The range of personal data collected by the case studies

Item	The Guardian	BBC	Washington Post	CNN
Name	✓	✓	✓	✓
Email	✓	✓	✓	✓
Postal Address	✓		✓	✓
Telephone Number				✓
Fax Number				✓
IP Address		✓	✓	
Credit Card Number			o	✓
Geo-location via mobile			✓	✓
Date of Birth			✓	o
Gender			✓	o
Job Title			✓	
Professional Networks	✓		✓	
Photo				o
Third Party Social Media Profile			o	o

°identified in the January 2017 data update.
Source: Author.

The *Washington Post* and CNN (commercially-oriented) are collecting more personal data than *The Guardian* and the BBC (public oriented) and a wider range of data. All the firms say they comply with the self-regulatory recommendations of their nation or region. It is alarming how much personal data is being harvested. Requests to gain access to users' external social media profiles indicates an urgent need for intervention. *The Washington Post* and CNN are also tracking users using location systems such as GPS tracking via mobile phones. The tracking of audience movements and location is also being achieved through the use of cookies and beacons (Table 2).

Table 2: Tracking devices used by the case studies

Item	The Guardian	BBC	Washington Post	CNN
Cookies	✓	✓	✓	✓
Beacons			o	✓

°identified in the January 2017 data update.
Source: Author.

Cookies are small applications placed on a user's computer by a web server that collect user-preferences and enable ecommerce, such as maintaining the persistence of a shopping cart's contents. Cookies can also be used to store user data between sessions. A definition of beacons and their use is provided by Stuart (2014):

> A beacon is a low energy Bluetooth chipset known as Bluetooth Smart which has its own integrated power source and emits a 2.4GHz signal which communicates with a smartphone to pinpoint your position to within 200 feet. The big opportunity for marketers is the ability to combine the location information derived from beacons with other customer information to generate personalised offers and communications, enhancing the customer experience and maximising marketing ROI.

Beacons are beginning to be used to deliver location-based advertising, for example they can be placed on a shop doorway to send an alert to a customer's mobile phone that their favourite jeans are on sale. The beacon can also provide additional information to guide the person to a specific section of a shop. The collection of the movements of users reflects the growing exchange of data between mobile devices and computing embedded in objects, referred to as the 'Internet of Things' (IoT). The classic illustrative example of the IoT is the fridge that informs you when it is empty.

Having considered *the collection* of personal data we now move on to look at *how* personal data is being used (Table 3).

Table 3: The purpose of the data collection by the case studies

Item	The Guardian	BBC	Washington Post	CNN
Personalization	✓	✓		
Enable participation	✓	✓	✓	✓
Contact users	✓	✓	✓	✓
Obtain user data in order to improve services	✓	✓		
Understand how services are being used	✓	✓		
Identify opportunities for selling advertising	✓		✓	✓
Market services to users	✓		✓	✓
Target adverts			✓	✓
Supply products				✓
Notify users of offers			✓	
Obtain permission to act for other agents			✓	
Subscription purposes				✓
Enable social networking				✓

Source: Author.

The declared uses of personal data appear to be far narrower than is evidenced. This is particularly true of *The Washington Post* and CNN. *The Guardian* and the BBC are collecting data in order to improve and personalize services whereas their US counterparts are prioritizing marketing, commerce, and conversion activities. One of the most worrying trends is the industry acceptance that it is the user's own responsibility to check the privacy policies for any embedded third party services. This is partly mitigated by an increase between June 2015 and January 2017 in the amount of information being provided for the public on their websites. All the organizations assume a level of media literacy and some understanding of the law. Yet, privacy policies are written for producers rather than audiences. Certainly young people, who are arguably most at risk, would find them impenetrable. The final Table illustrates how personal information is used by the firms. As in Table 1, CNN has expanded its use of PA and BT since June 2015.

Table 4: Third party use of personal data by the case studies

Item	The Guardian	BBC	Washington Post	CNN
Share personal data within the organization, group, or sub-contractors	✓	✓	✓	✓
Share data with others, with consent			✓	
May collect anonymised user data				✓
Collect data from public sources on users			✓	o
Not responsible for the practices of third parties			✓	o
Share data without prior consent				o

°identified in the January 2017 data update.
Source: Author.

In all the cases, the firms – whether they are oriented towards public service or commerce – are trading access to more customized services in return for sequential requests for personal information. Alarmingly, CNN state that if they are acquired by another business, users' personal details may be transferred along with other company equity.

The Washington Post and CNN are more likely to share both data with others and a wider range of data; for CNN this had expanded by January 2017 to include personal game scores. From the Terms and Conditions it is not clear whom *The Washington Post* are sharing data with, conversely Time Warner – CNN's parent company – provides a detailed list of the companies within the conglomerate.

There is a growing use of the disclaimer in this self-regulated landscape. In 2015, *The Washington Post* declared it could not be held responsible for any embedded third party service. In January 2017, CNN also adopted this position, making it clear that any user accessing services from outside the US does so at their own risk. In 2015, CNN noted that they are a global company therefore "it is necessary to transfer your information internationally (…) The data protection and other laws of other countries, such as the United States, may not be as comprehensive as those in your country" (CNN, 2015). In 2017, CNN's Privacy Policy now takes a more emphatic stance stating "If you are located outside of the US, you use this service at your own risk" (CNN, 2017).

The aim of this study was to find out whether PA and BT might be useful for public service media. Yes, undoubtedly this is the case, particularly if mediation by machine is framed as being a fresh distribution method. However, there are challenges that come with its use, firstly ensuring the privacy of the public is taken into consideration, second – and of no small consideration – there will be a need for investment in technology and training. To summarise the overall findings:

1. Machine mediation can deliver content to the right platform at the right time to suit users' preferences.
2. Machine mediation disrupts 'natural' browsing patterns and can result in a narrowing of information returned creating knowledge silos.
3. Data journalism can offer a widening of information around topics.
4. The use of personal data is often not clear, particularly agreeing to the cross-referencing – and even collection of data – from within users' social media accounts.
5. There is a strong need for media outlets to encourage literacy in the use of personal data using audience-specific forms of address.
6. The public is commodified and their personal data is reduced to 'assets' that can be acquired.
7. North American and European self-regulatory frameworks appear to be similar.

Machine mediation is growing and this is partly due to the ability of computers to learn (machine learning) and the ease with which they can sort, sift, and deliver content to identified locations. Having experienced Google and Wikipedia's ability to return highly accurate searches, and perhaps not knowing a world before the internet, young people *expect* their media to be on the right platform at the right time, on demand. They may accept they have to trade personal information in exchange for more personalized services, or simply be unaware of the implications. Who is collecting what and for which purpose is not at all clear, which suggests a need for public service intervention at policy and industry levels. Furthermore, there is a part for PSM to play in the future development of such technologies and practices as they are becoming an intrinsic part of digital media distribution.

We have been looking at PA and BT, acknowledging that these activities have a wider function than the audience analytics of broadcasting. To demonstrate the growing enmeshing of audience data with the mechanics of media delivery see Table 5.

Table 5: Audience analysis and the delivery of digital media

Media Type	Audience Analytics	Use
Broadcast Channels	• Audience Ratings • Audience Share • Audience Reach	• To judge the popularity of individual programmes and channels. • Adjust scheduling to maximize audiences. • Analyze regional location.
Web-based Media (Websites and also media delivered to SMART TV and mobile devices via internet Protocols).	• Personal Details • Browsing Patterns • Browsing Preferences • Purchasing Details • Location	• Track user-engagement into/out of and between websites/Web-based media. • Define audience interests. • Group audiences into similar interest 'segments'. • Supply appropriate media to suitable platforms. • Offer ecommerce. • Define user location. • Collect user location data.
Towards Media Embedded in Objects (The 'Internet of Things').	• Personal Details • Browsing Patterns • Browsing Preferences • Purchasing Details • Purchasing Preferences • Location • Pervasive user-sensing (proximity via wearable devices).	• To judge where to send media – which platform device, or object. • To define the location of the audience. • To judge how the media was received in order to nuance future delivery. • Monitor user's presence. • Collect user location data.

Source: Author.

In summary, as the delivery of media becomes linked with our understanding of the audience, their devices, and their movements, we have moved far beyond analysis of sentiment and audience numbers. The high volume of data (big data) that is now indicative of the almost live nuancing of digital media production and delivery, requires mediation by machine. These processes can no longer be done by hand. So is mediation by machine good, bad, or just inevitable?

Conclusions

The 'mediascape' is extending beyond the confines of television and radio channels, and beyond websites and web-based media delivered to mobile devices towards the 'Internet of Things.' This is the delivery of media and information to web-enabled objects such as cars, household appliances and via beacons placed strategically in doorways. Media is also beginning to be offered for downloading to accompany exhibitions or historical walks via QR Codes. This, of course, challenges the very definition of media. The volume of content being diffused through the network of networks (the internet) and particularly via the browser-based World Wide Web is of such volume that we are moving into the realm of data science. Mediation by machine is a dominant and intrinsic part of web-based media. Mediation by machine is therefore inevitable.

From a positivist perspective, PA and BT offer a highly responsive solution to supplying audiences with whatever media they want, how they want it, when they want it. The ability of web-based tracking and delivery systems offer multi-way, multi-dimensional distribution. There is also the opportunity to use the 'return path' to develop deeper relationships with the public and to understand more about them as a mass, a group, or an individual. For audiences there is the opportunity to support PSM through crowd-sponsorship and crowd-thinking, if PSM enthusiastically explores the possibilities.

For PSM there is a dependency on starting up or extending existing data management departments, on data management planning, and in the acquisition of skilled data scientists and analysts. Commercial media such as Amazon, Netflix and YouTube are industry leaders as they have had these structures in place for many years. However, there are indications that PSM is beginning to catch up. There is a high dependency on national regulators and policy makers understanding the importance of encouraging PSM to enhance and extend their web-based activity. Conversely, there is a lack of intervention by PSM in the way PA and BT is developing, and this is worrying. PSM needs to act as a counter and strong foil to commercial outlets in the media data sphere. There also continues to be debates on the use of personal data online, and this is something that should be the natural province of PSM as a protector, educator and guardian of the citizen in the sphere of media and communications.

We have been arguing for a higher presence of PSM in digital media networks in order to counter any narrowing of news and information resulting in knowledge silos. Networked media requires public service algorithms and machine driven PSM systems that continue to challenge the known, in exactly the same way that PSM functioned in the broadcast era. Until PSM engages with data science and data systems, commercial media (e.g. Netflix, Amazon Prime and so on) will retain an advantage. Fuelled by the commercial systems offered via online trading, commercial media are able to plough these funds into becoming purveyors of high quality media.

Acknowledgements

The paper presents indicative findings from 3-year international study (2015–2018), entitled "Organizational culture of public service media in the digital mediascapes: people, values and processes" which is funded by the Polish Science Foundation (NCN), SONATA 8. For more information: www.creativemediaclusters.com.

References

Adstandards.com (2016). *ASC Online Behavioural Advertising Compliance Procedure.* Retrieved January 1, 2017 from https://adstandards.com/en/OBA/index.html.

BBC (2011). *IBM's Watson supercomputer crowned Jeopardy king.* Retrieved January 1, 2017 from http://www.bbc.co.uk/news/technology-12491688.

BBC News (2015). *Social Media 'Outstrips TV' as News Source for Young People.* Retrieved January 10, 2017 from http://www.bbc.co.uk/news/uk-36528256.

BBC News Labs (2017). *Behind the BBC's Messenger News Bot.* Retrieved January 14, 2017 from http://bbcnewslabs.co.uk/2016/11/16/mundo-for-messenger/.

Bolter, J., and R. Grusin (2000). *Remediation: Understanding New Media.* Cambridge MA & London, England: MIT Press.

Brynjolfsson, E., and A. McAfee (2014). *The Second Machine Age. Work, Progress, and Prosperity in a Time of Brilliant Technologies.* New York, London: WW Norton & Company.

Castells, M. (2009). *Communication Power*, Oxford University Press: Oxford.

Cochran, A. (2016). *Interview*, September 15, 2016, Toronto, CA.

Cushion, S. (2012). *The Democratic Value of News: Why Public Service Media Matter*, Houndmills. UK: Palgrave MacMillan.

Davenport, T. (2014). *Big Data @ Work: Dispelling the Myths, Uncovering the Opportunities*. Boston MA: Harvard Business Review Press.

Digital Advertising Alliance (2015). *Digital Advertising Alliance Announces Mobile Privacy Enforcement to Begin September 1, 2015*. Retrieved January 23, 2017 from http://digitaladvertisingalliance.org/press-release/mobile-privacy-enforcement.

Ess, C. (2009). *Digital Media Ethics: Digital Media and Society Series*. Cambridge UK and Malden MA: Polity Press.

European Commission (2016). *Reform of EU Data Protection Rules*. Retrieved April 7, 2016 from http://ec.europa.eu/justice/data-protection/reform/index_en.htm.

Freedman, D. (2014). *The Contradictions of Media Power*. London and New York: Bloomsbury Press.

Gloor, P. (2006). *Swarm Creativity: Competitive Advantage through Collaborative Innovation Networks*. Oxford: Oxford University Press.

Głowacki, M., and L. Jackson (eds.) (2014). *Public Media Management for the Twenty-First Century: Creativity, Innovation and Interaction*. London and New York: Routledge.

Głowacki, M., and L. Jackson (2016). *The Significance of Fluidity in the Network: Organisational Structures within Digital Clusters*. Retrieved January 21, 2017 from http://ripeat.org/library/2016/7053-significance-fluidity-network-age-organisational-structures-within-digital.

Graham, M., and S. De Sabbata, (2013) *The Age of Internet Empires*, Retrieved June 2, 2016 from http://geography.oii.ox.ac.uk/?page=age-of-internet-empires.

Hurrell, B., and A. Leimdorfer (2015). *The Data Journalism Handbook*. Retrieved June 20, 2015 from http://datajournalismhandbook.org/1.0/en/in_the_newsroom_1.html.

Internet Advertising Bureau (2009). *IAB Handbook: A Guide to Online Behavioural Advertising*. Retrived January 23, 2017 from https://iabuk.net/sites/default/files/OnlineBehaviouralAdvertisingHandbook_5455.pdf.

Iyengar, S., and D.R. Kinder (2010). *News That Matters: Television and American Opinion* (Updated Edition). Chicago: The University of Chicago Press.

Jenkins, H., S. Ford, and J. Green (2013). *Spreadable Media: Creating Value and Meaning in a Networked Culture*, New York and London: New York University Press.

Lievrouw, L., and S. Livingstone (2002). *The Handbook of New Media*. London: Sage Publications.

MacCormick, J. (2012). *9 Algorithms That Changed the Future: The Ingenious Ideas That Drive Today's Computers*. Princeton NJ and Woodstock Oxfordshire: Princeton University Press.

McKinsey (2015). *An Executive's Guide to Machine Learning*. Retrieved June 3, 2016 from http://www.mckinsey.com/industries/high-tech/our-insights/an-executives-guide-to-machine-learning.

Manovich, L. (2013). *Software Takes Command*. London: Bloomsbury Academics.

Meier, P. (2015). *Digital Humanitarians: How BIG DATA is Changing the Face of Humanitarian Response*, London and New York: CRC Press.

Merriam-Webster.com (2016). *Algorithm*. Retrieved January 1, 2017 from http://www.merriam-webster.com/dictionary/algorithm/.

Miller, P. (2010). *Smart Swarm*. London: Collins.

Pariser, E. (2012). *The Filter Bubble: What the Internet is Hiding From You*. London: Penguin Books.

Provost, F., and T. Fawcett (2013). *Data Science for Business: What you need to know about data mining and data-analytic thinking*. Sebastopol CA: O'Reilly.

Pyle, D., and C. San Jose (2015). *An Executive's Guide to Machine Learning, McKinsey Qarterly: June, 2015*. Retrieved June 29, 2015 from http://www.mckinsey.com/Insights/High_Tech_Telecoms_Internet/An_executives_guide_to_machine_learning?cid=Digital-eml-alt-mkq-mck-oth-1506.

Rogers, S. (2015). Why Data Journalism is the new Punk. In: T. Felle, J. Mair, and D. Radcliffe (eds.), *Data Journalism: Inside the global future*. Bury St Edmonds, UK: Abramis Academic Publishing.

Siegel, E. (2013). *Predictive Analytics: The Power to Predict who will Click, Buy, Lie, or Die*. Hoboken, New Jersey: John Wiley and Sons.

Silverstone, R. (2007). *Media and Morality: On the Rise of the Mediapolis*. London: Polity Press.

Skeggs, B., and S. Yuill (2016). *Values and Value*. Retrieved 15 January, 2017 from https://values.doc.gold.ac.uk/about/.

Solon, O., and J. Wong (2016). *Facebook's Plan to Tackle Fake News Raises Questions over Limitations*. Retrieved December 19, 2016 from https://www.theguardian.com/technology/2016/dec/16/facebook-fake-news-system-problems-fact-checking.

Stuart, D. (2014). *The Marketers Guide to Beacons and Other Location-based Services*. Retrieved April 13, 2016 from http://digitalmarketingmagazine.co.uk/articles/the-marketers-guide-to-beacons-and-other-location-based-services/937.

Tanenbaum, A., and D. Wetherall (2014). *Computer Networks* (fifth edition). Harlow, UK: Pearson Education Limited.

Vitale, C. (2014). *Networkologies: A Philosophy of Networks for a Hyperconnected Age – A Manifesto*. Winchester UK & Washington USA: Zero Books.

Williams, O. (2015). Google adviser calls on tech giant to create a separate organisation for data, *The Guardian*, 25 March, 2015. Retrieved July 6, 2015 from http://www.theguardian.com/media-network/2015/mar/25/google-sandy-pentland-separate-organisation-data.

Anja Stević and Emil Čančar

University of Zagreb, Croatia

Public service media in Croatia: virtues and flaws of media transformation

Abstract: This chapter discusses the historical, legislative and organizational framework of Croatia's public service media Hrvatska radiotelevizija (HRT) in order to provide a background for changes which occurred due to changing mediascape and transition of public service media to Web 2.0, as an interactive public social media. HRT's transition and transformation from state-owned media to public service enterprise with all the downsides eventually led to the formation of a convergent public media, which is slowly adapting to new media platforms and challenges. Multi-platform content and technological improvements remain HRT's top priorities so that the organization can serve democratic values and fulfil its goal as an accountable source of information. After observing and examining the main features of public service media and its adaptation to the evolving online environment it remains clear that there is still a lot to be achieved.

Keywords: media transition, convergence, new media environment, online journalism, adaptation, Hrvatska radiotelevizija.

Introduction

"There is nothing more important in a democracy than a well informed electorate!" – cries MacKenzie McHale, an executive news producer in the Aaron Sorkin-penned series premiere of HBO's *The Newsroom*. Even though taken from a drama series, the quote pretty much sums up the *raison d'etre* of providers of public service broadcasting (PSB). To inform, educate and entertain, the John Reith formula for the PSB has carried weight and dictated the course of the work of media professionals for decades. Their values were set high: to use PSB to give the necessary information to their citizens, information that they needed to function in a democratic society. It has already been said many times, but things are changing rapidly. With the proliferation of channels and new media platforms, the PSB is at a 21st century turning point, to paraphrase Jakubowicz (2008).

In today's media environment we are witnessing negative assumptions about the existence of traditional media outlets, such as television and radio, whose power no longer prevails. Instead, new media players have emerged. The new fluid and fast-changing media environment evolved in only a few decades and public service media (PSM) can no longer resist adjusting, adapting and changing (in both internal and external ways). Taking into consideration growing market competition, the spread of Internet news portals, mobile news applications, social media etc., we can agree that it is a demanding media environment in which PSM strives to stay at the top as a main source of news and information (Perišin, 2010: 49–50; Peruško, 2011: 65, 75).

The goal of this chapter is to show the main features of the Croatian PSM – Hrvatska radiotelevizija (HRT), its legal background, its organization (and governance processes) as well as to outline its new strategy to remain a key media player in the digital environment. Croatia was one of the first countries in Central and Eastern Europe (CEE) to establish a radio station on May 15, 1926. Croatian television appeared thirty years later and it was the first television station in that part of Europe, and it was considered a phenomenon[1]. Comparing it with Western Europe, where PSM still dominated the audience shares in countries like Germany, the Netherlands, Belgium, Spain and Italy, the PSM in Croatia really did enjoy the position as a leader in the media system by 2010 (Roller, 2010:156). It has gone through many obstacles, changed political regimes and government systems since it started, to become an independent PSM organization serving the population.

Overview of historical and legislative background

Hrvatska radiotelevizija is a legal entity that has the status of a public institution whose activity, function and content of public services, financing, management, supervision and mode of operation are regulated under its own law and regulations. The founder of this public institution is the Republic of Croatia and the Croatian Government exercises the founding rights[2]. Its goal is to serve Croatian society in an independent and autonomous way, funded by public money. It is the only Croatian PSM and it operates under its own Act – the Law on HRT, which has been changed several times since it was introduced. HRT was based on the Yugoslav state RTV Zagreb, which changed its name to HRT in June 1990[3]. It sustained heavy losses to its broadcasting array and technological infrastructure during the War for Independence (1991–1995) and it falls into the category of the systemic model of PSM introduction. The systemic model means that PSM

1 *HRT – The evolution of Croatian Radio and Television*. Retrieved April 23, 2015 from http://www.hrt.hr/hrt/evolution-croatian-radio-and-television/.

2 Zakon o HRT-u, NN 76/12.

3 *Povijest HRT-a*. Retrieved April 21, 2015 from http://www.hrt.hr/hrt/povijest-hrt-a/.

in Croatia was introduced along with the transition to democracy and all related processes (Jakubowicz, 2008: 17).

The transformation of the state radio-television broadcasting into a public service did not start simultaneously with the declaration of independence of the Republic of Croatia. War and the strong influence of the conservative ruling party, HDZ (CDU: Croatian Democratic Union) delayed this transformation for a decade (Popović, 2004: 18). The HRT remained as a state media organization until 2003. The change process started in 1997, with *Forum 21*, a group of journalists who drafted 'Resolution 21' that called for the transformation of HRT into a public service organization (Popović, 2004: 18). After the change of government in 2000 the Law on HRT was enforced in line with European democratic standards, which ensured the direct election of the members of the HRT Council. The HRT Law came into effect in 2001 and it was the first law which had real influence on the content from civil society, through the Programme Council, whose task was to promote and protect the public interest by monitoring and improving the quality of PSM programmes. The 2001 Law on HRT offered democracy on paper (privatizing the third channel, editors could not be party members, strengthening the HRT Council and introducing civil society into its fold) but it allowed politicians and Parliament to appoint supervisors. Therefore, while civil society had oversight over the programmes, the state controlled the HRT management (Popović, 2004: 22). There was no alternative but to create and introduce a new bill. The Organization for Security and Co-operation in Europe (OSCE) Mission to Croatia sought the assistance of the Polish media expert Karol Jakubowicz to advise the government on the new piece of legislation (Popović, 2004: 23). The new law saw the light of day in February 2003 and its contents regarding professionalism, programmes and human rights were impeccable. The law recognized that members of the Council could not be affiliated with other news groups, state officials etc., but did not set any limitations regarding party membership (Popović, 2004: 25). Car (formerly Popović), an Assistant Professor at University of Zagreb, was a member of the HRT Council in 2011 and for some of 2012. She resigned from the HRT Council in 2012, publicly criticizing the Council's work: the members used their positions for personal gain, censorship, and non-action in relation to the Council's fundamental task – supervising the HRT's programme scheme and protecting the public interest. Car suggested discussions on children, minorities and gender issues in the programme content, but was ignored by the members of the Council.

Another change in the media law took place in 2010. Again, it was not satisfactory, so in 2012 it was amended and the new organizational structure of the public service board was confirmed – the creation of a Supervisory Board and a

Management Board. The 2012 legal additions to the HRT Act gave more authority to the Director General and the election into bodies of management was put in the hands of the Parliament. These changes were designed to facilitate the functioning of the HRT and as a prelude to its restructuring and future development of the PSM for providing new audio and visual services (Popović, 2004).

The programme guidelines, as prescribed by the Law, are broad. The HRT needs to meet the interests on national, regional and local levels. Its program must contain informative, cultural, entertaining, children, sport, educational and artistic content. By doing so, the PSM is obliged to promote national interests, basic human rights, patriotism, tolerance, to understand and respect diversity, democratic values and institutions, civil society, and to promote a culture of public dialogue (Law on HRT, 2010: Article 6).

The funding of HRT is based on the dual model of PSM financing. Most of the revenue is obtained from the mandatory licence fee that citizens pay if they possess a radio or a TV receiver[4]. A smaller portion of PSM is funded through advertising revenue. The license fee is paid directly to HRT and the argument for this is financial and programme independence (HRT Law, 2010; art. 17, subsec. 2–3). The fee is 80 kuna per month for each household (roughly 11 EUR), which is divided between a number of units, such as television and radio programmes, the Croatian Audiovisual Centre, and the Fund for Promoting Pluralism and Diversification of Electronic Media etc. Every five years the contract between the Government and HRT is renewed and the level of the fee is decided, depending on the media's programme production intensity (HRT Law, 2010: art. 13). The Supervisory Board determines the fee, and the 2010 Law prescribed a maximum fee of 1.5 percent of the average salary, based on statistical calculations (HRT Law, 2010: article 33). Additional revenue is collected by selling advertising space, but the Law on HRT specifies the length of advertisements and special time slots for them. For example, programmes for children and religious programmes must not contain any advertisements. The contract between the government and HRT is also made public through the HRT website[5] and the contract currently in force was signed in 2013.

The changes that were introduced to the Law in 2012 reorganized the HRT and now it consists of three bodies: the Council, the Supervisory Board and the Management Board. A Director General heads the Management Board, and is

4 *Pristojba*. Retrieved April 24, 2015 from http://www.hrt.hr/pristojba/.

5 *Ugovor izmedu Hrvatske radiotelevizije i Vlade Republike Hrvatske*. Retrieved April 30, 2015 from http://www.hrt.hr/uploads/media/UGOVOR_HRT_I_VLADA_RH_2013-2017.pdf.

appointed after a public call for candidates and from Directors of HRT Units (HRT amended Law, 2012: Article 21a). A person with political or diplomatic immunity cannot serve as a member of the Management. The tasks that fall under the authority of the Management Board include managing the finances and property, creation of internal Acts and documents and the appointment of editors (HRT Law, 2010: art. 20–21). The Director General's authority was increased by the 2012 law amendment and included running the management, supplying the other bodies with necessary documentation for their work, proposing the financial plan and the final financial bill and carrying out all other duties as prescribed by the Statute of the PSM. The Supervisory Board consists of five members, one of whom represents the HRT workers, three (along with the president) are appointed by Parliament (*Sabor*) and the party in opposition selects at least one (HRT Law, 2010: art. 22). Unlike the Council, the members of the Supervisory Board can be compensated for their work, while the Council's work is voluntary. The function of the Supervisory Board is self-explanatory; it oversees the financial operations, ledgers, approves loans and handles other similar work. The mechanism by which the PSM is accountable to its publics is the Programme Council of the HRT (HRT Council). It is a body of 11 members, nine of whom are appointed by Parliament after a public call for candidates and two are chosen by employees of the HRT (HRT amended Law, 2012: Article 25). One may be appointed a member of the Council if he or she is a well-known and respected academic, intellectual, an artist or another expert who has promoted democratic values, rule of law, has been a defender of human rights and advocate of civil society, a promoter of culture and science or a protector of free media and freedom of speech (Law on HRT, 2010: art. 25/s9). A person cannot be appointed as a member of the Council if they work for the PSM or any other media organization, if they are employed in a political party or as a public official, or if they have any business ties with the HRT (Law on HRT, 2010: art. 25/subsec. 10–13). The Council's duties include overviewing the programmes, appointment of editors-in-chief and informing the Management and the editors if professional or programme codes have been violated. The Council also appoints the person responsible for user relations who, in order to be chosen, must meet all of the criteria necessary to be appointed to the Council[6]. The person appointed, the user's Commissioner, receives user's complaints and suggestions and reports to the Council at least twice a year (Law on HRT, 2010:

6 The report on user suggestions, complaints and comments is issued to the HRT Council and is made public on the HRT website. Retrieved April 25, 2015 from http://www.hrt.hr/278668/hrt/izvjestaj-povjerenika-za-razdoblje-od-1-sijecnja-do-31-prosinca-2014-godine.

article 32). In order to maintain the freedom of the press, the Council cannot view media content before it goes on air (Law on HRT, 2010: art. 26/4). The Council's work is transparent.

Control over the laws regarding HRT is one of the main tasks of the Electronic Media Agency. Via its Electronic Media Council the main goal of the Electronic Media Agency is to carry out the duties of a regulatory body in the area of electronic media. As stated: "Electronic Media Act regulates the rights, obligations and responsibilities of legal and natural persons that provide audio and audiovisual media services and services of electronic publications by electronic communication networks, and the interest of the Republic of Croatia in the field of electronic media"[7]. As can be seen from the distillation of the Law, it regulates the work of HRT extensively. It outlines the programme and democratic values, establishes the management and governing bodies of HRT and it also refers to questions of accountability and establishes the institution of the users' Commissioner. The legal framework that prescribes the values and norms resonates somewhat with the official documents of the Council of Europe (2012) that dictate the standards for PSM such as *Recommendation of the Committee of Ministers to member States on public service media governance*. The similarities are not surprising as, for its accession in 2013, Croatia was obliged to adjust its legislation (and media policy) to meet with EU standards. Besides the Law on HRT, the PSM has its own acts such as the organization's Statute and various regulations monitoring the elections, special coverage of events and rules of quizzes and other entertainment content. In addition, the work of HRT is regulated by the Contract between the Government of Croatia and the PSM. The Director-General of HRT and the Minister of Culture signed the Contract currently in force in 2013 for a four-year period. The contents of the Contract include programme breakdown, financing and strategic development and technical improvements related to the new media and communication practices (Contract between the Government and HRT, 2013).

Organization, audiences and market competitors

There are two key tasks of public television in a liberal democracy. First, to support the democratic government and the rule of law, which is at the same time a guarantee of its independence and freedom. Second, to provide accurate and comprehensive information and an egalitarian and free public forum for debating major social issues for the public (Popović, 2004). HRT operates three national

7 *Agency for Electronic Media. Legal documents*. Retrieved April 23, 2015 from http://www.e-mediji.hr/en/aem/legal-documents/.

and eight regional radio channels, four terrestrial TV channels and one satellite TV channel broadcasting in the Croatian language. It consists of two national television programmes HRT1 and HRT2 and two specialized programmes, both established in 2012, HRT3 for film and culture and HRT4, a news channel. The news channel HRT4 was the first to start cooperating with the radio. It is based on combining radio interviews with live broadcasting and is presented daily. HRT as PSM also includes eight regional radio stations and eight regional HRT centres. Radio and television programmes have also broadcast internationally, digitally via satellite, since 1997. The two international radio programme channels, *The Voice of Croatia* and the Internet radio programme *Speaking contents* provide general and specialized information newscasts in English, Spanish and German for Croatians living abroad, as well as for the international public. The international television programme broadcasts selection form HRT4's regular news programme. All listed programmes are broadcast throughout Europe and beyond, especially in countries with large Croatian communities, such as Australia, New Zealand and North and South America. Croatian Radio broadcasts three special Internet programmes and due to new media platform developments, *The Voice of Croatia* has been extended to a video content and TV news edition which can be found on their interactive website.

Until the commercial TV stations appeared, the central HRT's newscast was the only source of information for Croatians; audiences had to wait until 19:30 to tune in and get their daily news (Perišin, 2013: 156). Nowadays, the commercial television company, Nova TV, has overtaken HRT in ratings shares (Perišin, 2013). Television is the most important and powerful media (Car, 2010: 95, Car and Andrijašević, 2012: 19) but still, in the Croatian media environment, radio and print hold their ground. The "Trust in Media" study carried out in 2009 by Faculty of Political Science and Media Metar Agency showed that 57 percent of the population watches television often or regularly, confirming television as the most popular medium in Croatia. Television is followed by the Internet, which is very rarely or rarely used by 55 percent of those surveyed (Car and Andrijašević, 2012: 19). The latest results of the *Croatian TV Market Analysis,* carried out in 2013 by the agency Ipsos Plus, in cooperation with Media HUB and AGB Nielsen, showed that television is still the number one source of information for 59 percent of the population (AEM, 2013). HRT with its four channels, eight regional radio stations and a web edition has the most diverse media platforms. Nova TV has one additional TV channel, as RTL does (mostly light topics and entertainment shows) with the exception that on RTL there is a cartoon channel for toddlers.

In their regional report "The importance of media integrity" Petković, Hrvatin and Popović (2014: 95, 119) claim that despite its public role, HRT has resorted to mechanisms similar to those used by commercial television (in terms of changing formats, the trivialization of content, sensationalism, etc.) in order to compete with competitors. However, the share of news in the channels with national concessions shows that HRT has the highest percentage of news programmes. As stated in Petković, Hrvatin and Popović (2014: 119), HRT1 has 26.6 percent, Nova TV 13.5 percent and RTL 12.8 percent of news programmes and these statistics support HRT's public role in providing news content. Studies show that topics such as civil society, children and young people, people with disabilities, senior citizens, national minorities, non-governmental organizations (NGOs), asylum seekers, gender rights and the rights of sexual minorities, are mainly covered by HRT. Despite the difficulties, HRT is an institution with a long tradition of quality production and it has specific content that is not available elsewhere. It also has a stable financial framework (compared to other types of media) thanks to the license fees, so this advantage should be used accordingly (Petković, Hrvatin and Popović, 2014: 95).

The audience shares for HRT began to drop with the emergence of commercial TV stations in 2003 and according to HRT Restructuring program (2013: 7) every other Croatian household has several dozen TV channels at its disposal and these are delivered to them by telecom operators using cable and satellite transmissions[8]. The ratings shares of HRT are dropping fast and declined from 50 percent in 2006 to less than 30 percent by the end of 2012 (HRT Restructuring program, 2013: 8). The latest data provided by Roller (2014: 155) state that the audience share peaked at a mere 22 percent at prime time in 2013. Roller (2014: 155–56) also highlights that, even though the public service lost more than half of its audiences, it still produces and broadcasts programmes that reflect the public interest throughout its broadcasting. The internal strategic report also admits that the PSM no longer appeals to its younger audiences and recognizes that the competition has successfully used new technologies, such as HDTV. The audiences for HRT are well educated and the older population (Roller, 2014). Those data have already been academically prophesied, as Jakubowicz (2008: 15–16) stressed that most PSM organizations have trouble attracting younger audiences. The report also describes its current audiences as older, educated, urban and predominantly male (HRT Restructuring program, 2013: 12). Such an audience structure is described as not

8 Examples of cable TV in Croatia are MaxTV and B-net.

beneficial in the Restructuring report, which, even though it is published on the HRT official website, is classified as 'confidential.'

It also has to be emphasized that the *Video on Demand* service on the HRT website has been used more than 2 million times for the top 10 shows in the second half of 2014 alone (Roller, 2014: 157). Roller consequently notes that future research should take into account the non-linear usage of content *online*. The research still does not take into account the significant number of users when it comes to dealing with traditional audience shares, which place HRT as being less successful than its competitors. Roller (2014: 163) considers that alternative light entertainment programmes have lured away audiences from the PSM, but not from its main competitors.

At the end of 2012 the PSM provider published a new set of rules and regulations and announced its reorganization. The new HRT is primarily looking for a new approach to the media and wishes to show that a public service is no longer just radio and television, but a joint effort, which acts as new media. The new organization aims to use of all the platforms and media to produce a high-quality, authentic and varied programme. High quality, trusted news and current affairs content on all of the platforms is one of the first goals (Perišin, 2013: 155–156).

Transition to PSM 2.0

Public service media is a term that is used instead of the out-dated term public service broadcasting to indicate that public service is no longer limited to the traditional media, but is shifting to other platforms, as well as the Internet (Jakubowicz, 2008: 1). The value of universality should no longer be perceived as broadcasting on a couple of channels and radio stations, but rather as a "presence on all relevant media platforms with significant penetration" (Jakubowicz, 2008: 11), and this is the reason for PSM's shift and expansion. As already noted, HRT is losing its younger audiences. Today's trends in society, such as fragmentation, individualization, and networking and personalization of media usage, combined with the levelling of educational and social differences have all led to the "rejection of traditional PSM assumption" (Jakubowicz, 2008: 4). Moreover, in order for PSM (and HRT) to survive, a shift has to take place from a mainly transmission mode to a communication mode and the inclusion of the civil society. The PSM organizations are, so it seems, pretty stubborn when it comes to relocating their services to multiple platforms and the new media. Jakubowicz (2008: 12) explains the sociological aspect of their resistance in perceiving only citizens (not consumers or clients) and the out-dated Reith formula *inform-educate-entertain* as well as ignoring hybrid programmes. In this new context, a new term *public social media* – a PSM interacting with its users and audiences in an online environment – seems a welcome one. It should denote cornerstone goals and values of PSM carried out in a new setting, via new media platforms, with the inclusion of its users.

In the context of the transition of the Croatian PSM to a fully digital environment, the article *Convergence Journalism and the Public Interest: The Case of Croatian Public Radio Television* written by Tena Perišin is an invaluable source of information. Perišin is an Associate Professor in the Faculty of Political Science at the University of Zagreb and an award-winning journalist and used to work as an editor at HRT[9]. Her academic and insider participant role at the HRT documented all the efforts and ambitions, as well as setbacks, concerning convergence, new philosophies and reorganization. Perišin considers that HRT's main goal, after announcing reorganization in late 2012, was the production of high quality, trusted news and current affairs on all platforms (Perišin, 2013).

HRT was one of the first to launch nonlinear media web services. In 2000 it was ranked first among other providers of such services, and was also internationally known and recognized. However, because the development of this medium was stopped, and insufficient consideration was given to it, between 2001 and 2012, the position of the HRT web portal fell below 30th place. At the end of 2012, due to the improved application of media synergy effects, its rating began to increase and by March 2013 it was 19th of all web portal services (*HRT Restructuring program*, 2013).

Given that today's content should be born digital and stay digital and the system should be based on multi-platform publishing, with many different outputs from one input, what is needed is a fully-integrated multi-platform organization, underpinned by digital infrastructure (Jakubowicz, 2008: 12). During 2013, in an effort to strengthen its output, HRT began integrating its many media platforms (Freedom House, 2015). Director-General Goran Radman came up with a new strategy, including a new organizational structure. Different programme schemes resulted in a good foundation for the further development of a convergent newsroom. The main innovation is a new service that consists of all media combined together. In the *News Media Service*, radio, television and online media are fused into a single news media service. This type of organization will allow for a faster and better public news service and will, at the same time, make better use of reporters' competences and technological resources and optimize the cross-platform use of multimedia news content (Perišin, 2013: 160). Content is

9 See: http://fpzg.academia.edu/TenaPerisin/CurriculumVitae and https://hr.linkedin.com/pub/tena-perisin/12/590/907 (Retrieved April 26, 2015).

produced in one place and spread across all of the media platforms that make up the PSM. As Perišin (2013: 171) stated, convergence is not only a means for HRT to become more efficient, to produce more news and high-quality programmes, and to keep their employees, it is also a survival kit for the PSM in Croatia.

The HRT website has been redesigned, and offers fresh news with embedded videos (mostly from newscasts)[10]. The *Video on Demand* service is available for all of its shows, which are uploaded minutes after being broadcast. The app for following HRT is available, but is not in widespread use. The interface is counter-intuitive and users on iTunes only rated it with two stars. Facebook pages are created for almost all channels and shows. The central Facebook page is *Novi Mediji, Hrvatska radiotelevizija*[11] and the main activities highlight the programme content of the day. The same task is being handled by HRT on Twitter[12], although the feed sometimes links news from the HRT portal or HRT's YouTube promo spots[13]. Another Twitter account (@hrtvijesti) was launched in September 2013 and it really does deliver timely news in 140 characters. Although it is still active, the original Twitter account is still operating in the old transmission mode, without interacting with users and audiences. The same can be said for audience created content – HRT still clings to its traditional transmission mode in that arena. Unlike the BBC, which targets younger audiences with short news videos on Instagram[14], HRT is nowhere to be found.

After announcing their restructuring, but moving forward slowly, HRT decided to bring in an outside expert. David Brewer, a former BBC news editor came to Zagreb and worked along with Digilab (a group of HRT frontrunners combining people from different platforms and paving the way for convergence) to provide his insights to the company's medium and senior management (Perišin, 2013: 167). After leaving HRT in March 2013 he left a report that stated, among

10 The HRT portal is very trustworthy. The common practice in Radio Student, the Faculty of Political Science's community radio, is to check it regularly for news. They are written in a professional manner, without hidden agendas or bias and editors encourage young radio journalists to use HRT as their source.

11 See: https://www.facebook.com/HRTnovimediji/timeline.

12 See: https://twitter.com/novimedijihrt. The Twitter account was activated in 2010 and is updated on a daily basis.

13 See: https://www.youtube.com/user/HRTnovimediji/videos The YouTube channel offers various short videos, from stories, newscasts to promotion spots.

14 *BBC tries Instagram video to deliver daily news.* Retrieved April 27, 2015 from http://www.theverge.com/2014/1/22/5333812/bbc-instafax-instagram-video-news-experiment.

other things, that HRT is a renowned brand with good journalists who wish to implement changes in their practices and, perhaps most importantly, that there is adequate space in which to build a converged news room (Perišin, 2013). Unfortunately, the management did not see his advice as important. The focus is still on the central news show *Dnevnik*[15] while other TV news outlets and platforms are being neglected, even though the Contract between the Government and HRT stipulates that there should be innovation, creativity and communication with citizens on new platforms and new media (Perišin, 2013: 167–169; Contract between the Government and HRT, 2013: 8, 57).

Conclusions

The cry that the executive news producer made at the beginning of this chapter about the well-educated electorate quickly received an answer. After a fierce debate on the news, the fictional anchor, Will McAvoy, shouts at her: 'People choose the facts now!' It is an apt illustration of the media environment in which we exist. Car, referring to Ramonet (2010: 97) writes that the estimates of the amount of information produced in the last three decades of the 20th century surpasses the amount of information produced in the last 5,000 years. Put another way, the Sunday edition of the New York Times contains more information than an educated 18th century citizen could have accumulated in a lifetime! These estimates were made in 2001 and it is not hard to imagine the increase in today's flow of information, which comes from personalized media use, media accessible from one's pocket and multiscreening, anytime, anywhere.

We cannot argue that HRT is not carrying out its obligations, at least it is trying very hard, but somehow it fails to achieve its main goal, to truly serve the public. The clear evidence for that is in its declining audience shares; commercial and private media are taking over. HRT has no alternative but to adjust to its market and its competitors and that is the reason for big structural and internal changes which started to take place in 2013. The biggest shift occurred in 2015 when a traditional and famous information newscast, *Dnevnik*, changed its traditional broadcasting time from 19:30 to 19:00. This was significant and a big step towards adapting to a commercial television style, which is not typical for a public service. Reinventing their approach to news reporting (news sensationalism, soft news, dual anchor newscasts) still does not increase audience ratings to those of

15 *Dnevnik* was re-launched in February 2015 and for the first time in history it was moved from its original (and trademark) time slot. It airs now at 19:00 (instead of 19:30), 15 minutes before its rival Nova TV and with two anchors.

commercial television. Another disadvantage is the unwillingness of HRT staff to embrace the new vision of a converged newsroom. The management and other media professionals are still blind to the new trends in the media sphere. Most of them are sceptical, which slows down the integration of radio, television and new media (Perišin, 2013: 155). The focus is still on the main TV newscast, *Dnevnik*, and the employees still cling to old media habits (Perišin, 2013). However, despite the problems of HRT's structural organization, an online technological change happened in 2015, when a new application, HRTi for viewing radio and TV content, was launched and made available for Windows, Android and iOS devices. HRT will always have an advantage, as it is the only national medium serving other interests, such as religion, minorities, culture, sports, special programmes, international channels, educational shows and children's programmes.

Even though the PSM is present on social media, the interaction between HRT and its users is weak, if not non-existent. Despite the traditional Commissioner for users' praises and complaints, it seems that the media still sticks to its traditional one-way transmission. There is no practice of user-generated content or citizen journalism. The opportunities that come from two-way communication could transform the PSM into a medium that political philosophers dream about: publics forming around issues, publics as the element of democracy, with a Web 2.0 twist (Clark and Aufderheide, 2009: 11). Due to the interactivity they enable, the individual is no longer a passive user of the media content but, rather, becomes an integrated part of the whole media system, especially via social networks.

The most recent 2015 Freedom House report which categorizes Croatia as partly free when it comes to media, slams the HRT for programme censorship, lacking transparency, failure to meet professional standards and points out that senior management has been accused of being in conflict of interest due to the fact they are appointed by the parliament (Freedom House, 2015). In 2015 as well, a change of government introduced a series of political interventions in the PSM, such as firing journalists and the dismissal of the Director General of the HRT by Parliament (OSCE, 2016). In addition, the long expected overarching project by the former government's Ministry of Culture, concerning media regulation and dubbed "Media strategy," never saw the light of day in its proper form (Jindra, 2014). The Law makes little reference to the progress of PSM in the sense of the changing mediascape. The internal documents available on the HRT website stress that multi-platform content and technological improvements are the number one priority until 2017, as does the Contract between HRT and the government. However, as academic studies show, the reality is different. To underline this claim, it is hard to imagine that the commercial media services of the future will have the incentive to remedy social inequality or serve universally (Clark and Aufderheide, 2009: 9).

So, what will it be? A well-informed electorate or an electorate picking content from the media tree using phones, tablets, laptops and on-demand services? The claim that people choose the facts they want now is exaggerated. They do, however, choose the news and content that they watch. Luckily, they will still have a safe haven to keep them afloat in the media storm. That is, if the safe haven that is HRT comes to its senses and hops on the convergence ship. Instead of the PSM that dominated the media system for decades and just recently lost its flagship position, it would be a welcome change if the HRT quickly and adequately (partly) transformed itself into a *public social media* and set the example for media in the CEE region. Luckily, that ship hasn't sailed. Not yet.

References

AEM/Agency for Electronic Media (2013). *Croatian TV Market Analysis*. Retrieved July 14, 2016 from http://www.e-mediji.hr/hr/pruzatelji-medijskih-usluga/istrazivanja-i-analize/odrzano-predstavljanje-studije-analiza-tv-trzista/.

Car, V. (2007). Digital Television in Croatia: Is Television Becoming a New Media? *Medijska istraživanja*, vol. 13, no. 2: 5–21.

Car, V. (2010). Television in a New Media Environment. *Media Studies*, 1(1–2): 91–104.

Car, V., and I. Andrijašević (2012). *Mapping Digital Media: Croatia*. Open society foundations. Retrieved January 19, 2016 from https://www.opensocietyfoundations.org/reports/mapping-digital-media-croatia.

Clark, J., and P. Aufderheide (2009). *Public Media 2.0. Dynamic, Engaged Publics*. American University: Center for Social Media. Retrieved April 7, 2015 from at http://www.cmsimpact.org/sites/default/files/documents/pages/publicmedia2.0.pdf.

Contract between the Government of Croatia and HRT for the time period 2013–2017. Retrieved April 29, 2015 from http://www.hrt.hr/uploads/media/UGOVOR_HRT_I_VLADA_RH_2013-2017.pdf.

Council of Europe (2012). *Recommendation CM/Rec(2012) 1 of the Committee of Ministers to member Stateson public service media governance (Adopted by the Committee of Ministers on 15 February 2012 at the 1134th meeting of the Ministers' Deputies)*. Retrieved July 20, 2016 from https://wcd.coe.int/ViewDoc.jsp?id=1908265.

Freedom House (2015). *Croatia*. Retrieved April 7, 2015 from https://freedomhouse.org/report/freedom-press/2014/croatia#.VUErJyGqqko.

HRT Act (2010). Retrieved April 29, 2015 from http://www.hrt.hr/uploads/media/Zakon_o_HRT_2010.pdf.

HRT Amended Law (changed portion only) (2012). Retrieved April 29, 2015 from http://www.hrt.hr/uploads/media/Zakon_o_izmjenama_i_dopunama_Zakona_o_HRT-u_2012.pdf.

HRT's Business and Development Strategy 2013–2017 (2013). Retrieved April 29, 2015 from available at http://www.hrt.hr/uploads/media/HRT_s_Business_and_Development_Strategy_2013-2017.pdf.

HRT Restructuring plan (2013). Retrieved April 29, 2015 from http://www.hrt.hr/uploads/media/Program_restrukturiranja_HRT-a_8.7.2013.pdf.

Jakubowicz, K. (2008). *Participation and partnership: a Copernican revolution to re-engineer public service media for the 21st century.* Retrieved April 7, 2015 from http://ripeat.org/wp-content/uploads/2010/03/Jakubowicz.pdf.

Jindra, J. (2014). *Strategija koja to nije*. Retrieved July 14, 2016 from http://www.h-alter.org/vijesti/strategija-koja-to-nije.

OSCE (2016). *Independence of public broadcaster and broadcast regulator must be respected, says OSCE Representative following events in Croatia*. Retrieved July 14, 2016 from http://www.osce.org/fom/226861.

Perišin, T. (2010). *Televizijske vijesti* [Television news]. Zagreb: Biblioteka Budi novinar. Naklada Medijska istraživanja.

Perišin, T. (2013). Convergence Journalism and the Public Interest: The Case of Croatian Public Radio Television (HRT*). Croatian Political Science Review*, vol. 50, No. 5: 155–172.

Peruško, Z (2011). Kategorija 2. Pluralizam i raznolikost medija. In: Z Peruško (ed.), *Hrvatski medijski sustav prema UNESCO-ovim indikatorima medijskog razvoja*. Zagreb, 57–89.

Petković, B., S. Hrvatin, and H. Popović (2014). *Značaj medijskog integriteta, vraćanje medija i novinarstva u službu javnosti.* Zagreb: Centar za istrazivačko novinarstvo.

Popović, V. (2004). HTV: Public Television? HRT's Programme Council: Institution of public Scrutiny or Political Control? *Politička misao*, vol. XLI, no. 2: 17–29.

Radman, G. (2012). Program rada i upravljanja HRT-om 2013–2018. *Medijska istraživanja*, Vol. 18, No. 2: 73–120.

Roller, V. (2014). The New Age of Television in Croatia: Genres, Audiences and the Public Interest. *Politička misao*, vol. 51, no. 4: 142–171.

Alicja Jaskiernia and Katarzyna Pokorna-Ignatowicz
University of Warsaw, Poland
Andrzej Frycz Modrzewski Cracow University, Poland

Public service media vs. sovereign national media: transition of public service media in Poland

Abstract: The chapter contributes to research into the current changes of the model of the public service media (PSM) in Poland. This study focuses on radical regulatory and practical changes that the new government have announced and introduced. The intention behind the changes is to transform the PSM into a national media (NM). The new NM model may lead to a break away from the concept rooted in European standards, which require PSM to serve the interests of the whole, diversified and polarized, society. By analyzing the changes in Poland's PSM, the article might act as a warning for Europe's PSMs. The failures of Poland's PSM are clear: to reform funding structures, to accept the realities of the challenges posed by private media and under appreciation of the demographics of audiences and their desire as stakeholders to participate. The failure of Poland's public service media may rapidly deprive them of public status and legitimacy.

Keywords: Poland, media system, media law, media policy, public service media, media reform.

Introduction

The transformation of Poland's public service media (PSM), both radio and television broadcasters, resembles a ship sailing on rough sea with very inexperienced crew. The recently recruited ones have declared the new course they have set is one of 'healing' and 'depoliticizing' for the PSM. The changes, however, revolve around extensive personnel change not only amongst managers, but also among journalists and regular employees, and around the concept of servitude towards the 'good change.' This two words slogan of Prawo i Sprawiedliwość (PiS – the Law and Justice political party), which has governed since the autumn of 2015, remains an ideological banner under which the party has been conducting a variety of reforms: political, social and cultural. Apart from having a parliamentary majority and having established a single-party government, the party is also supported by having a PiS President. Thereby the governing politicians are convinced they have a strong democratic legitimacy to perform radical reforms in practically all sectors, which they have been expressing by messages directed towards both Poles and the international community. Several weeks after the election, acting at a speed that ruled out any substantive discussion, the Sejm (Parliament's Lower Chamber) passed the so-called 'small amendment' to the Broadcasting Act, without consulting either the creative communities or the media. The amendment changed the procedure of media companies submitting open tenders for appointments to the three-person supervisory boards of the 20 joint stock companies (spółka akcyjna in Polish, henceforth SA) of the two broadcasting branches, TV and radio, of the PSM. The amendment bypassed the PSM's regulatory organ the Krajowa Rada Radiofonii i Telewizji (KRRiT, the National Broadcasting Council) and allowed the government to make widespread personnel changes at all levels. During January 2016, the government replaced, those people who had gained their appointments through the open tender system, with people closely associated to the PiS party. The government also with great haste devised a package of legislative acts, which changed the structure, management form, financing and supervision of the PSM. The reach of the package also extended to the nation's most important state news agency, Polska Agencja Prasowa (PAP, Polish Press Agency). The political opposition and private 'commercial' media companies, as well as international organizations, were critical towards the authorities, deeming the action to be an attack on media. Although the authorities promoted their decisions as "returning media to the nation" and the rolling-back of the "anti-Polish narrative," the apparent pro-government bias and the government-friendly agenda on PSM reminded the older audience of media from the communist period. Given the circumstances, the announcements of the 're-polonization of private media' were even more menacing. Private media companies have so far kept their autonomy partly due to their sources of income but also because, in many cases, they have foreign owners.

This article will analyze the projects of the Poland's PSM reform and assessments of those reforms by various internal groups and important international institutions. The hypothesis is that in the countries of unconsolidated and poorly rooted democracy, and not too high a level of political culture, PSM may easily become a 'political bounty.' The weakness of the PSM in Poland was its excessive commercialization, brittle autonomy and feeble social participation in the management. Thereby the legitimization of the Poland's PSM as 'public' in terms of ownership, funding and control is weakly grounded in common social consciousness. Consequently, the ruling party had few problems when 'hijacking' the PSM to serve its own agenda despite the protests by the opposition, civil society and international institutions. The overall aim of this chapter is, that by analyzing the situation of Poland's PSM, to sound a warning for Europe's PSM sector so that do not make the same mistakes.

Transformations of public service media in Poland

The story of PSM in Poland starts in the last decade of the 20th century with the fall of communism and the ensuing system transformation. During the communist period, in accordance with media doctrine Poland's radio and television broadcasters were separate institutions and monopolies, which responded directly to the government and the communist party organs. Legislation during the communist period did not provide for the possibility of other broadcasters being in operation (Pokorna-Ignatowicz, 2003). The state-party monopolistic model of the media market was questioned in Poland's Round Table Agreement, which was a political contract drawn up between the socialist authorities and the opposition on April 5th, 1989. The implementation of the Round Table Agreement started democratization processes throughout society and all economic sectors.

While the changes to press publishing rules typical of democratic countries took place immediately afterwards in the summer of 1989, the work on developing the regulatory infrastructure for innovative digital media lasted three more years. In the transitional period (1989–1993), when many projects of legislative solutions were being presented and rejected, the media market was developing itself despite the lack of regulations. As early as January 1990, the first commercial radio station (RMF FM) began broadcasting from Cracow, and soon after other commercial and religious radio broadcasters became active, followed by television broadcasters. It was a peculiar form of market deregulation, in which broadcasters acted without concessions but their frequencies were assigned and they paid broadcasting taxes (Mielczarek, 2007; Pokorna-Ignatowicz, 2012). This pioneer period in the ad hoc development of new media infrastructures came to an end on December 29, 1992, when the Broadcasting Act was passed (Broadcasting Act, 1992).

The Broadcasting Act introduced a dual audiovisual media model consisting of two sectors: PSM and private commercial media. Furthermore, the Act created a regulatory organ KRRiT (the National Broadcasting Council), to which the broadcasting market is subject. Moreover, the new regulations reshaped the structure of PSM sector. State broadcasters became public broadcasters and from January 1st, 1994, operated as joint-stock companies owned by the state. The Broadcasting Act of 1992 over several amendments designated a mission statement for the public broadcasters' tasks and activities. All public service media had to provide reliable information, support and popularize the national cultural heritage, have consideration for minorities etc. There was, however, a controversial clause on the responsibility to "respect Christian values on the basis of universal ethical values". The remit of programming requirements, were formulated in very general terms, and eventually led to the commercialization of the content and problems with the European Union's rules of state aid (Klimkiewicz 2014: 275).

Under the Broadcasting Act, the PSM sector in Poland comprises 19 joint-stock companies owned by the state (see Table 1).

Table 1: The structure of Poland's PSM sector state-owned joint-stock companies and proportions of national media markets (viewers and listeners)

	TELEVISION	RADIO
Parent Company	Telewizja Polska S.A. (TVP)	Polskie Radio S.A. (PR)
Regional Divisions	16	17 regional programs - Audytorium 17
Nationwide Channels	TVP1 TVP2 TVP HD TVP Regionalna (16 regional programmes)	Jedynka (Program 1) Dwójka (Program 2) Trójka (Program 3) Polskie Radio 24 (Program 4)
International Channels for: Byelorussians Polish Diaspora	TV Belsat TV Polonia	Radio Poland
Specialized Channels	TVP Info (news and regional) TVP Kultura (cultural) TVP Seriale (drama) TVP Rozrywka (entertainment) TVP ABC (children's channel) TVP Sport TVP Historia (history) TVP Parlament	–

Source: Authors.

There is one television enterprise Telewizja Polska – Spółka Akcyjna, (TVP) and 18 radio enterprises: Polskie Radio S.A. and 17 regional public broadcasters. Poland's Television (Telewizja Polska – Spółka Akcyjna, TVP) owns two countrywide channels of universal character (TVP1, TVP2), TV Polonia for the Poles abroad, TV Belsat in Belarussian and ten specialized channels, including a 24-hour news channel, sports and others (historical, cultural, parliamentary and for young viewers). 16 regional divisions of TVP located in big Poland's cities broadcast their own programmes. Despite the increasingly big competition from private broadcasters, the public broadcaster's share in the television market is still about a third, but in 2016 the competition has overtaken it more and more often.

In the post-communist era, Poland's public service broadcaster (TVP) managed to maintain for 23 years, against private media competition, a significant share of the market (circa 33 percent). The reforms of 2015 had a major and negative impact on TVP's ability to maintain its share of the market. For example, the viewing figures for POLSAT (a private media company) in 2016, overtook TVP1's for the first time. In the context of radio broadcasting, the four State-owned channels (Programs 1–4) have an aggregate 18 percent share of the market. The two most popular private (commercial) media companies broadcasting radio are RMF – FM with a 24.9 percent share and Radio ZET with 13.7 percent.

Between 1992 and the end of 2015, the management of the State-owned SAs were appointed through the process of open tenders. As a result of the PiS party's so-called post-election 'small amendment,' also named the 'bridge' act, or even the 'personnel' act, which was passed with extreme haste in January 2016, the tendering procedure for appointing PSM's management was replaced by a system of 'political' nominations from the Treasury Minister.[1]

While the government and opposition were setting the new operating rules for the PSM's broadcasting SAs in the early 1990s, another equally serious debate concerned the issue of their funding (Braun, 2007; Jakubowicz, 2007). A mixed system was agreed upon, in which the income from subscriptions (license fees) would be supplemented by advertisement and sponsorship revenues. The decision was not only a result of the dire financial situation of the SAs after the collapse of communism, but also of the willingness of government to provide them with the ability to compete with the private commercial broadcasters, which were gaining popularity. The funding decision initially enabled the SAs, especially the television broadcasters to become both serious players in the advertising market and a threat to the private commercial broadcasters. Nevertheless, the share of license fees is only about 30 per cent of the overall income of Telewizja Polska S.A. (TVP) (see Table 2), which is one of the lowest in Europe. The paucity of this state funding begs the question as to whether the funding package for TVP follows the standards of PSM funding since most of the funds come from commercial activities. By contrast, the licence fee income is still the main source of public funding for Polskie Radio S.A (see Table 2).

1 The Ministry of Treasury was liquidated in 2017. Its competence toward PSM was taken by the Ministry of Culture and National Heritage.

Table 2: Public television and radio funding in Poland 2016 (as planned)

	Licence fee. Proportion of total income (percent)	**Licence fee-Proportion of the funding of mission (percent)**	**Licence fee. Income PLN millions**
Telewizja Polska	30	32	335
Polskie Radio S.A.	68	75	170
Regional radio broadcasting	80	87	150

Source: Authors based on the data from the KRRiT (KRRiT, 2016d).

Any future reform of the PSM's broadcasting SAs must be aware that the subscription collection is very poor; about 70 per cent of households with radio and television receivers do not pay the license fee (KRRiT, 2016d).

Public service media and political entanglement

The entanglement between the PSM and politics remains the key problem. Efforts have been made to separate them from direct political influence through adopting legislative solutions based on models from Western Europe. Complete independence, however, has never been achieved. Winners of Poland's general elections have always treated the PSM broadcasters, especially television, as "political bounty" (Pokorna-Ignatowicz, 2010: 39–48). All players from the Polish political scene have always sought to gain influence over TVP. Some have done it openly, others behind the scenes, some more violently, others more subtly. With every change government, the winners have not only mentioned PSM reclamation because the activity was supposed to favour the winners. Reclamation involved immediate changes to key personnel, and often to journalists as well. Over the past 21 years, 15 chairmen have managed TVP. Polskie Radio has faced a similar situation. This PSM staff madness prevents the permanent non-political management from designing and implementing long-term strategies for the broadcasting SAs.

Within a few months of PiS initiating the new PSM regulations in December, 2015, many journalists, publicists, and various programme hosts, not always associated with information or politics, were fired or left on their own accord. PiS considered them as either supporters of the previous government or simply as unable to assure PiS of an appropriate, obeisance of PiS' instructions. "The good change" affected everybody, from the most popular anchors to young reporters, and even the favourite weatherman. Media personnel from niche right-wing oriented media (TV Republika) and the Catholic (TV Trwam) who were associated with PiS replaced the PSM's professional journalists. The effect of these staffing reforms has been a drop in public television viewing figures specifically of TVP's news programmes, which are losing out to commercial channels' news (KRRiT, 2016a). Journalists working in such unstable employment conditions are constantly anxious about losing their jobs, which does not foster journalistic independence, editorial autonomy or community solidarity.

The government's behaviour towards PSM in the legislative-organizational and content spheres are indicative of a clear change in paradigm and evolution from developing a model of relatively independent PSM. The new direction involves submitting the PSM to one political vision, which is paternalistically fulfilling its 'mission' of shaping society in terms of homogeneous political ideals mostly linked to conservative and Catholic values. Ideas of pluralism, openness to different beliefs and standpoints have been set aside. Indeed, these concepts cannot survive, even in residual form, in this PSM model of one ideological option. Unfortunately, other post-communist countries like Hungary and Croatia have adopted this type of PSM model. The common denominator of these countries is the lack of political culture tradition accompanied by low organizational culture and journalism standards, as well as lack of vision regarding the tasks of depoliticized PSMs (Bergant 2016: 5–11).

From public service media to national media

The next step in the PiS-inspired transition process occurred in June 2016. Work on the 'little amendment' was still in progress, when the government passed, on June 22nd 2016, the National Media Council Act, which provides for creation of a new regulatory supervising body, the Rada Mediów Narodowych (RMN; the National Media Council) for both PSM broadcast SAs and PAP (The National Media Council Act, 2016). The legislation in the pipeline to be passed concern changes in funding and structural modes. The key plank of this upcoming legislation is the Draft of the National Media Act, which amounts to the termination of the *public* service media (PSM) model and the emergence of the *national* media (NM) model (Draft of the National Media Act, 2016). The NM model contains three key elements:

a) the transformation of the hitherto legal form of commercial partnerships of the SAs and PAP into nationalized companies (i.e. the stock is wholly owned by the State), which become "institutions of culture";
b) replacement of KRRiT's open tender system of approving nominations to the boards of the PSM's SAs with enabling the newly created 5-person politically

appointed RMN (National Media Council) to operate a wholly opaque system of appointing parliamentary and Presidential nominations;
c) modifying the mixed sources funding system with the addition of an audio-visual fee.

Substantial changes to the mission sphere and the structure of the previous PSM were planned. Stated reasons for the draft argue the previous status of public broadcasters, the SAs, was driven in the opening phase of the post-communist period by a "distinctive fetishization for limited companies," whereas their changed status is more similar to cultural institutions and it "is more conducive to fulfilling their public mission than it would be in the form of a limited company" (Draft of the National Media Act: 24). Chief executive officers (CEOs) who will also be editors-in-chief, as defined by the Press Law Act, will manage these institutions (The Press Law Act of January 26th 1984). The Act provides that the tasks which have so far required an approval from the supervisory board or general meeting will now require an approval by the RMN (National Media Council). The supervisory organ not only appoints the companies' boards, but it also supervises and approves some of the decisions and legal actions in accordance with the law and their efficiency. The RMN will thus replace the previous 19 three-person supervisory boards of the former SAs. The proponents notice the analogy of a holding structure comprising a parent company overseeing subsidiaries.

Undeniably, the key role for NM will be played by RMN's board of five-persons, of whom the Sejm will appoint three and the President the other two. The RMN will become the main organ defining the NM's tasks and supervising their execution, as well as managing through delegation of power to appoint employees to key positions. The RMN's pluralistic character is to be guaranteed by one seat being reserved for a member appointed by the parliamentary opposition. Depoliticization, on the other hand, is to be assured by the clause in the Act that excludes certain people from being considered for an RMN appointment: individuals working in executive power organs, government administration or local government, as well as in KRRiT. Members of Parliament are not excluded. Indeed, politicians or members of all political parties are not excluded. The RMN was vouchsafed full authority over the members of the outlets' supervisory boards. The Chairman of RMN will appoint the outlets' CEOs and their deputies, after a tender process, for a two-year tenure that may be extended without a repeat tender. The regulations do not specify the restriction on repeat tenures. The most significant issue the RMN will manage is the National Media Fund, which through deductions for administrative purposes, will also be used to fund the RMN's work. A qualitatively new element of the national media management will be Społeczne

Rady Programowe (SRP; the Community Programming Councils), which will advise on schedule matters and – more importantly – personnel matters. The SRPs will present mission fulfilment evaluations to RMN and CEOs, as well as any clear conclusive assessments, be they positive or negative. The SRPs also act at the regional and international television level and programmes. The Central Community Programming Council consists of 9–15 members chosen by RMN from among candidates proposed by non-profit social organizations, creative associations, academia, Churches, trade and employer unions and, in the case of regional radio stations, national and ethnic minorities. The SRPs and people constituting them indirectly partake in the game of filling the most important seats in the NM companies because the Act grants them with the power to propose candidates to tender for seats on those companies boards, which are not open to the general public.

Mission of the national media

One of the tasks of the RMN is to define the standards regarding the tasks of an outlet's public mission and its funding with reference to the requirements resulting from EU legislation. A preliminary opinion of Ministers in charge of culture and national heritage, Polish EU membership and public finance will be necessary, as well as that of the Office of Competition and the President of Consumer Protection. Both the RMN and the SRPs supervise the fulfilment of the NSM's mission.

The NM's mission, generally described in Article 3, was developed as a list of tasks in Article 9. The mission consists of some obvious tasks regarding acquisition and dissemination of reliable information and access to diversified radio and television programmes and other services associated with information, opinion journalism, culture, education, sports and entertainment, to arouse and satisfy the comprehensive interests of viewers. The role of the viewers was also the obligation to create the conditions for a pluralistic debate on public issues as well as promotion of civil activity. Programmes are to be impartial, pluralistic, independent (Art. 3, Draft of the National Media Act, 2016) and of high quality in terms of the substance, professionalism and ethics (Art. 4, ibid.). The existing regulation on respecting Christian values, the basis for which shall be universal ethical values, was kept (ibid.).

Amongst 23 tasks explained in detail in the Act, the NM is obliged to enrich historical consciousness and prevent the image of Polish history being contorted, as well as disseminating knowledge about Poland abroad. The regulations are consistent with the current Polish debate on controversial topics related, for instance, to Polish society's vision of Holocaust or to the comments about

"Polish concentration camps" instead of "Nazi" or "German" which have appeared in foreign media and met with public indignation. The issues are in accord with the opinion often presented by the right wing that the activity to date in the artistic sphere of the Polish media and cinematography have presented elements which cast a shadow on Poland's image. Issues regarding the reassertion of Polish families by presenting the values of family life and protecting children and teenagers from demoralization have also become important elements of the mission. The mission is also a result of the conservative world-view, which currently dominates in the mainstream ideological debate that PiS has fostered, supported – more or less clearly – at the same time by the Catholic Church. The Act also emphasizes the NM's tasks directed at Poles living abroad regarding information and sustaining a connection with Poland.

Programme pluralism is to be achieved by enabling citizens and organizations to participate in public life through the presentation of diverse opinions and beliefs, as well as the execution of liberty, of social control and criticism, and also acknowledging the informational and cultural needs of national and ethnic minorities living in Poland. The obligation to present in the media opinions which are expressed in conversation, announcements and speeches by representatives of political parties, trade unions and employers' unions in crucial public matters also adds to the pluralism of the programming. A similar commitment is to allow non-profit organizations to tell the media of their activities free of charge, depending on their significance for the community (Draft of the National Media Act, 2016).

The mission's important elements shall be media educational activities including shaping pro-health attitudes, promoting ecological consciousness and counteract social pathologies, as well as media education. The national media mission "for common good and for personal good" is to take place in cooperation with national authorities, the Catholic Church and other Churches and civil institutions. In the case of chief national authorities, cooperation is also expressed by obligatory representations of the posts of the Speaker of the Sejm, the Speaker of the Senate, the President of Poland and the Prime Minister. PAP, on the other hand, is obliged to include the full text of the standpoints of the Sejm, the Senate, the President of Poland or the Council of Ministers. The latter raises doubts in the light of Art. 5 on self-reliance and independence, which reads that national media shape "the content and form of the information they present in accordance with the editorial independence rule" (Draft of the National Media Act, 2016). The Council of Europe documents that guarantee the independence of public service broadcasting should especially be mentioned since the Council of Europe treats the guarantee for public authorities to access airtime practically without restrictions, as a limitation of the media independence and thus it should be limited to extraordinary cases referred to in the regulations (Council of Europe, 2006). The Council of Europe creates detailed standards on the matter, including making the time available for the parliamentary opposition and their right to respond (Council of Europe, 1996).

The NM's mission will be fulfilled by countrywide programmes, 24-hour radio and television news programmes, both local and directed at Poles living abroad (Art. 10, Draft of the National Media Act, 2016). In Article 11, a range of activities was complemented with a widened broadcasting spectrum anticipating internet platforms and paid television. In other words, so called specialized programmes, audiovisual programmes on demand and other new forms made possible by new technologies (interactive services). The NM is allowed to take different actions than simply broadcasting, including producing, servicing and trading, also export and import in relation to audiovisual creativity. The Act lacks regulations (or their announcement) regarding the use of the old PSM's possessions including access to the abundant archives of PR and TVP.

Funding

Subscription fees and revenue from commercial activities are the main sources of funds for the PSM, but the level of received income never satisfied the needs of the SAs. Poland has the least effective licence fee payment system in Europe. Only a tenth of households pay the licence fee on time and many social groups (about 43 per cent of registered obligated payers) are exempt from paying the license fee (Wp.money.pl, 2016). When Prime Minister Donald Tusk called the license fee 'extortion' in 2008, revenue decreased substantially. A reform of the national media funding matter had long been necessary. The Act's draft appoints a new institution with company status, which is financially separated from the Treasury, called the National Media Fund. The Fund Statute is appointed through the regulation of the Speaker of the Sejm upon the RNM's request, however, the RNM will be the supervising organ. Its aforementioned role is to carry out tenders for CEOs, appoint them to the position and establish rules for the institutions' executive personnel's remuneration. The CEOs are responsible for the programme-financial plans, which will be subject to preliminary public consultations and made available for "the ministers in charge of cultural matters, national heritage protection and public finance" (Draft of the National Media Act, 2016). Changes to financial plans require the opinion of Sejm's commissions competent in NSM matters and public finance, but the regulation does not determine the binding character of such an opinion. The regulations clearly suggest that the means acquired through public funding will be at the disposition of an organ controlled by the RNM and government administrations (Ministries) with advisory functions to parliament.

The NM's revenue maintains the mixed character and may come from both the National Media Fund and income from commercial activities, including advertising and sponsoring revenues. The statutes of the national outlets of radio and television may contain regulations on advertisement and trade content emission limitations referred to in the Broadcasting Act. Targeted subsidies from the government budget are also provided for and are to be given to activities related to the educational mission, including the dissemination of knowledge of Poland abroad. A field for different types of particular Ministries' activities related to national public relations or public affairs is thus open, which may align some programmes of national broadcasters with typically national channels. In order to reach such consensus, the RNM's agreement will be necessary. It should be pointed out here that each case of additional public aid is subject to the European Commission notification.

In the place of licence fee, an audiovisual fee is expected to be added to the electricity bill. The legislator expects the Fund's annual income from the audiovisual fee to be PLN2 billion, which is the current cost of public radio and television broadcasting (TVP S.A., 2015: 24). If collection of the audiovisual fee reaches 80 per cent efficiency, the revenue may be as much as PLN2.5 billion. The change in funding was planned by the authorities to become effective as early as January 2017. However it must be subject to the European Commission notification as a new public aid, which the authorities forgot to take into account. Since the change involves both the entity and the beneficiaries (PAP), the Fund should start operating only after the completion of the procedure mentioned. Nevertheless, each funding model leaves a margin, which allows the PSM/NM and personnel policy to be influenced and politically pressured to lose independence. Structural uncertainty of funding, however, has always been the basic tool of making media dependent upon policy makers. Indeed, one of the most malicious forms of control and political corruption (Bergant, 2016: 9) comes from government/state advertising abusing the unclear rules of the advertisement market.

National, not public service media: controversies and consequences

The changes, which were indeed made at express pace, have especially negatively influenced television, which has seen a drop in viewing figures (KRRiT, 2016a), and a decrease in the quality of news programmes and programmes of editorial character. After the changes introduced in the beginning of 2016, a survey was conducted which assessed the level of pluralism and impartiality in the main news programmes of the three biggest television providers (*Wiadomości* in TVP1, *Fakty* in TVN and *Wydarzenia* in Polsat). The survey showed that the news programme on public service television had become the most biased, it tends to polarize the information and lacks balance between the image of events seen from the vantage point of authorities and critical opinions since the latter, expected of the opposition, are not given (Mrozowski and Popadiak-Kuligowska: 68–71; 100–102). Foreign media have published awareness of the manipulation of information presented in public television programmes. *The Washington Post* has accused the flagship programme, *Wiadomości* of TVP1, of having presented President Barack Obama's statement on the state of democracy in Poland during the NATO summit in Warsaw in July, 2016, dishonestly, leaving out the critical overtone of the remark. Similarly, an incomplete report was given on the public television website (Birnbaum, 2016). The programme has seen a record drop in the number of viewers, over half a million in a year.

The adopted Act of the National Media Council and drafts of further changes have caused strong objections not only from the opposition, but also from lawyers, NGOs and international organizations. The suggested changes have been questioned because they show willingness to introduce mechanisms of media instrumentalization, inconsistency with the Constitution, as well as failing to meet the European standards resulting from membership in organizations such as the Council of Europe. European documents obviously do not prejudge the model, but the binding paradigm is thought to be of legal ethics, which is also expressed in relations between different bodies that constitute the PSM structure. The Council of Europe's recommendations and resolutions on the guarantee of public service broadcasting independence (Council of Europe, 1996, 2006, 2012a, 2012b) may be referred to here because they clearly describe desired competence of supervising bodies and executive bodies, as well as public service values and principles adopted by EBU in 2012 (EBU, 2012). Both adopted and planned Polish reforms are more and more often seen as a step backwards in the PSM development in Europe.

We recognize that Poland's PSM have for many years been seen as a political pawn and a prize for the governing party. This must stop. Nevertheless, past wrongs do not justify the passage of legislation that conflicts with international standards for press and media freedom. The amendment clearly falls short of these standards and represents a step backward for public broadcasting in Europe (IPI-EFJ-ECMPF, 2016).

Various groups have protested against the drafts, which in fact provide for PSM subordination to Polish authorities. The radio and television broadcasting market regulator, KRRiT (the National Broadcasting Council), has issued an announcement in which PiS's actions have been deemed "a violation of the principles of media self-reliance, pluralism and independence," and the PSM new authorities' actions, which include removing journalists from their posts, have been considered "a political purge executed on behalf of the governing party" (KRRiT, 2016c). Non-governmental organizations have made pleas for media 'departyization' and an amendment carried out in dialogue with viewers, creators and managers which would consider "citizens' legitimate interest," but they have not been responded to (Obserwatorium Demokracji, 2016).

According to the Helsinki Foundation for Human Rights, the draft "may be a threat to the constitutional freedom of expression" and may exacerbate the existing pathologies in the way PSM operate and lead to their dependence on the authorities (Helsińska Fundacja Praw Człowieka, 2015: 5). The EU and the Council of Europe's regulatory acts and documents are not conclusive on the solutions regarding forms of management and the desired legal status of public broadcasters. The solutions are present in the models of joint-stock companies or companies subject to government administration (France, Finland, Italy, Slovakia), public companies not subject to government administration (the Czech Republic, Estonia, Ireland, Germany) or in models which are difficult to classify: non-profit organization (Switzerland), public limited company (Belgium), public corporation (the United Kingdom, Catalonia), a company which belongs to a foundation created by the state (Sweden) or a public service Fund/Foundation created by the government (Hungary). Hitherto Poland's PSM model was similar to France's and now, with the status planned, as an organization unit with legal personality whose property belongs to the state and whose range and organization of financial plans are defined by the Minister of Treasury, it may be exposed to becoming dependant on government administration. Nonetheless, the Council of Europe have numerous times pointed out that a state's influence on PSM activities and its control over them cannot turn into "quasi-monopolisation" of the media by the authorities (The Venice Commission, 2005). The changes introduced are deemed as being in complete opposition to the values and commitments resulting from Declaration and Recommendation of the Committee of Ministers of the European Council from February 15, 2012 on PSM governance (The Council of Europe, 2012a, 2012b).

Indeed, taking away KRRiT's competences in the field of national media authorities' nominations, supervision of public mission's tasks execution and passing them to the RMN (National Media Council) has been a source for concern to constitutional law specialists. It will lead to a partial overlap of the two institutions' competences. The Helsinki Foundation for Human Rights (2016: 3) opines that the draft may be treated in this respect as an attempt to bypass the Constitution and to weaken KRRiT (the National Broadcasting Council), which is a constitutional body. It is true that the group can easily be accused of being politicized because the way its members are appointed allows it, nor have the people who have sat on it always been fully competent and separated from on-going politics. Nevertheless, an attempt to deprive a constitutional body of some substantial functions without a change to the Constitution may be recognized, at the very least, as controversial by numerous legal bodies. The Act's initiators justify the substantial change, which deprives the regulator of prerogatives regarding the appointment of PSM companies' authorities, with a negative assessment of KRRiT's combining "the function of electronic media market regulator, which should be impartial towards all participants on the market, with the function of a body executing the rights in the ownership supervision sphere" (The Draft of the Act of National Media, 20162). In their opinion, only the former – the function of the media market regulator – is based on its constitutional status, and "the Constitution does not provide for any particular competences of KRRiT regarding the public media" (ibid.). It should be pointed out that the drafts of the Act of national media and audiovisual fee provide for a further limitation of KRRiT's role through abolishing a regulation from the Broadcasting Act from 1992, which imposes on the regulator the obligation to plan, in consultation with the Prime Minister, the directions of media policy regarding radio and television broadcasting. The regulation has been deemed historical and practically dead (The Draft of the National Media Act, 2016: 1). Its abolition might mean that any cooperation between KRRiT and numerous government institutions in terms of regulation drafting, co-regulation and the flow of information on media market will not be possible.

The drafts prove to be inconclusive or the solutions suggested are unclear regarding many essential matters. National media viewers' complaints are to be dealt by RMN, but the Act's draft does not contain sanction indications, so both the institutions' role – KRRiT's and RMN's – is not well established in this regard. The matter of representing Poland in different foreign bodies (ERGA, EPRA, Contact Committee of the Audiovisual Media Services Directive, etc.) is also not stated. It is not clear whether the only representative will still be KRRiT or if it will be joined by RMN.

Conclusions

The drafted regulations imply a radical system change in all aspects of the PSM activities in Poland, including their structure, management, funding and control, as well as significant elements of the mission. The mere change in the name from PSM to NM clearly indicates the intentions of the change initiators. Media should serve the national interest and as such should be subordinate to authorities chosen by the sovereign body – which is the nation – in democratic elections. It is true that the Polish PSM, especially television, have been influenced by growing commercialization for the last two decades, and that a prominent politician of the party which governed the country for eight years (Civic Platform, Platforma Obywatelska – PO) called the subscription an extortion, and that the subscription collection efficiency has been the lowest in Europe. The current plan of transformation the PSM, which started with a clear break with the past, is partly a break with some good practices and quality standards developed in the last 25 years.

The lack of civil consultations of the project, its non-transparent preparation and the pace of proceedings in the parliament wasted a chance for a serious, extensive debate on the PSM reform in Poland which has not been undertaken by any past ruling parties. The Council of Europe's offer of expertise preparation and discussion on new regulations was rejected. Numerous European institutions, including the Council of Europe, are worried about the new drafts. In a report by the Commissioner for Human Rights of the Council of Europe, issued after a visit in Poland in February 2016, concerns were expressed regarding the true nature of changes in the PSM (Commissioner for Human Rights of the Council of Europe, 2016). Initial doubts were raised by the so-called 'small media' act from December 2015 (The Personnel Act, 2015). The Commissioner for Human Rights suggested back then that the amendment, by passing the competence of nominating the board of directors' members to the Minister of Treasury, is a threat for the PSM's independence. The Council of Europe does not accept the pace at which the changes to the legislature were performed either – within merely three days, without any consultations and *vacatio legis*, ignoring critical opinions from within the country and abroad. The opinions were stated by all prominent organisations handling human rights matters in the scope of media freedom: EBU, EFJ, Reporters without Borders, OSCE or the Helsinki Foundation (EFJ, 2015). In their announcement, European regulators group ERGA (2016) indicates that depriving KRRiT, which is an independent competence body in the PSM authorities' nomination sphere, of its competences raises concerns about politicizing the whole process.

Could the execution of the PSM transformation plan lead to termination of the PSM in Poland due to their replacement with NM, which may become the government or party media? Such media, controlled by parliamentary majority or by government, that falls short of the standards referred to in European institutions' documents, has been present in various European countries (Jakubowicz, 2007; Jaskiernia, 2006). The model of the NM being introduced in Poland causes the opposition's concerns, especially since the legislative and executive powers are in the hands of the same political party. The fear is that the media will become subject to the interests of one side of the political stage and will become entirely instrumentalized. The governmental-parliamentary model, which gives one seat in a five-person Council to the opposition, predetermines the reality of its feeble pluralism. Apart from statutorily guaranteed standards for pluralism and independence, the issue of the execution of provisions, which depends highly upon political culture and the level of democracy consolidation, remains. It should be recall, according to the European standards, the PSM should be characterised by pluralism and diversity, support culture and cultural identity, foster social coherence and be related to democratic society's needs (Amsterdam Protocol, 1997). Currently, the work in progress NM model, partly sovereign according to European standards, may amount to breaking with the concept rooted in European standards, which ensure PSM serve the interest of the whole, diversified and polarized, society. The Polish PSM, just like those in many other European countries, are undeniably at a turning point, which shall influence the model of their actions for many years, or even decades. The government or hybrid model with public-governmental features, may head towards media atrophy in the social debate because they will be viewed as the authorities' propaganda instrument. Regardless of the creation of an attractive mission, a diversion from both infotainment and unsophisticated entertainment, the key role of PSM is always building a public agora, seeking social consensus, and serving the values of pluralism and inclusivity. Copying the case of Fox News Channel onto Polish reality is perilous and risks marginalization of their function, regardless of the best decision-maker intentions.

References

Amsterdam Protocol (1997). Treaty of Amsterdam amending the Treaty on European Union, the Treaties establishing the European Communities and certain related acts – Protocol annexed to the Treaty of the European Community – Protocol on the system of public broadcasting in the Member States. *Official Journal C 340, 10/11/1997 P. 0109.* Retrieved November 25, 2016 from http://eur-lex.europa.eu/LexUriServ/LexUriServ.do?uri=CELEX:11997D/PRO/09:EN:HTML.

Bergant, B. (2016). Quo vadis public broadcasting, *ORF TEXTE, Public service media in Europe. Why independence matters*: 5–11.

Birnbaum, M. (2016). *Obama slammed Polish democracy on Friday. Here's how Polish TV proved him right*, "The Washington Post", July 9, 2016. Retrieved November 25, 2016 from https://www.washingtonpost.com/news/worldviews/wp/2016/07/09/obama-slammed-polish-democracy-on-friday-heres-how-polish-tv-proved-him-right/.

Braun, J. (2008). *Telewizja publiczna w czasach transformacji* [Public Television in the Times of Transformation]. Warszawa: Wydawnictwa Akademickie i Profesjonalne.

Commissioner for Human Rights of the Council of Europe (2016). *Report by Nils Muižnieks, Commissioner for Human Rights of the Council of Europe, Following his visits from 9 to 12 February 2016, Strasbourg, 15 June 2016, CommDH (2016) 23*. Retrieved November 25, 2016 from https://wcd.coe.int/com.instranet.InstraServlet?command=com.instranet.CmdBlobGet&InstranetImage=2924182&SecMode=1&DocId=2376250&Usage=2.

Council of Europe (1996). *Recommendation No. R (96) 10 of the Committee of Ministers to Member States on the guarantee of the independence of public service broadcasting adopted on 11 September 1996*. Retrieved November 25, 2016 from https://rm.coe.int/CoERMPublicCommonSearchServices/DisplayDCTMContent?documentId=090000168050c770.

Council of Europe (2006). *Declaration of the Committee of Ministers on the guarantee of the independence of public service broadcasting in the member states, adopted on 27 September 2006*. Retrieved November 25, 2016 from https://search.coe.int/cm/Pages/result_details.aspx?ObjectID=09000016805d7431.

Council of Europe (2012a). *Declaration of The Committee of Ministers on Public Service Media Governance adopted on 15 February 2012. The Council of Europe*. Retrieved November 25, 2016 from https://search.coe.int/cm/Pages/result_details.aspx?ObjectID=09000016805cb4b4.

Council of Europe (2012b). *Recommendation CM/Rec(2012)1 of The Committee of Ministers on Public Service Media Governance adopted on 15 February 2012*. Retrieved November 25, 2016 from https://search.coe.int/cm/Pages/result_details.aspx?ObjectID=09000016805cb4b4.

EBU (2012). *Public Service Values. Editorial Principles and Guidelines*. Geneva: European Broadcasting Union. Retrieved November 25, 2016 from https://www.ebu.ch/files/live/sites/ebu/files/Publications/EBU-Public_Service_Values.pdf.

EFJ (2015). *Poland: we are outraged by the abolition of safeguards for the pluralism and independence in public service media*. Retrieved November 25, 2016 from http://europeanjournalists.org/blog/2015/12/30/poland-media-organisations-to-oppose-abolition-of-safeguards-for-pluralism-and-independence-in-public-service-media/.

ERGA (2016). *Statement of the European Regulators group for Audiovisual Media Services (ERGA) on the necessity of Independent media*. Retrieved November 25, 2016 from https://ec.europa.eu/digital-single-market/en/news/statement-european-regulators-group-audiovisual-media-services-erga-necessity-independent-media.

Helsińska Fundacja Praw Człowieka [Helsinki Foundation for Human Rights] (2015). *Uwagi Helsińskiej Fundacji Praw Człowieka do poselskiego projektu ustawy o zmianie ustawy o radiofonii i telewizji, Warszawa, 30 grudnia 2015* [A comment by the Helsinki Foundation for Human Rights on the change to the Broadcasting Act, Warsaw, December 30, 2015]. Retrieved November 25, 2016 from http://obserwatoriumdemokracji.pl/wp-content/uploads/2016/03/PL_Helsinki_ustawa-o-mediach.pdf.

Helsińska Fundacja Praw Człowieka [Helsinki Foundation for Human Rights] (2016). *Uwagi Helsińskiej Fundacji Praw Człowieka do projektu ustawy o Radzie Mediów Narodowych oraz zmianie niektórych ustaw, Warszawa, 14 czerwca 2016* [A comment by the Helsinki Foundation for Human Rights on the draft of the National Media Council act and changes to various acts, Warsaw, June 14, 2016]. Retrieved November 25, 2016 from http://www.hfhr.pl/wp-content/uploads/2016/06/HFPC-opinia-ustawa-o-Radzie-Mediow-Narodowych.pdf.

IPI-EFJ-ECPMF (2016). *Poland: IPI-EFJ-ECPMF urge government to guarantee public broadcasting independence*. Retrieved November 25, 2016 from http://ipi.freemedia.at/newssview/article/poland-ipi-efj-ecpmf-urge-government-to-guarantee-public-broadcasting-independence.html.

Jakubowicz, K. (2007). *Media publiczne. Początek końca czy nowy początek* [Public service media. The Beginning of an End or a New Beginning]. Warszawa: Wydawnictwa Akademickie i Profesjonalne.

Jaskiernia, A. (2006). *Publiczne media elektroniczne w Europie* [Public Electronic Media in Europe]. Warszawa: ASPRA-JR.

Komisja Wenecka [The Venice Commission], (2005). *Opinion on the compatibility of the Laws "Gasparri and "Frattini" of Italy with the Council of Europe standards in the field of freedom of expression and pluralism of the media adopted by Venice Commission 10–11 June 2005*. Retrieved November 25, 2016 from http://www.venice.coe.int/webforms/documents/?pdf=CDL-AD(2005)017-e.

Klimkiewicz, B. (2014). *A Polyvalent Media Policy in the Enlarged European Union*. Kraków: Jagiellonian University Press.

KRRiT (2015). *Informacja o podstawowych problemach radiofonii i telewizji w 2014 roku, Warszawa marzec 2015* [Information on elementary problems in radio and television broadcasting in 2014, Warsaw, March 2015], Retrieved November 25, 2016 from http://www.krrit.gov.pl/Data/Files/_public/Portals/0/konferencje/sprawozdania/informacja-www.pdf.

KRRiT (2016a). *Rynek telewizyjny w II kwartale 2016 roku* [Television market in the 2nd quarter of 2016]. Retrieved November 25, 2016 from http://www.krrit.gov.pl/Data/Files/_public/Portals/0/kontrola/program/tv/kwartalne/rynek-telewizyjny-w-ii-kw.-2016.pdf.

KRRiT (2016b). *Udział w rynku i wielkość audytorium programów radiowych w III kwartale 2016 roku* [The share in the market and the size of auditorium of radio programmes in the 3rd quarter of 2016]. Retrieved November 25, 2016 from http://www.krrit.gov.pl/Data/Files/_public/Portals/0/kontrola/program/radio/kwartalne/rynek_3_kwartal2016.pdf.

KRRiT (2016c). *Stanowisko Krajowej Rady Radiofonii i Telewizji w związku z zagrożeniem wolności słowa w mediach publicznych z dnia 26 stycznia 2016 r.* [A standpoint of the National Broadcasting Council with regards to a threat to freedom of speech in the public media from January 26th, 2016]. Retrieved November 25, 2016 from http://www.krrit.gov.pl/krrit/aktualnosci/news,2208,stanowisko-krrit-w-zwiazku-z-zagrozeniem-wolnosci-slowa-w-mediach-publicznych.html.

KRRiT (2016d). *Podział środków na 2016 r.* [Allocation of funds for 2016]. Retrieved November 25, 2016 from http://www.krrit.gov.pl/krrit/aktualnosci/news,1976,podzial-srodkow-na-2016-rok.html

Mielczarek, T. (2007). *Monopol, pluralizm, koncentracja. Środki komunikowania masowego w Polsce w latach 1989–2006* [Monopoly, Pluralism, Concentration. Means of Massive Communication in Poland Between 1989 and 2006]. Warszawa: Wydawnictwa Akademickie i Profesjonalne.

Mrozowski, M., and T. Popadiak-Kuligowska (2016). *Ekspertyza programów informacyjnych głównych wydań TVP1 Wiadomości, TVN Fakty, Polsat Wydarzenia z okresu 4.02.2016 r. do 11.02.2016 r. Raport Końcowy* [Expertise on the chief news programmes TVP1 Wiadomości, TVN Fakty, Polsat Wydarzenia between February 2nd, 2016, and February 11th, 2016], Warsaw, March 2016. Retrieved November 25, 2016 from http://www.krrit.gov.pl/Data/Files/_public/Portals/0/komunikaty/12.04.2016/krrit_eksperyza.pdf.

Obserwatorium Demokracji [Democracy Observatory] (2016). *Obywatelski Pakt na rzecz Mediów Publicznych, 14 marca 2016* [Civil Pact for the Public Media, March 14, 2016]. Retrieved November 25, 2016 from http://obserwatoriumdemokracji.pl/wp-content/uploads/2016/05/Pakt_na-rzecz_Medi%C3%B3w_Publicznych_14.03.16.pdf.

Pokorna-Ignatowicz, K. (2003). *Telewizja w systemie politycznym i medialnym PRL: między polityką a widzem* [Television in Political and Media Systems of the Polish People's Republic: Between Politics and Viewer]. Kraków: Wydawnictwo Uniwersytetu Jagiellońskiego.

Pokorna-Ignatowicz, K. (2010). Polska telewizja publiczna jako "łup polityczny" [Polish Public Television as "Political Bounty"]. *Studia Medioznawcze*, nr 2: 39–48.

Pokorna-Ignatowicz, K. (ed.) (2012). *The Polish Media System 1989–2011*, Kraków: Oficyna Wydawnicza AFM.

Prawo prasowe [Press Law Act] (1984). Ustawa Prawo prasowe z dnia 26 stycznia 1984 r. – Prawo prasowe (Dz. U. Nr 5, poz. 24, z późn. zm. [The Press Law Act of January 26th, 1984].

Projekt ustawy o mediach narodowych [Draft of the National Media Act] (2016). Retrieved November 25, 2016 from http://orka.sejm.gov.pl/Druki8ka.nsf/Projekty/8-020-177-2016/$file/8-020-177-2016.pdf.

TVP S.A. (2015). *Sprawozdanie Zarządu z wykorzystania przez Telewizję Polską S.A. wpływów z opłat abonamentowych na realizację misji publicznej w 2015 roku, Załącznik do Uchwały Nr 134/2016 Zarządu Spółki TVP S.A. z dnia 15 marca 2016 roku* [A report by the Board of Directors on the use by Telewizja Polska S.A. of the income from the subscription fees to fulfil the public mission in 2015, Attachment to the resolution No. 134/2016 of the Board of Directors of TVP S.A. from March 15, 2016]. Retrieved November 25, 2016 from http://centruminformacji.tvp.pl/.

Ustawa o radiofonii i telewizji [The Broadcasting Act] (1992). Dz.U. 1993 nr 7 poz. 34.

Ustawa kadrowa [The Personnel Act] (2016). Ustawa o zmianie ustawy o radiofonii i telewizji [The amendment to the Broadcasting Act]. Dz. U. z 2016 r. poz. 25. Amending the Public Broadcasting Service Law of 1992 was adopted by the Polish Parliament 106.on 30 December 2015 and signed by the President on 7 January 2016.

Ustawa o RMN [The National Media Council Act] (2016). Ustawa z 22 czerwca 2016 r. o Radzie Mediów Narodowych [The National Media Council Act from June 22nd, 2016], Dz. U. z dnia 29 czerwca 2016 r. poz. 929.

Venice Commission (2005). *Opinion on the compatibility of the Laws "Gasparri and "Frattini" of Italy with the Council of Europe standards in the field of freedom of expression and pluralism of the media adopted by Venice Commission 10–11 June 2005*. Retrieved 25, 2016 from http://www.venice.coe.int/webforms/documents/?pdf=CDL-AD(2005)017-e.

Venice Commission (2015). *Opinion on Media Legislation of Hungary, adopted by Venice Commission June 19–20, 2015*. Retrieved November 25, 2016 from http://www.venice.coeint/webreforms/documents/?pdf=CDL-AD(2015)015-c.

WP.money.pl (2016). *Abonament rtv płaci w terminie zaledwie 10 proc. Polaków. „Skandaliczny wynik“* [Radio and television subscription fee is paid on time by merely 10 per cent of Poles. "An outrageous result"]. Retrieved November 25, 2016 from http://www.money.pl/gospodarka/wiadomosci/artykul/abonament-rtv-polacy-placenie-w-terminie,57,0,2164025.html.

Päivi Maijanen
Lappeenranta University of Technology, Finland

The blessing and curse of being public: managing change in public service media in Finland

Abstract: This study contributes to the emerging research on public service media management by analyzing how the dimensions of publicness – consisting of public ownership, public funding, and public control – affect the strategic thinking and strategy making process. The analysis is based on semi-structured interviews conducted with managers in the Yleisradio (the Finnish Broadcasting Company, Yle). In handling the shift toward the digital online world, managers seem to be constantly balancing between traditional broadcast logic and new online logic. The analysis shows that publicness complicates and further deepens the challenges that managers perceive and face as decision-makers. Furthermore, the study shows how the Yle's tax-based funding – launched in 2013 – made managers more sensitive toward the expectations of the politicians and demands of the tax-paying public. In addition, managers felt more obliged to serve media users and provide value for society.

Keywords: public service media, management, digitalization, change, publicness, dominant logic, Yle, tax-based funding.

Introduction

This study explores how the public status of public service media (PSM) companies affects managers' pursuits of change. The study sheds light on how "the publicness" (Bozeman, 1987) – being publicly owned, funded, and controlled – affects the strategy making process of PSM managers in addressing the radical changes taking place in the competitive media environment. Empirically, this study is based on the analysis of managers' perceptions in the Finnish Broadcasting Company (Yleisradio – Yle). Related to the topic, the study aims to analyze in which ways managing a publicly owned, funded, and controlled company is a blessing and/or a curse.

Despite many similarities, there are fundamental differences between managing private media companies and PSM companies. Whereas private media's strategies are driven by pursuits of profit, the focus of PSM is to fulfil its public service task. In addition and especially during the recent years of digital transformation, PSM managers have been required to think also in new competitive terms in order to address increasing media competition, radically changing media behaviour, and technological development (Nissen, 2014). As a result, managers of PSM companies are managing change on two fronts: their companies have to be both competitive in the media market and, at the same time, fulfil their public service task (Lowe and Martin, 2014). PSM companies carry features typical for public (civic owned) organizations. Public service tasks link the PSM companies to the wider socio-political context with specific tasks and obligations, confirmed by legal regulations and supported by public funding. To analyze managerial challenges, public management literature offers a useful approach to highlight the consequences of the publicness on change management in PSM (e.g. Walshe et al., 2010). The renewal process that is taking place in PSM is a shift from the traditional broadcast model toward the new digital multiplatform content production model (Bardoel and d'Haenens, 2008; Lowe, 2010; Maijanen and Jantunen, 2014). As Głowacki and Jackson (2014: xxvii) note, PSM companies are "between two models, the broadcast and network paradigm." They are in a situation where the old and new world co-exist or/and collide. Managers have to simultaneously deal with the old and new paradigm. In this challenging situation the managers are confronted by path-dependent organizational rigidities typical to incumbent organizations with long traditions. In addition to this difficult task, managers have to take into account the obligations and expectations related to PSM's role as a public service institution. This, as studies of PSM management show, often tends to put constraints on managerial actions as well.

This study approaches the managerial challenges in the PSM by applying two theoretical concepts. The dual situation of the old and new logic will be approached by means of the concept of dominant logic. Dominant logic is the way managers define the organization's core approach to the business (Bettis and Prahalad, 1995; Bettis and Wong, 2003; Prahalad and Bettis, 1986). In this research, the concepts of an "old" and "new" dominant logic will be used. Old dominant logic refers to the traditional broadcast logic and new dominant logic to the new digital online logic. The other used theoretical approach is based on public management research, which offers a frame to analyze how "the publicness" (Bozeman, 1987) affects change management in public service organizations. The publicness is defined as consisting of three dimensions: public ownership, public funding and public control (Andrews et al., 2011; Bozeman, 1987; Piening, 2013). Even if there are no univocal answers, recent studies in this field suggest that public enterprises or organizations do differ and publicness does matter in issues of how the organizations are managed and how they renew themselves (Walshe et al., 2010; Andrews et al., 2011; Piening, 2013).

The main research question is how the publicness of PSM companies affects the management. More concretely, the study analyzes how managers perceive the effects of public ownership, funding, and control of their work of managing strategic change toward the new digital dominant logic. The empirical analysis is based on semi-structured interviews with top-level managers at the Finnish Broadcasting Company (Yle) during the winter of 2013–2014. At the time of the study, Yle was implementing new strategies and organizational reforms launched in 2011. The reforms were to accelerate the digital transformation. The analysis shows that publicness imposes affects that managers perceive as both as a blessing and a curse in their work. The results confirm that the features related to publicness complicate and further deepen the challenges that arise from the co-existence of the new and old dominant logics. This particularly applies to the new tax-based funding – launched in 2013 – which has created extra pressures on these challenges, which has, for example, increased the audience's awareness of their right to demand services and content. On the other hand, managers perceive that the steady funding base makes it possible to execute long-term planning.

Theoretically, this study contributes to the emerging research field of PSM management (Arriaza Ibarra, 2015; Głowacki and Jackson, 2014; Gulyás and Hammer, 2013). For a long time, there has been a gap in the studies of the challenges facing PSM management (Nissen, 2013). The growing interest among media scholars in the PSM has been focusing on such questions as funding (Lowe and Berg, 2013), the role of public (Głowacki, 2015; Lowe, 2010), regulations (Donders and Moe, 2011) and public value assessment (Lowe and Martin, 2014) to name a few. This study contributes to the multitude of research areas by focusing on the perspectives of the managers and by approaching the challenges from the PSM management perspective. As to managerial implications, this study will provide more understanding on the complexity of challenges that the managers of PSM are coping with in their pursuits of change. By showing how clearly the public ownership, control and funding manifest themselves in the managerial decision-making, this study gives real life evidence for the tight link between PSM and publicness.

Theoretical framework

The concept of dominant logic

The concept of dominant logic is linked to the managerial and organizational cognition research tradition in strategy research. One of the main research questions of this tradition deals with the question of how the managers' interpretations of the business environment and the organization's role in it affect an organization's renewal capacity and performance (Kaplan, 2011; Tripsas and Gavetti, 2000). According to dominant logic, individuals, groups, and organizations create knowledge structures (Walsh, 1995) – known as mental models (Porac et al., 1989) or schemas (Bartunek, 1984) – acting as simplified models of the complex reality. Dominant logic is a managerial-level knowledge-structure manifesting an organization's approach to its business (Prahalad and Bettis, 1986; Walsh, 1995). According to the definition launched by Prahalad and Bettis (1986: 490), dominant logic refers "to the way in which managers conceptualize the business and make critical allocation decisions." The concept incorporates the fundamental beliefs about the organization's role and mission, which underlie other elements such as customer relationship, products etc. (Von Krogh et al., 2000). As a simplified world view, dominant logic facilitates information processing and decision-making (Bettis and Prahalad, 1995; Bettis and Wong, 2003). Strategically, the basic idea of dominant logic is that it is gradually adopted by the organization, thus turning from managerial into an organizational phenomenon (Bettis and Wong, 2003; Côte et al., 1999; Kor and Mesko, 2013; Lampel and Shamsie, 2000; Oblój et al., 2013).

Following the evolutionary view of organizational behaviour (March and Simon, 1959; Nelson and Winter, 1982; Teece, 2012), dominant logic also evolves over time through successes and failures and becomes gradually embedded in the organizational structures, routines, processes and capabilities (Bettis and Wong, 2003; Côte et al., 1999; Teece, 2012). Dominant logic brings consistency for the organization's behaviour as long as the environment stays stable or encounters only minor changes. However, when facing radical changes, the old must be questioned and either redefined or replaced by a new one. Due to the organizational path dependencies (Schreyögg and Sydow, 2011; Sydow et al., 2009), the transition from the old to the new dominant logic is a gradually evolving, often pain staking process. The process often creates a situation, in which the two logics co-exist: the old continues in the organizational practices, routines and thinking at the same time as the new, which gradually takes space through learning processes initiated by new strategies.

The co-existence of the old and new dominant logics inevitably challenges managers and their decision-making capabilities. Managers have to be able to balance between the two simultaneously competing and complementary world views. Both dominant logics have to be taken into account for both internal and external reasons – to address both existing and arising future demands.

Dimensions of publicness

To study how the public service company status affects change management in PSM, this study will apply the model launched by Bozeman (1987), and applied in later studies of public management (e.g. Andrews et al., 2011; Piening, 2013). Based on the model, publicness consists of three dimensions, which are public ownership (state vs. private ownership), public funding (tax-based vs. consumer payments), and public control (political vs. market control). Organizations vary in their level of publicness, and in fact, as Bozeman (1987: 83) states, "all organizations are public, but some are more public than others." Furthermore, organizations may be more public in one dimension, but less public in another. Bozeman regards public control as the most relevant feature of public organizations i.e. the main question is to what extent an organization is subject to political authority. As to organizational renewal, the higher level of publicness is assumed to correlate to barriers of change (Andrews et al., 2011; Piening, 2013).

Based on the literature of public management, it is important to highlight some consequences that a higher degree of publicness has on change management and renewal capacity in public organizations. Public ownership means that the organization has a task to enhance public value, such as to promote equality, democracy and welfare. However, because of the ambiguous and vague goals whose achievement is difficult to measure, the public organizations lack the underlying bottom line of profit making that drives the private firms to innovations (Boyne, 2002; Harvey et al., 2010; Klein et al., 2013; Rainey and Bozeman, 2000).

Furthermore, public funding may provide a certain level of security that may reduce an organization's sensitivity to customers' needs, because success does not depend on their preferences (Andrews et al., 2011). On the other hand, the organizational slack (i.e. over-abundant resources) can also be regarded as an important precondition for innovations (Penrose, 1959). Some recent studies suggest, though, that a higher degree of publicness mainly tends to moderate the positive effect of organizational slack (Klein et al., 2013; Piening, 2013). In addition, excessive tax-based slack can create a feeling of security under which "decision makers are likely to favour stability" instead of allocating resources to creating innovations and enhancing organizational learning (Salge and Vera, 2013: 160).

Public control is closely related to fulfilling expectations and accountability demands of external stakeholders (Bryson et al., 2007) who are often politicians with short-term targets (Boyne, 2002; Piening, 2013). The dependency on external stakeholders' goal-setting may reduce managers' initiatives, autonomy, and pursuits of long-term changes (Fernandez and Rainey, 2006; Piening, 2013; Salge, 2011). Correspondingly, the accountability demands – which are justified by the public funding – tend to increase cautiousness of managers and discourage them from risk taking (Ferlie et al., 2003).

Yle in light of publicness and dominant logic

Yle as a public company

The specific features of public organizations and public management can be applied in the case of the Finnish Broadcasting Company – as well as in the PSM companies in general. They are publicly owned, publicly funded (often combined with private income), and publicly regulated (Lowe and Berg, 2013; Nissen, 2013). Yle can be regarded as having an exceptionally high level of publicness. Yle is state-owned, parliamentary controlled and regulated, and it is one of the few PSM companies which is 100 per cent publicly funded. Yle is also exceptional because of its current tax-based funding model. The historical decision concerning the levying of a PSM-tax was taken in 2013 (around a year prior to the dates, on which the interviews for this study were conducted) to replace the earlier license fee model by an earmarked Yle tax (Engblom, 2013; Lowe and Berg, 2013). As to the publicness, the decision to levy a mandatory Yle-tax (on income earners) can be seen as an act to increase Yle's level of publicness. It is also important to point out that despite many challenges and changes in the media sector, Yle maintains a dominant position in the Finnish media market (Carlsson, 2013). At the time of the interviews, the share of Yle's daily TV viewing was 42 percent and radio listening 51 percent.

Concerning public control, Yle's position and its public service tasks are defined by law and the company is supervised by a Parliament appointed Administrative Council, which decides "on issues concerning considerable restriction or expansion of the activities or significant changes in the organization of the company" (*Act on Yleisradio Oy* 1380/1993). However, it is justifiable to say that Yle enjoys editorial independence (Lowe and Berg, 2013). Nevertheless, the disputes and debates on Yle's position and remit raised by politicians and private media companies before the final funding decision indicated the company's closed relationship to the political sphere. The funding decision was a strong political statement being a manifestation of public (political) control as well.

Furthermore, it can be presumed that the public status of Yle imposes similar effects on management as in public service sector organizations in general. They are not motivated by making profit, but by providing public value to society in line with the Act on Yleisradio, which defines Yle's remit and public service task. The strategic targets for the years 2012–2014 are illuminating: "Yle serves all

Finns," "Yle provides value to society" (*Yle's annual report*, 2012). The managers are supposed to fulfill obligations determined by law, expectations of political stakeholders, and needs of the tax-paying public. As Lowe and Berg (2013: 81) explain: tax funding "implies rights: Every citizen paying the tax has a right to expect the same quantity and quality of service as anyone else paying that tax."

Yle in the context of the old and new dominant logic

Based on the preceding reflections on dominant logics, specified characteristics can be applied in the context of PSM. As pointed out, the present disruption caused by digitalization has created a situation, in which organizations are coping with the old and new dominant logics. The former in the context of content production culture represents the traditional broadcast and the latter represents the new online multiplatform (Głowacki and Jackson, 2014; Maijanen and Jantunen, 2014).

As mentioned previously, dominant logic is deeply rooted in an organization's history. The concept evolves through successes and failures thus becoming embodied in the organization's way of thinking and acting. In the case of PSM, the roots are in its heritage of "the social project of enlightenment mission" (Lowe, 2011: 22). Traditional broadcasting – one-way communication for large audiences – has its origins in this pedagogic mission of distributing information to citizens. Another historical characteristic feature of public service broadcasting (PSB) corporations is related to their privileged status (Lowe, 2010; Nissen, 2014), which has secured them abundant resources, stability and self-sufficiency. This tradition together with the enlightenment mission that underlays the traditional broadcast dominant logic of PSB companies has now been questioned and radically changed because of the disruptive consequences of digitalization in the media business. Therefore PSM companies need to redefine their traditional dominant logic or gradually replace the old dominant logic with a new one that defines their role and mission (that underlays decision-making, audience relationship, content production etc.) in the digital media business environment. Naturally, the dominant logic of PSM has gradually evolved along with the deregulation of media markets. But during the times of digitalization and exponential increases in media competition and individualization of media usage habits, the dominant logic is now facing radical changes. The PSM companies have collectively become "just" one player in the global media with the challenge of satisfying the constantly changing individualized needs of media users. These changes are challenging because they question the established ways of thinking and doing (Picard, 2012) rooted in the past heritage of broadcast culture (Arriaza Ibarra, 2015).

Methodology

The empirical analysis is based on semi-structured interviews with 16 managers at Yleisradio (Yle) during 2013–14. The interviews were conducted at a time of active strategic changes taking place in the company. A broad organizational reform and new strategies were launched in 2011. In the organizational reform, six sub-units were established on the basis of different functions. Three sub-units were content units: the News and Current Affairs unit, the Creative unit, and the Swedish Yle unit. Three other units were the Media unit (responsible for the general planning and coordination of content), the Operations unit (responsible for larger productions and technological infrastructure), and the Joint Operations unit (a matrix unit consisting of such units as HR, Strategy, Legal Affairs, etc.). The purpose of the organizational reform was to diminish the barriers between technologies – radio, TV, and internet – and to make Yle more flexible and customer-centered, for instance, by creating services and content for younger media users (to improve its quite modest reach among the young audiences), developing internet work, and opening up access for partnerships.

The interviewees (N=16) represent the aforementioned sub-units and different tasks, ages, and work experience groups (measured in years). The main criteria for the selection of the interviewees was their active involvement in long term development and strategy work. All the interviewees represent strategy-level management, but seven were *members of the management group* (MG), and nine represented the management level below called *upper middle managers* (UMM) in the analysis. Half of the interviewees (n=8) were 50 or more years old, and the other half (n=8) were less than 50 years old. The interviewees' work experience at Yle ranged from less than 10 years' experience (n=4), 10–20 years (n=2), 20–30 years (n=8) and more than 30 years (n=2). The female:male gender ratio was 7:9. In order to preserve their anonymity, the interviewees were coded numerically by management level, e.g. MG1 and UMM9 (the numbering follows the interview schedule of both management groups).

The interviews that lasted from 60 to 90 minutes were structured but informal as Eriksson and Kovalainen (2008) suggests in order to create an open and friendly atmosphere. The interviewees were asked to concretely and freely tell about the past changes, e.g. what their role has been in managing change, what kinds of strategically important decisions they have made and how they have made these decisions, how they think the changes have succeeded, what kinds of challenges they have been facing in implementing these changes, and how they see the future in terms of opportunities and threats.

The interviews were taped, transcribed, and analyzed using a thematic coding method (Patton, 2002; Miles et al., 2014). Initially, all expressions referring to any of the dimensions of publicness (public ownership, funding, and control) were coded. In the coding process, attention was also paid to how the interviewees perceived the effects of publicness (whether it had increased obligations and constraints or possibilities and opportunities etc.). The coded expressions were then grouped thematically. The key aspect of categorization were the issues which the publicness affects. As the interviews were concerned with managing change, the thematic categories were then grouped into broader upper-level themes according to how they relate to the strategy making process.

Findings from qualitative analysis

Figure 1 summarizes the main results of the empirical analysis, of which the main aim was to analyze how – according to the interviewee's perceptions – the dimensions of publicness (public ownership, funding, and control) affect the management of strategic change. Figure 1 shows the thematic categories which were obtained by analyzing and grouping the codes used. The effects of publicness on change management can be grouped into two upper-level themes that relate to the strategy making process. These two themes are *strategy formulation* and *strategy implementation*. In the former, the effects of publicness can be further grouped into two thematic categories, which are *audience and content* and *strategic repositioning*. The latter consists of two thematic categories which are *decision-making* and *the speed and nature of change*.

The following section analyzes and describes more specifically the obtained thematic categories. The analysis follows the two upper-level themes going from strategy formulation to strategy implementation and covering each thematic category.

Figure 1: The results of the empirical analysis

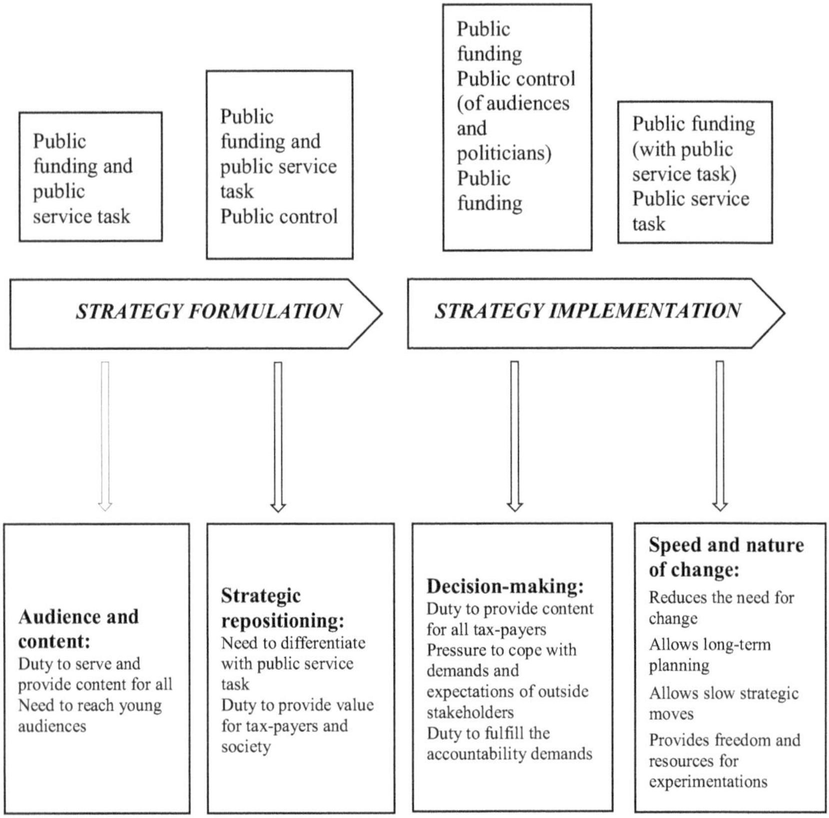

Source: Author.

The effects of publicness on strategy formulation

In the context of *strategy formulation*, the first category of *audience and content* relates to the duty to serve and provide content for all Finns, covering media users of both traditional broadcast (old dominant logic) content and new online content (new dominant logic). Managers perceive that this duty was emphasized by funding from tax and the public service task to be fulfilled: everybody has to get services and content for the tax money, as one manager describes the situation:

> So, I personally, frankly think that, if all Finns working and getting paid pay Yle tax they should be provided at least with something they would enjoy. [UMM6]

The task to serve all Finns means that Yle is in a situation, which as an interviewee from the management group (MG1) points out, is not an either/or world, but having both worlds at the same time. According to the manager (MG1), the co-existence of both broadcasting (old dominant logic) and new internet dominant logic adds a burden to, and slows down, the process of change.

The duty to serve and provide content for all tax-paying media users causes a conflicting pressure. The challenge in the context of content production culture is in finding the right balance between the traditional broadcast (old dominant logic) and new multiplatform online (new dominant logic). Serving the old and loyal audience maintains the old broadcast logic, but at the same time there is more and more pressure to serve and reach better young audiences following a new content production logic:

> First, we have to find something relevant for all. (…) Because otherwise they pay for nothing, which means that the challenge with younger people is even bigger. Because if they don't perceive that they get something for the Yle tax, then…we are not doing well. [UMM4]

Strategic repositioning (see Figure 1) refers to managerial concerns about Yle's position and task in the media environment. Both public funding and public service task create pressures to focus on the public service task as an asset, which differentiates Yle from the private media. The interviewees said that one of the strategic focus areas was the creation of value for society. After the launch of the Yle tax, the differentiation in respect of value creation has become more strongly emphasized:

> We want to provide value for the society (…) that is what we have always wanted but we haven't really put it into words. Now we say it loud and we are thinking a lot of these do good -projects and other this kind of things (…) It could be a motor in the change itself (…) To clarify the public service role and to somehow underlie it could be the competitive edge for us. [UMM8]

The differentiation in respect of the public service task is also seen as an opportunity: Yle is allowed – and expected – to do things that others do not do. Furthermore, Yle does not have to worry about not getting large audiences all the time:

> Ten years ago, we made much more the same kind of things [as the private companies – Author]. I think the tax model is that we can take it very easy and make, for example, live TV broadcasts from the Music Centre to every home (…) None of the private media does this. Here we can say 'this is our task', and no one needs to grit their teeth. [MG1]

To fulfill the task of providing value for the society, one of the goals is to enhance creative industries with partnerships and collaboration. This leads to the opening up of the traditionally closed boundaries of the PSM.

> But how the value is created, well, it is not created by closing up. Instead, it means that we have to open up, we have to make these resources [of Yle – Author] available for everyone, we have to do things together with others, we have to enhance that more jobs are created in the media sector and so on. (…) Let's do less alone, let's do more with others. [MG7]

The emphasis on the importance of creating value and differentiating with the public service task is also related to the private media and its criticism directed toward Yle. Managers are concerned that the new PSM tax might provoke tensions between Yle and private media companies. The latter has for some years actively lobbied policymakers and raised discussions and debates on Yle's role and position. The numerous demands and critiques, issuing from the public, may create cautiousness:

> [Yle] have a good position, and in general anything we do, someone begins to bark and say that Yleisradio can't do this and that, and it is not suitable for a tax funded organization and you disturb us [private media – Author] (…) so we maybe are a bit cautious. [MG5]

The effects of publicness on strategy implementation

In the context of *strategy implementation*, the category of *decision-making* (see Figure 1) relates to the way managers perceive that publicness enhances or hampers their ability to make decisions. One of the biggest concerns is to provide relevant content for all taxpayers irrespective of age. Despite one of Yle's strategic targets being to reach out better to younger audiences the interviewees were concerned that too much time and effort is allocated to the traditional broadcast viewers and listeners and too little to young internet users. The interviewees perceived the Yle tax as putting extra pressure on reaching the younger audience:

> [Yle-tax] challenges because more and more often you can hear in the corridors and meeting rooms that we have million Finns that are not using our services and our task is to reach everyone, provide something for everyone. …And in this way it [Yle tax – Author] was a pretty good solution, because it forces us to look more strongly for the audience that we don't have now. This lacking million. [UMM1]

The situation is perceived as troublesome and challenging because of the expectations and reactions of the outside stakeholders – audiences, politicians, and private media. Some of the interviewees claimed that audiences, since the decision to replace the license-fee with the tax-based funding, have become more critical and demanding toward Yle's content. Yle's decision-makers have to cope with occasionally harsh critiques, stringent demands and passionate reactions coming from loyal customers (who represent the traditional media usage habits):

> The critique from viewers and listeners has become stronger and it is terribly harsh, like I want this right now (…) like if you make me pay and then you don't show Here, Beneath the North Star [a Finnish drama film from 1968 – Author] because I want to see it now. [UMM9]

Accordingly, Yle's managers have to cope with both the reactions and expectations of policymakers, as well as pressures coming from the private media companies. The managers consider that these pressures are related to Yle's task and remit and inevitably constrain their abilities to make radical moves:

> During these years of media disruption, there has been a lot of social and political pressure around what we are allowed to do and what we are not allowed to do, there is an ongoing discussion on what we are allowed to do on the internet (…) But all these factors affect how we progress and the decision-making and so on. [UMM2]

Furthermore, Yle as a publicly owned, funded, and controlled company is by definition accountable for the use of money collected from the media users. The interviewees perceive that the Yle tax places more obligation than the license fee to be accountable of their decisions:

> And then, this transparency is important, the nature of tax money is that how it is directed, that it is used in the right way that we can justify that this matter is important in relation to the task given to us. [MG7]

In addition, the economically difficult situation of private media puts further pressure on Yle to use its money in a reasonable way:

> The economic crisis of our business environment obliges us to bargain and to learn to do things inexpensively and in that sense competitively (…) we must not build for ourselves that kind of operating processes (…) which makes things terribly expensive, or that we put out just one exceptional product a year. [UMM2]

In addition to the challenges facing Yle's decision-makers, they also reflect on how the publicness affects *the speed and nature of change* (see Figure 1). The interviewees perceive that both public funding and the public service task impact on strategic change. Some interviewees think that the public funding creates stability and a feeling of security which may reduce the desire or need for change:

> Our traditional saying is that you cannot save a thriving firm. So, Yle is doing somewhat too well, that is if there was a some kind of crisis in some place it would start making an effort. [MG3]

On the other hand, there is the perception that stable funding carries positive effects on the change. For example secure funding makes it possible to make long-term planning and carry out innovative experiments:

> In a certain way, our funding model (…) it makes possible, really anything, and really long-term planning – no one else has the possibility for such long-term planning, of course, our funding model can change, but for the private neighbor it can change in a one-month cycle. [UMM2]

In line with this, some managers point out that the public service task allows Yle to take more deliberate moves than the private media companies, which enables Yle to avoid making too prompt and risky changes that could harm its customer relationship:

> What has somewhat improved our position is that we haven't had commercial pressures to panic (…) in other words, this kind of conservatism, at least relative conservatism in comparison to what private media have done. This has created trust [among the public – Author] and stability, and improved our image. [MG2]

Conclusions

The purpose of this study was to analyze how the publicness of PSM companies affects managing change in these organizations. In this study, the PSM companies are defined as organizations, which are publicly owned, funded, and controlled (Andrews et al., 2011; Bozeman, 1987; Piening, 2013). The study exams how these dimensions of publicness affect PSM managers' endeavours to foster organizational renewal in order to address the disruptive changes in the media environment caused by digitalization. In terms of the Prahalad and Bettis' (1986) concept of dominant logic applied in this study, the key issue is a shift from the old broadcast dominant logic towards the new online dominant logic. The analysis approaches the question by exploring how managers perceive the effects of publicness – whether it enhances the shift or hinders it, whether it creates new possibilities or constraints etc. Empirically, the study explores the research question by using semi-structured interviews to get the opinions of a representative sample of senior managers of Yleisradio (Yle; the Finnish Broadcasting Company).

The study shows that the publicness of PSM companies affects both the strategy formulation and strategy implementation. The interviewees express the effects especially in issues related to customer relationship, the company's role and mission, and managerial decision-making. Concerning the dimension of publicness, the interviewees emphasize the effects of *public funding* and *public control*. They seldom mention the notion of public ownership. One reason could be that the style of ownership is regarded as being integral to public funding and public control. In addition, the interviewees often emphasize the public service task by linking it to the public funding and control.

The most striking findings arise from the consequences of Yle's new tax funding model launched in 2013. The findings not only confirm that the public funding has many effects on management (Bozeman, 1987; Piening, 2013), but they also highlight what happens when the level of publicness increases. Yle is an excellent case to study this issue, because the tax funding can be seen as an increase in the level of publicness. In addition, as the interviews for this study were conducted quite soon after the launch of Yle's tax, this study was able to capture fresh reflections. The tax funding seemed to increase both the pressures and challenges facing Yle's managers. For example, they believed the tax obliges Yle to serve all tax paying Finns. This has created extra pressure to serve young audiences, amongst whom Yle traditionally have had low levels of penetration. Managers also perceived that tax funding hardened the critique and demands of especially older audiences (who represent the old broadcast logic), who feel that as taxpayers they have the right to get the kind of content they want. These demands were mirrored by private media companies, which continued to question Yle's role, especially on the internet. In addition, the tax funding more than the license fee obliged Yle's managers to be more accountable for their decisions. Related to this obligation, the issue of the kind of content Yle is allowed to produce with tax money becomes more relevant than before. All these demands, expectations, and public and political debates put extra pressure on managers to reflect on Yle's role in the media environment and in society in general. One issue in strategy formulation was to emphasize the public service task as an asset in media competition and a way to differentiate Yle from private media companies. The public service task was regarded as the ultimate source of legitimacy that justified the tax funding.

Public control is the other dimension of publicness that is often mentioned by managers. The findings show that public control is not only the control of politicians as emphasized by Bozeman (1987) but also, in Yle's case, audiences. Furthermore, private media can be regarded to practise public control. The interviewees claimed they have to constantly cope with many demands and expectations of audiences and politicians and with the critique of private media. Furthermore, the analysis shows that the public control is closely interrelated with the funding issue. The funding decision increased the impact of the public control. Indeed, the correlation between public funding and public control is logical, because the tax funding decision was a political decision.

Referring to the title of this chapter, the effects of publicness can be seen as both a blessing and a curse for managers. Their main curse consists of the pressures and challenges that managers encounter when coping with the expectations of all the social and political stakeholder groups. This made managers more cautious, and in hampering the shift from the old dominant logic towards the new enforced the naturally path-dependent nature of organizational behaviour. This impact accords with those studies of public management, which suggest that a higher level of publicness tends to raise barriers to innovations and renewal (Andrews et al., 2011; Piening, 2013). On the other hand, as the Yle shows, the public service task and funding can be seen as a kind of a driver towards the new dominant logic as managers are forced to seek innovative ways to reach younger audiences.

The blessings and curses related to publicness are highlighted in the way managers perceive the effects on the speed and nature of strategic change. Public funding may create a feeling of security, which makes people happy with the situation and moderates any needs for urgent changes. On the other hand, the counter-argument is that the security resulting from this type of funding enables both long planning and innovations.

Finally, this study contributes to the research of PSM management by highlighting the managerial perspective. The study shows the kinds of challenges and pressures the role of public service institution has on management. Importantly, the study highlights the consequences managers face when a sudden increase in the level of publicness takes place.

References

Act on Yleisradio Oy 1380/1993. Unofficial translation, Ministry of Transport and Communications of Finland. Retrieved February 25, 2016 from https://www.finlex.fi/en/laki/kaannokset/1993/en19931380.pdf.

Andrews, R., G.A. Boyne, and R.M. Walker (2011). Dimensions of publicness and organizational performance: A review of the evidence. *Journal of Public Administration Research*, 21(Suppl. 3): 301–319.

Arriaza Ibarra, K. (2015). Management and organization of public service media companies: Basic concepts related to efficiency and failure in European public service media, with two case examples (Germany and Spain). In: K. Arriaza Ibarra, E. Nowak, and R. Kuhn (eds.), *Public service media in Europe. A comparative approach*. Abingdon/New York: Routledge, 147–169.

Bartunek, J.M. (1984). Changing interpretive schemes and organizational restructuring: The example of a religious order. *Administrative Science Quarterly*, 29 (3): 355–372.

Bardoel, J., and L. d'Haenens (2008). Reinventing public service broadcasting in Europe: Prospects, promises and problems. *Media, Culture & Society,* 30(3): 337–355.

Bettis, R.A., and C.K. Prahalad (1995). The dominant logic: Retrospective and extension. *Strategic Management Journal*, 16(1): 5–14.

Bettis, R.A., and S. Wong (2003). Dominant logic, knowledge creation, and managerial choice. In: M. Easterby-Smith and M.A. Lyles (eds.), *Handbook of organizational learning and knowledge management.* Oxford: Blackwell Publishers, 343–355.

Boyne, G.A. (2002). Public and private management: What's the difference? *Journal of Management Studies*, 39(1): 97–122.

Bozeman, B. (1987). *All organizations are public.* San Francisco: Jossey-Bass.

Bryson, J.M., F. Ackerman, and C. Eden (2007). Putting the resource-based view of strategy and distinctive competencies to work in public organizations. *Public Administration View*, 67 (4): 702–717.

Carlsson, U. (ed.) (2013). *Public service media from a Nordic horizon. Politics, markets, programming and users.* Göteborg: Nordicom.

Côte, L., Langley, A., and J. Pasquero (1999). Acquisition strategy and dominant logic in an engineering firm. *Journal of Management Studies*, 36(7): 919–952.

Donders, K., and H. Moe (eds.) (2011). *Exporting the public value Test.* Göteborg: Nordicom.

Engblom, L.-Å. (2013). Public service financing in the Nordic countries. In: U. Carlsson (ed.), *Public service media from a Nordic horizon. Politics, markets, programming and users.* Göteborg: Nordicom, 93–106.

Eriksson, P., and A. Kovalainen (2008). *Qualitative methods in business research.* London: Sage.

Ferlie, E., J. Hartley, and S. Martin (2003). Changing public service organizations: Current perspectives and future prospects. *British Journal of Management*, 14 (Suppl. s1): 1–14.

Fernandez, S., and H.G. Rainey (2006). Managing successful organizational change in the public sector. *Public Administration Review*, 66(2): 168–176.

Głowacki, M., and L. Jackson (eds.) (2014). *Public Media Management for the Twenty-first Century. Creativity, Innovation, and Interaction.* New York, London: Routledge.

Głowacki, M. (2015). Governance of public service media in Poland: The role of the public. *Media and Communication*, 3(4): 26–34.

Gulyás, A., and F. Hammer (eds.) (2013). *Public service media in the digital age: International perspectives.* Newcastle upon Tyne: Cambridge Scholars Publishing.

Harvey, G., C. Skelcher, E. Spencer, P. Jas, and K. Walshe (2010). Absorptive capacity in a non-market environment. A knowledge-based approach to analysing the performance of sector organizations. *Public Management Review*, 12 (1): 77–97.

Kaplan, S. (2011). Research in cognition and strategy: Reflections on two decades of progress and a look to the future. *Journal of Management Studies,* 48 (3): 665–695.

Klein, P.G., J.T. Mahoney, A.M. McGahan, and C.N. Pitelis (2013). Capabilities and strategic entrepreneurship in public organizations. *Strategic Entrepreneurship Journal*, 7 (1): 70–91.

Kor, Y.Y., and A. Mesko (2013). Research notes and commentaries: Dynamic managerial capabilities: Configuration and orchestration of top executives' capabilities and the firm's dominant logic. *Strategic Management Journal*, 34(2): 233–244.

Lampel, J., and J. Shamsie (2000). Probing the unobtrusive link: Dominant logic and the design of joint ventures at General Electric. *Strategic Management Journal*, 21(2): 593–602.

Lowe, G.F. (ed.) (2010). *The public in public service media, RIPE@2009*. Göteborg: Nordicom.

Lowe, G.F. (2011). Respecting the PSB heritage in the PSM brand. *International Journal on Media Management*, 13(1): 21–35.

Lowe, G.F., and C.E. Berg (2013). The funding of public service media: A matter of value and values. *International Journal on Media Management*, 15(2): 77–97.

Lowe, G.F., and F. Martin (eds.) (2014). *The value of public service media. RIPE@2013*. Göteborg: Nordicom.

Maijanen, P., and A. Jantunen (2014). Centripetal and centrifugal forces of strategic renewal: The case of the Finnish Broadcasting Company. *International Journal on Media Management*, 16(3–4): 139–159.

March, J. G., and H.A. Simon (1958). *Organizations.* New York: John Wiley & Sons.

Miles, M.B., A.M. Huberman, and J. Saldaña (2014). *Qualitative data analysis. A methods sourcebook* (3rd edition). Thousand Oaks: Sage Publications.

Nelson, R.R., and S.G. Winter (1982). *An evolutionary theory of economic change.* Cambridge, MA: The Belknap Press of Harvard University Press.

Nissen, C.S. (2013). What's so special about public service media management? *The International Journal on Media Management*, 15(2): 69–75.

Nissen, C.S. (2014). Organisational Culture and Structures in Public Media Management – in Search of a Model for the Digital Era? In: M. Głowacki and L. Jackson (eds.), *Public Media Management for the Twenty-first Century. Creativity, Innovation, and Interaction*. New York, London: Routledge, 81–102.

Oblój. K., M. Weinstein, and S. Zhang (2013). Self-limiting dominant logic: An exploratory study of Chinese entrepreneurial firms. *Journal of East-West Business*, 29(4): 291–316.

Patton, M.Q. (2002). *Qualitative research and evaluation methods* (3rd edition). Thousand Oaks: Sage Publication.

Penrose, E.T. (1959). *The theory of the growth of the firm*. Oxford: Oxford University Press.

Picard, R.G. (2012). The changing nature of political case-making for public service broadcasters. In: G.F. Lowe and J. Steemers (eds.), *Regaining the initiative for public service media, RIPE@2011*. Göteborg: Nordicom, 27–44.

Piening, E.P. (2013). Dynamic capabilities in public organizations. A literature review and research agenda. *Public Management Review*, 15 (2): 209–245.

Porac, J., H. Thomas, and C. Baden-Fuller (1989). Competitive groups as cognitive communities: The case of Scottish knitwear manufacturers. *Journal of Management Studies*, 26 (4): 397–416.

Prahalad, C. K., and R.A. Bettis (1986). The dominant logic: A new linkage between diversity and performance. *Strategic Management Journal*, 7 (6): 485–501.

Rainey, H.G., and B. Bozeman (2000). Comparing public and private organizations: Empirical research and the power of the a priori. *Journal of Public Administration Research and Theory*, 10(2): 447–469.

Salge, T.O. (2011). A behavioral model of innovative search: Evidence from public hospital services. *Journal of Public Administration Research and Theory*, 21(1): 181–210.

Salge, T.O., and A. Vera (2013). Small steps that matter: incremental learning, slack resources and organizational performance. *British Journal of Management*, 24 (2): 156–173.

Schreyögg, G., and J. Sydow (2011). Organizational path dependence: A process view. *Organization Studies*, 32 (3): 321–335.

Sydow, J., G. Schreyögg, and J. Koch (2009). Organizational path dependence: Opening the black box. *Academy of the Management Review*, 34(4): 689–709.

Teece, D.J. (2012). Dynamic capabilities: Routines versus entrepreneurial action. *Journal of Management Studies*, 49 (8): 1395–1401.

Tripsas, M., and G. Gavetti (2000). Capabilities, cognition, and inertia: Evidence from digital imaging. *Strategic Management Journal*, 21 (10–11): 1147–1161.

Von Krogh, G., P. Erat, and M. Macus (2000). Exploring the link between dominant logic and company performance. *Creativity and Innovation Management*, 9(2): 82–93.

Walsh, J.P. (1995). Managerial and organizational cognition: Notes from a trip down Memory Lane. *Organization Science*, 6(3): 280–321.

Walshe, K., G. Harvey, and P. Jas (eds.) (2010). *Connecting knowledge and performance in public services. From knowing to doing.* Cambridge: Cambridge University Press.

Yle's annual report (2012). Retrieved February 15, 2016, from https://docs.google.com/a/yle.fi/file/d/0BwuyxSDWW6WwbVZ5Z3ZYOFVON2M/edit?pref=2&pli=1.

Michał Głowacki and Alicja Jaskiernia
University of Warsaw, Poland

Conclusions: towards public service media renewal

Abstract: Through examination of the findings from studies published in the "Public Service Media Renewal: Adaptation to Digital Network Challenges" collection, the goal of this chapter is to map the conditions for the reinvention of public service media in rapidly changing mediascapes. By highlighting the continuous importance of public service media, the chapter offers a framework for the analysis of public service media renewal through the lenses of selected drivers and obstacles for adaptation and change – systemic, regulatory, financial, technological, organizational, societal and mental. In the conclusions, we map ten indicators of public service media adaptivity, each of which might be treated as a tool to test how evolved public service media have become. The chapter ends with a set of recommendations for potential topics when discussing and studying the future of public service media in the digital network reality.

Keywords: adaptation, evolution, public service media renewal, policy-making, change management.

Introduction

The goal of this collection has been to investigate the evolution of public service media (PSM) in the digital network age. The authors have taken a holistic approach to investigate the ways in which PSM extend and modernize in order to adapt to the rapidly changing mediascapes, which are typified by collaborations with independent producers, multiplatform projects, transmedia forms, aggregation of high technology and creative firms, and so on. Overall, it has been argued that current changes in media and society offer scope for the reinvention of PSM. Thus, we have suggested looking at PSM from the perspective of its renewal – our core term that highlights internal and external strategies and which has the potential to make PSM strong, efficient and innovative.

PSMs were largely created in the 20th century to encourage an engaged and informed citizenry, but also to serve national informational needs such as audience participation and a knowledge-based society. They were tasked with producing high quality content, representing increasingly diverse publics, and combating market failure. The contribution of PSM to democracy and pluralism in the media has been emphasised in media studies and policy documents for years. The importance of maintaining PSM has been recognized by the European Union (Protocol to the Amsterdam Treaty on Public Service Broadcasting, 1997; European Parliament, 2010), the Council of Europe (2007, 2012a, 2012b) and in the national media regulation of the EU's member states. Searching for the ways in which PSM could continually evolve, respond, adjust and advance, has been regarded as critical for PSM to fulfil its tasks, legitimate its operations and act as a counterpart to the dominance of global media enterprises (Siune and Hultén, 1998; Nissen, 2006; Jakubowicz, 2010; Lowe and Steemers, 2012; Suárez Candel, 2012; Krichels, 2014; Głowacki and Jackson, 2014; Jaskiernia and Głowacki, 2015). The European Broadcasting Union (EBU) defined the core values of PSM and conducted a set of initiatives and projects to assist policy-makers and leaders in public service to adapt to the digital realm (EBU, 2012, 2014, 2015). Primarily, PSM in Europe were given tools to assist their current impact. The PSM were also called to make massive shifts in production, governance processes and mindset, either or both when it comes to opportunities and obstacles for successful adaptation and change.

In this concluding section, we aim to develop a framework for conditions fostering PSM renewal. Referencing to the findings in the studies that form the "Public Service Media Renewal: Adaptation to Digital Network Challenges" collection, we build on comparative research and case study analyzes on PSM in Australia, Austria, Belgium (Flanders), Croatia, Finland, Poland, United Kingdom and the U.S.A. All the chapters published in the book provide examples of successful and less successful and ineffectual strategies to evidence how evolved public service media might become. By mapping several challenges, we argue for a multi-layered analytical prism through the lenses of which systemic, regulatory, financial, technological, organizational, societal and mental dimensions may be viewed. The chapter closes with a list of indicators of public service media adaptivity and also recommendations for potential subjects for future studies on the evolution of PSM.

Mapping selected drivers for public service media renewal

Overall, a call for public service media renewal is tightly connected to the rise of new media and technologies, and changes in publics' behaviours as well as in PSM's surroundings, all of which have caused the clustering and emergence of innovation ecologies. In order to find its place in a complex reality, PSM needs to extend its operations and adjust to new market demands at all levels.

Nicole Gonser, Markus Grammel, Johann Gründl and Gisela Reiter explain the public's attitude towards the programming offered by ORF, Austria's PSM.

The authors argue that representatives of the publics attribute a high degree of importance to PSM, especially when being asked about ORF's contribution to society. Although the study has further noted that ORF is still seen as a credible and high quality news provider, there is a growing need to reconnect with younger media users who often abstain from consuming the media through traditional radio and TV means. Audience fragmentation, the rise of the networked publics and technologies, is viewed by Tiziano Bonini as one of the ways to move forward. Bonini argues a participatory turn is necessary for PSM to remain relevant and to efficiently deliver public service media content via online platforms, mobile devices, and so on. In order to build citizen-generated and citizen-centered PSM, the publics need to have an opportunity to co-create, co-decide and explore new ways to support them financially (crowdfunding). Bissera Zankova contends that enhancing public participation has the potential to strengthen the PSM's position as a central media institution in the digital age. The notions of harvesting ideas from creative publics, and public involvement in the processes of governance might contribute to the innovation potential of PSM. Therefore, it should be treated as a critical point when searching for future approaches to media regulation.

Technology not only offers a wide range of opportunities for public engagement but also a better understanding of the needs of contemporary media users. In the Preface to this book, Roberto Suárez Candel argues for the evolution of public service media towards the data paradigm. Lizzie Jackson explains why PSM firms need to engage with predictive analytics and behavioural targeting in order to bring relevant content to diverse audiences online as well as to remain visible and findable. A core argument is that exploration of machine mediation techniques might improve the PSM's ability to act as counterparts to commercial and global media firms, such as Netflix, Amazon Prime and YouTube. Research conducted by Jonathon Hutchinson has discovered evidence that PSM can when using the idea of algorithmic participation engage with microinfluencers and super-users via social media. Jonathon Hutchinson also suggests data sets can inform collaborative production practices and have the potential of strengthening relations with users who actively produce and consume culture.

Opportunities for PSM reinvention have also been found when looking at public service media as a part of wider media ecology. In this context, Tim Raats and Karen Donders argue that partnership systems and collaboration between PSM and their surrounding agents become crucial in the network environment. Tim Raats and Karen Donders have mapped several examples, in which PSM enterprises in Europe have increased their innovation potential through commissioning practices and relations with universities, creative industries and startup communities. Referring to discussions on multi-stakeholder approaches to public service media in Flanders, Tim Raats and Karen Donders note that due to systemic and long-term collaborations PSM might become a key player in innovation and a 'market strengthener,' which is of particular importance in small democracies. Similarly, Michał Głowacki calls PSM enterprises to interact with high technology and creative media clusters. Referring to a case study of public service media ecology in Estonia, Michał Głowacki also indicates that partnership systems and collaboration with external stakeholders might strengthen both the overall ecology and the position of PSM – its competitiveness and effectiveness. In addition, partnerships and collaborations have the potential to speed-up PSM renewal from the structural and managerial perspectives.

Mapping selected obstacles for public service media renewal

In addition to mapping opportunities that support the idea of public service media renewal, the authors in this collection indicate a set of potential barriers for change. Through case studies analyzed in the book, these barriers mostly appeared when looking at current regulatory and organizational settings, insufficient funding, path-dependencies as well as the mindset which might limit the ways in which PSM adapt.

Bissera Zankova argues that policy-makers in Europe and beyond are still taking advantage of existing international standards and regulations that foster extension of PSM to new platforms, partnership systems and participation. For instance, while European media regulation and studies by the Council of Europe and the European Broadcasting Union suggest fundamental shifts from traditional broadcasting models, the practice in many countries has shown that legal norms adopted by the member states do not fully reflect on rapid developments in media and technology. A prime example, as Michał Głowacki notes, is media regulation in Estonia that is still mostly focused on radio and TV. This limits the potential of the Estonian Public Service Broadcasting to innovate. Similarly, Anja Stević and Emil Čančar argue that PSM in Croatia uses its online services mostly as a 'bolt on' to traditional broadcasting means. This, in turn, results in only a few examples of platforms fostering citizen journalism, user-generated content and other participatory practices that could support shifts from one-way communication towards so-called 'public social media.'

Several authors in the chapters in this collection argue that the current performance of PSM (programming included) often results in the lack of understanding of PSM's role, which may have a negative impact on public support towards public service media. Users, in order to support PSM, need to have a feeling that public service content is independent, diverse, universal, innovative and of high quality, and that the voice of the public in decision-making processes is being heard by policy-makers, leaders and managers at PSM. However, Tim Raats and Karen Donders note that during the discussions on policy framework for PSM in Flanders the interests of audience might have been neglected. The same can be said about recent changes in media law in Poland, where the government passed the new media regulation without organizing public consultations. Alicja Jaskiernia and Katarzyna Pokorna-Ignatowicz further note that the Polish model of public service media has recently been replaced by that of a 'sovereign' national media. Indeed, the new regulatory framework did not include discussions on the ways, in which PSM could adapt to the digital network environment but focused on the management bodies of public radio and public TV, who were politically appointed. As a result, public service media is a governmental tool for propaganda with biased reporting, which has stopped or put on hold the evolution of PSM in Poland. Similar tendencies were observed by Tiziano Bonini who writes about media reforms in France and Hungary. A PSM serving one political ideology is likely to lose the support of diverse communities and might have an impact on the financial situation of that PSM. Tiziano Bonini further notes that the evasion rate of licence fee payers has contributed to financial problems of public service media in several countries. The lack of sufficient public funds has a negative impact on PSM quality, distinctiveness and innovation potential. As Michał Głowacki notes insufficient public funds in Estonia are among the critical factors that limit the PSM's engagement with high technology and creative clusters, which consequently might not regard public service media as being an attractive partner for collaboration.

Finally, attempts have been made to analyze PSM's adaptation from the internal perspective. Bearing in mind that in order to adapt to digital network challenges, PSM enterprises need to evolve themselves, several authors have mapped limitations caused by management systems, alongside their organizational setting and design. For instance, a low level of technology awareness by Croatia's PSM has been explained by Anja Stević and Emil Čančar as resulting from the late transformation and only recent attempts to integrate previously separated newsrooms. In fact, Croatia might not be the only case where internal restructuring should be seen as a starting point for the PSM renewal. Roberto Suárez Candel claims that the problem of many PSM enterprises is the necessity of dealing with over-sized, outdated and poorly governed structures. Although there is a need and willingness to embrace post-industrial approaches, as demonstrated by strategic re-organizations, there is an interplay between old and new media logic. In line with this, Päivi Maijanen shows that managers of public service media in Finland found it problematic to simultaneously manage and introduce internal change, as well as dealing with the path-dependent nature of organizational behaviour. Tiziano Bonini explains internal changes often accompany job cuts, and changes in the size of a PSM enterprise. Lizzie Jackson found another barrier for internal adaptivity. Lizzie Jackson notes that PSM staff might not currently have the right skillset to deal with data analytics and data management. This is why thinking outside the box and having a supportive attitude towards public service media evolution becomes critical. Both Roberto Suárez Candel and Bissera Zankova argue that thinking outside the box, based on core values and overcoming path-dependencies, shall be seen as a starting point for any discussion on PSM going forward.

Conditions for public service media renewal

Referencing all the challenges related to PSM in the digital network era, we suggest a set of dimensions which, we argue, are necessary for PSM renewal. Public service media is adaptive, and thus, likely to renew if:

1) It extends its operations beyond traditional radio and TV broadcasting;
2) Offers the publics the opportunity to participate in content creation;
3) There is a continual awareness of technology trends and skillsets to experiment with new techniques and processes, such as big data, data management, predictive analytics, behavioural targeting, and so on;
4) It is building partnerships with creative and high technology firms;
5) It is exploring new ways for funding to have a wider and safer economic base;
6) It has a flattened and flexible organizational structure, where there is integration of previously separated units and departments and the culture of experimentation;
7) It fosters multi-stakeholder dialogue and takes advantage of the expertise of European institutions, publics (public consultations), networks of researchers, and so on;
8) It has a strategy to deal with uncertainties and transparent management structures;
9) It has supportive leaders and managers who are able to think beyond broadcasting models;
10) It aspires to be a key player in the overall innovation ecology.

We invite testing of the framework of public service media renewal and to challenge it when examining the evolution of specific PSM case studies. Above all, we also call for more extensive debates and inclusion of new subjects related to future PSMs. For instance, we have learnt from this collection that there are still insufficiently covered topics, such as discussion on the ways in which PSM experiment with big data and public-private partnership. We believe that an investigation in this regard would require more in-depth analysis of skillsets, internal communication systems and processes, working patterns and strategies for staff motivation and development. Similarly, we think that future approaches to PSM might require more in-depth diagnosis of management systems and the personalities of leaders who are to lead change in public service media enterprises. In addition, we think that a systemic investigation of the public perception of PSM is of importance when combining it with the setting and implementation of PSM's strategic goals.

We argue that one of the biggest challenges will be to answer the question of how much of the old logic could (or should) remain when searching for approaches to change? Finally, from several examples examined in this collection, we have learnt that any reinvention of PSM might not necessarily mean its improvement because late technological adaptation together with illiberal tendencies might challenge the core values of PSM, including diversity, universality and independence. Thus, one of the biggest goal for future discussions will be to answer the question of identifying the means to find a balance between novelty and tradition; how to communicate the urgency of media reform and to maintain the traditional ethos of PSM at the same time?

References

Council of Europe (2007). Recommendation CM/Rec(2007)3 of the Committee of Ministers to member states on the remit of public service media in the information society *(Adopted by the Committee of Ministers on 31 January 2007 at the 985th meeting of the Ministers' Deputies).* Retrieved January 31, 2017 from https://search.coe.int/cm/Pages/result_details.aspx?ObjectID=09000016805d6bc5.

Council of Europe (2012a). *Declaration of the Committee of Ministers on public service media governance.* Adopted by the Committee of Ministers on 15 February 2012 at the 1134th meeting of the Ministers' Deputies. Retrieved November 12, 2016 from https://wcd.coe.int/ViewDoc.jsp?id=1908241.

Council of Europe (2012b). *Recommendation CM/Rec(2012)1 of the Committee of Ministers to member States on public service media governance.* Adopted by the Committee of Ministers on 15 February 2012 at the 1134th meeting of the Ministers' Deputies. Retrieved November 12, 2016 from https://wcd.coe.int/ViewDoc.jsp?id=1908265.

EBU (2012). *Empowering Society. A Declaration on the Core Values of Public Service Media.* Geneva: European Broadcasting Union. Retrieved January 31, 2017 from https://www.ebu.ch/files/live/sites/ebu/files/Publications/EBU-Empowering-Society_EN.pdf.

EBU (2014). *Connecting to a Networked Society. Continuous Improvement of Trust and Return to Society. Full Report.* Geneva: European Broadcasting Union.

Retrieved January 31, 2017 from https://www.ebu.ch/files/live/sites/ebu/files/Publications/EBU-Vision2020-Full_report_EN.pdf.

EBU (2015). *Public Service Media. Contribution to Society. Geneva: European Broadcasting Union.* Retrieved January 31, 2017 from https://www.ebu.ch/files/live/sites/ebu/files/Publications/Restricted/MIS/Documents/EBU-MIS%20-%20PSM%20Contribution%20to%20Society%20-%20Report.pdf.

European Parliament (2010). *Report on public service broadcasting in the digital era: the future of the dual system (2010/2028(INI)).* Retrieved January 31, 2017 from http://www.europarl.europa.eu/sides/getDoc.do?type=REPORT&reference=A7-2010-0286&language=EN.

Głowacki, M., and L. Jackson (2014). *Public Media Management for the Twenty-First Century: Creativity, Innovation, and Interaction.* London, New York: Routledge.

Jakubowicz, K. (2010). PSB 3.0: Reinventing European PSB. In: P. Iosifidis (ed.), *Reinventing Public Service Communication: European Broadcasters and Beyond.* London: Palgrave MacMillan, 9–22.

Jaskiernia, A., and M. Głowacki (2015). *Democratization of media policy in the digital ecosystems—The case of Poland. Report from scientific seminar at the university of Warsaw (October 17, 2014).* Warsaw: University of Warsaw.

Krichels, T. (2014). *Public Media Models of the Future.* Retrieved January 31, 2017 from http://www.current.org/2014/02/pbs-examines-successes-in-public-service-among-stations/.

Lowe, G.F., and J. Steemers (2012). Regaining the Initiative for Public Service Media. In: G. F. Lowe, and J. Steemers (eds.), *Regaining the Initiative for Public Service Media.* Göteborg: Nordicom, 9–23.

Nissen, Ch. S. (2006). *Public service media in the information society. Report prepared for the Council of Europe's Group of Specialists on Public Service Broadcasting in the Information Society (MC-S-PSB),* Strasbourg: Media Division, Directorate General of Human Rights, Council of Europe.

Protocol to the Amsterdam Treaty on Public Service Broadcasting (1997). Retrieved January 31, 2017 from http://epceurope.eu/protocol-to-the-amsterdam-treaty-june-1997-on-public-service-broadcasting/.

Siune, K., and O. Hultén (1998). Does Public Broadcasting Have a Future? In: D. McQuail, and K. Siune (eds.), *Media Policy: Convergence, Concentration, and Commerce,* London: Sage, 23–37.

Suárez Candel, R. (2012). *Adapting Public Service to the Multiplatform Scenario: Challenges, Opportunities and Risks.* Retrieved January 31, 2017 from http://www.psb-digital.eu/docs/files/PSB-Digital_FinalReport.pdf.

List of figures

List of tables

Index

E

Notes on contributors

Editors

Michał Głowacki, Ph.D., is an associate professor at the University of Warsaw, Poland. He was the programme advisor to the Advisory Group on Public Service Media Governance at the Council of Europe in 2010. He has been involved in several research projects including "Media Accountability and Transparency in Europe" and "Organizational Culture of Public Service Media: People, Values and Processes." Michal has been awarded scholarships by the Danish Agency for Science, Technology and Innovation, the Swedish Institute, the Research Council of Norway and the Polish-American Fulbright Commission. His research interests are media policy, public service media and innovation culture.
E-mail: michal.glowacki@uw.edu.pl

Alicja Jaskiernia, Ph.D., is an associate professor at the University of Warsaw, Poland. Her research interests focus on media policy, media systems, international communication, media and democracy, the European Union and the Council of Europe media standards. Her publications include books, journal articles and book chapters on media policy, media in the U.S. and impact of the media on democratic systems. She was one of the Polish experts in Media Pluralism Monitor study (in 2015 and 2016) conducted by the Centre for Media Pluralism and Media Freedom at the European University Institute in Florence.
E-mail: a.jaskiernia@uw.ed.pl

Authors

Tiziano Bonini, Ph.D., is a lecturer in media studies at Siena University, Italy, where he teaches media sociology. He has published extensively on radio and new media, on public service media, digital culture and digital media audiences. In 2015 he co-edited the ECREA volume *Radio Audiences and Participation in the Age of Network Society* (Routledge). He has also done research for the European Broadcasting Union on European public service radio and social media. Since 2005, he also works as a freelance radio producer for public service radio (RTSI, RAI, RTÉ), community radio and commercial radio (Radio24).
E-mail: tiziano.bonini@unisi.it

Emil Čančar, holds a Master degree in journalism at the University of Zagreb, Croatia. Having majored in television and print media and writing several internationally acclaimed essays, for which he received the Rector's Special Acknowledgement, he has conducted research at the Social Science Research Center of the Mississippi State University. He spent a semester at the University of Warsaw on an Erasmus+ exchange, studying visual communication, media policy and public service media. His research interests are media and visual studies, photography and reporting on science.
E-mail: e.cancar@hotmail.com

Karen Donders, Ph.D., is a professor at the communications department and lectures policy analysis, political economy of journalism and European media markets at the Vrije Universiteit Brussel, Belgium. She is also a senior researcher at iMinds-SMIT and leads the Media Research Unit at IMEC-SMIT. Karen also acts as a consultant for the Flemish public broadcaster VRT. The opinions expressed in her chapter do not reflect the opinions of VRT.
E-mail: karen.donders@vub.ac.be

Nicole Gonser, Ph.D., is a key researcher and coordinator of media research at the Institute for Journalism & Media Management at FHWien University of Applied Sciences of WKW, Austria. She has completed her Ph.D. at the Department of Journalism and Communication Research at the University of Music, Drama and Media Hannover, Germany. Her work includes publications on public value, elderly people and media, the history of the broadcasting systems and media socialization.
E-mail: nicole.gonser@fh-wien.ac.at

Markus Grammel, holds a Master degree in Journalism and New Media. He researches and teaches at the Institute for Journalism & Media Management at FHWien University of Applied Sciences of WKW, Austria. He is particularly interested in the media literacy of young audiences.
E-mail: markus.grammel@fh-wien.ac.at

Johann Gründl, holds a Master degree in Communication at the University of Vienna, Austria. He is a research associate at the Journalism Research Center at the Institute for Journalism & Media Management at FHWien University of Applied Sciences of WKW. He is also a lecturer at the Department of Government at the University of Vienna. His research areas are political communication and social media.
E-mail: johann.gruendl@fh-wien.ac.at

Jonathon Hutchinson, Ph.D., is a lecturer in Online Media and Social Media Communication at the University of Sydney, Australia. He has recently completed his thesis investigating the role of user-generated content within the ABC. His current projects include the Everyday Social Media research group, the Sydney Cyber Security Network, the Charles Perkins Centre Health Humanities node, and Beyond Buzz: Understanding the impact of social media on PSM. Hutchinson has published widely nationally and internationally, and is the 2013 winner of the Australian and New Zealand Communications Association's Grant Noble Prize for Best Postgraduate Student Paper Award.
E-mail: jonathon.hutchinson@sydney.edu.au

Lizzie Jackson, professor, Ph.D., was one of the eight Advisors to the Council of Europe who drafted the current Declaration and Recommendation on the governance of public service media (2012). Lizzie launched the BBC's Online Communities in 1997 and she also managed the BBC's live streaming team and internet safety initiatives. Lizzie was named 'One of the 100 Innovators of the UK Internet Decade' in 2005 by NOP World and eConsultancy.com for her work developing the Social Media industry in the UK. She is Head of the Division of Creative Technologies at London South Bank University.
E-mail: lizzie.jackson@lsbu.ac.uk

Päivi Maijanen, Ph.D., is a post-doctoral researcher at the School of Business and Management at the Lappeenranta University of Technology, Finland. Her research interests are focused on strategic management and organizational change, particularly, on issues related to media management and digital transformation, such as changes in managerial and journalism practices and culture. Before starting academia, she had built a long career as a journalist and a manager at the Finnish Broadcasting Company.
E-mail: paivi.maijanen-kylaheiko@lut.fi

Katarzyna Pokorna-Ignatowicz, Ph.D., is an associate professor and a head of Department of Media Studies and Political Communication in Andrzej Frycz Modrzewski Krakow University, Poland. Her work includes research and publications on Polish media systems, history of media, journalism studies, relations between media and religion, media ethics. She is head of section of Mass Communication in The Polish Communication Association.
E-mail: katarzyna.pokorna@gmail.com

Tim Raats, Ph.D., is an assistant professor at the Vrije Universiteit Brussel, Belgium. He lectures Political Economy of the Cultural Industries, Media Policy and European Media and Communications policies. He is a senior researcher at IMEC-SMIT, focusing on public service media management and policy challenges and financing and production of television in small audiovisual markets.
E-mail: tim.raats@vub.ac.be

Gisela Reiter, holds a Master degree in Communication at the University of Vienna, Austria. She is a research associate at the Journalism Research Center at the Institute for Journalism & Media Management at FHWien University of Applied Sciences of WKW and a lecturer at the Department of Communication at the University of Vienna. She has participated in the research project "Public Value goes international" funded by Vienna Municipal Department 23 for Economic Affairs, Labour and Statistics. She has published on media usage and public value issues for Austrian audiences.
E-mail: gisela.reiter@fh-wien.ac.at

Anja Stević, holds MA degree in journalism, and BA degree in television studies from the Faculty of Political Science, Journalism Department of the University of Zagreb, Croatia. She has been a visiting scholar at the Social Science Research Center of the Mississippi State University. During her studies she has worked as a student teaching assistant in visual culture and photojournalism. She has completed an internship at the Croatian Radio-Television and Erasmus+ scholarship at the University of Warsaw. Her journalism experience has been gained around various European Union projects held by the Television Student and the Radio Student.
E-mail: anja.stevic1@gmail.com

Roberto Suárez Candel, Ph.D., is the Head of the Media Intelligence Service (MIS), the research unit of the European Broadcasting Union (EBU). He manages a team of international researchers responsible for data collection processes, the implementation of research and analysis projects and the publication of market reports. MIS' main goal is supporting European public service media across Europe in their daily operations, advocacy activities and strategic planning. Previously, Roberto Suárez worked as an academic researcher in Germany (Hans-Bredow-Institut für Medienforschung), Sweden (Stockholm University) and Spain (Pompeu Fabra University). His work focused on communication public policy, public service media and ecology of the media sector.
E-mail: suarez.candel@ebu.ch

Bissera Zankova, holds a Ph.D in Comparative Constitutional Law from the Central European University in Budapest, Hungary. For many years she has been a Council of Europe expert in the field of freedom of expression and media, a member of CDMSI and its Bureau. She has taken part in the Council of Europe missions in various European countries. Currently she is independent researcher and consultant as president of "Media 21" Foundation registered in Bulgaria. The foundation pursues projects and partnerships in new media and journalism. She has been also a member of the Bulgarian Commission on Media Ethics since 2015. She is particularly interested in media policy and media regulation and self-regulation.
E-mail: bzankova@gmail.com

Studies in Communication and Politics

Edited by Bogusława Dobek-Ostrowska and Michał Głowacki

Vol. 1 Bogusława Dobek-Ostrowska / Jan Garlicki (eds.): Political Communication in the Era of New Technologies. 2013.

Vol. 2 Michał Głowacki / Epp Lauk / Auksė Balčytienė (eds.): Journalism that Matters. Views from Central and Eastern Europe. 2014.

Vol. 3 Gunnar Nygren / Bogusława Dobek-Ostrowska (eds.): Journalism in Change. Journalistic Culture in Poland, Russia and Sweden. 2015.

Vol. 4 Bogusława Dobek-Ostrowska / Michał Głowacki (eds.): Democracy and Media in Central and Eastern Europe 25 Years On. 2015.

Vol. 5 Beata Ociepka: Poland's New Ways of Public Diplomacy. 2017.

Vol. 6 Michał Głowacki / Alicja Jaskiernia (eds.): Public Service Media Renewal. Adaptation to Digital Network Challenges. 2017.

www.peterlang.com